D0571578

OTHER BOOKS BY WILLIAM J. BENNETT

The Children's Book of Virtues
The Moral Compass
The Book of Virtues
The Index of Leading Cultural Indicators
The De-Valuing of America
Counting by Race (co-author Terry Eastland)
Our Children, and Our Country

WILLIAM J. BENNETT,

JOHN J. DiIULIO, JR.,

AND JOHN P. WALTERS

SIMON & SCHUSTER

BODY COUNT

MORAL POVERTY...

AND HOW TO WIN

AMERICA'S WAR

AGAINST CRIME

AND DRUGS

SIMON & SCHUSTER
Rockefeller Center
1230 Avenue of the Americas
New York, NY 10020

Designed by Karolina Harris

Manufactured in the United States of America

10 9 8 7 6 5 4 3 2 1

Library of Congress Cataloging-in-Publication Data
Bennett, William John.
  Body count: moral poverty—and how to win America's war against crime and drugs /
William J. Bennett, John J. DiIulio, Jr., and John P. Walters.
    p. cm.
  Includes bibliographical references and index.
  1. Violent crimes—United States. 2. Drug abuse—United States.
3. Criminal justice, Administration of—United States. 4. United States—Moral conditions.
I. DiIulio, John J. II. Walters, John P. III. Title.
HV6789.B45 1996
364.1'5'0973—dc20   96-32453
                                                          CIP

ISBN 0-684-83225-9

To the victims of violent

crime in America

and their families

CONTENTS

1

INTRODUCTION

It was almost exactly three years ago. One of the three authors of this book was in Pittsburgh, the first stop on a business trip. But the eyes of the nation, and many of the conversations in Pittsburgh, were focused on Florida. For in the "Sunshine State," the ninth foreign visitor had been murdered within a year. In that particular incident, two teenagers fired handguns through the car windows on both sides, hitting a young man from England in the neck, killing him, and wounding a woman in the arm and chest. The wounded woman made it to a pay phone and called 911. "I want an ambulance," she cried out. "My husband's dying. We've been shot. There's blood all coming out of his mouth and I think he's dying. . . . Please."

Four days earlier police had arrested three people and charged them with the ruthless murder of a German tourist. Uwe-Wilhelm Rake-brand was shot to death with a sawed-off .30-caliber carbine rifle while driving on a Miami expressway with his pregnant wife by his side. The suspects "hunted" their prey, the police said.

While flying to Dallas, the co-author read an article in *Newsweek* magazine about the murder of basketball star Michael Jordan's father. The article pointed out that one of the two eighteen-year-olds who were arrested for killing "Pops" Jordan was on parole for attempting to kill another man by smashing him in the head with an ax and putting him in a coma for three months, while the other was awaiting trial for bashing a sixty-one-year-old convenience store clerk in the head with a cinder block during a robbery, fracturing her skull and causing a brain hemorrhage.

When he arrived in Dallas, the talk of the city was not about the recent signing of their star running back Emmitt Smith. The city was stunned by the abduction from a city playground of a seven-year-old girl who had lived in suburban Plano. The young girl was taken while her parents were watching their soccer-playing son on an adjacent field. The girl was eventually found; she had been strangled to death. The man police arrested was on parole for a conviction on charges of burglary. He was also a convicted sex offender. In 1988 the suspect had broken into a North Dallas apartment and sexually assaulted an eleven-year-old girl. The co-author's next stop was Los Angeles. While being driven to his hotel, he read a story about the murder of a woman as she sat in the front seat of her car, waiting for her seventeen-year-old daughter outside a Bible study class. She was shot at close range, in front of her nine-year-old son, even though she complied with a demand by robbers that she give them her purse. Moments after the shooting the victim's son burst into the home and interrupted the study group. "My mother's been shot!" he cried, collapsing into tears. A dozen people attending the meeting rushed out to find her slumped in the front seat of her car. The young mother of three died a short time later.

He then landed in Chicago. He opened the paper to the local section of the *Chicago Tribune* and read about the murder of a seventeen-year-old at a high school football game. The young man was shot with a semiautomatic .25-caliber handgun in the right temple as he rode in a car, dressed as the school's mascot.

Then he arrived home to Washington, D.C.—known at that time as the "murder capital" of the nation—where there was a front-page story about a man indicted in the murder-for-hire slaying of a local builder. The man was fatally shot in the parking lot of an office building he owned. Police said the killer was hired by the victim's former father-in-law.

That trip and those murders gave birth to this book and its title.

• • •

Late-twentieth-century America has the distinction of being history's most violent "civilized" nation. But even the rapid pace at which it has become so is still gradual enough that we are no longer shocked by it. Like the frog who will jump out of scalding water but will allow itself to be parboiled in water that is heated slowly enough, much of the American public has become inured and desensitized to the horrors of violent crime.

To those who say of the business trip described above, "Crime has always been the stuff of headlines," we say: "Look behind the headlines. Look to the more than 10 million violent crimes committed annually in America. Look at the four- and fivefold per capita increases in violent crimes reported to the police since the late 1950s and early 1960s. Look at the fact that America—this 'shining city on a hill'—now leads the industrialized world in rates of murder, rape, and violent crime."

To those who say, "Don't worry, crime rates are dropping; we have passed through the worst; things will surely get better," we say: "We hope so. But don't count on it. Recent downward trends in crime mask an alarming rise in teenage violence—and there are a lot more teenagers on the way. We may be experiencing the lull before the coming crime storm. So there is a lot more that needs to be done."

And to those who call us alarmist, we say: "Sometimes the bells you hear are false alarms. And sometimes they are the chimes at midnight."

Body Count is our attempt to explain America's violent crime plague; to clarify why it is happening; to define its size, scope, and distribution; to show what the response of government has been; to explode the myths that dominate the crime and drug debate; to present profiles of what works; and to mark out new policy directions on how we can best contain it.

Body Count is about violent crime, drugs, and moral poverty—and about the manner in which the first two are created by the third. By "moral poverty" we mean the poverty of being without loving, capable, responsible adults who teach the young right from wrong. It is the poverty of being without parents, guardians, relatives, friends, teachers, coaches, clergy, and others who *habituate* (to use a good Aristotelian word) children to feel joy at others' joy; pain at others' pain; satisfaction when you do right; remorse when you do wrong. It is the poverty of growing up in the virtual absence of people who teach these lessons by their own everyday example, and who insist that you follow suit and behave accordingly. In the extreme, it is the poverty of growing up surrounded by deviant, delinquent, and criminal adults in a practically perfect criminogenic environment—that is, an environment that seems almost consciously designed to produce vicious, unrepentant predatory street criminals.

In Chapter 2, we argue that the nation's drug and crime problem is fueled largely by moral poverty, and put question marks over both some of the liberal litany of "root causes" (economic poverty, lack of government-funded social programs, racism) and over some of the conservative catechism of toughness (resortlike prisons, too few executions, too much gun control). We present powerful evidence about the connection between liquor, disorder, and crime. In Chapters 3 and 4, we argue that governmental responses to violent crime and drugs have too often failed not only to keep known, convicted criminals off the streets and drug dealers at bay. They have missed the true root cause of the problem—moral poverty—and so have failed to embody a clear, consistent, moral message about the punishment of criminals and the discouragement of drug abuse. A false premise has emasculated the criminal justice system: the notion that the first purpose of punishment is to rehabilitate criminals. We disagree. Strongly. The first purpose is *moral*, to exact a price for transgressing the rights of others. Indeed, we believe a society tells as much about itself by what it punishes as by what it praises; by what it condemns as by what it encourages; by what receives reprobation as by what receives approbation. The consequences of this false premise are documented here, and they are sobering and discouraging. But ours is not a counsel of despair. Rays of hope, from New York City to Houston to Charleston, shine through the depressing statistics of *Body Count*. And in Chapter 5 we examine the underlying causes, and cures, of moral poverty and social regression. We place our current crime plague in recent historical context and discuss today's lack of self-restraint and social norms, the breakdown of civil society, the attenuation of individual responsibility and commitments, and the importance of religious faith.

This book's recommendations are, of necessity, general. Some short-term public policy recommendations in the areas of incarceration, prisons, and policing are included; these are things that we can and should do right away. But the recommendations to alleviate moral poverty do not lend themselves very well to neat and tidy policy prescriptions. There are, after all, intrinsic limits on how much public policy can affect moral sensibilities.

Rigorous and empirical data are the foundation for our analysis and the discussion that follows. As you will see, this book is chock-full of the latest and most reliable facts, figures, charts, and graphs about violent crime and drugs. To you the reader we say: bear with us. These numbers are crucial—crucial because we believe that any fruitful discussion about crime and punishment in America should proceed from a proper regard for facts. This may seem to be an obvious point. And in fact it is. But for too long, the debate about crime and drugs in America has been dominated by a relatively small group of anti-incarceration advocates. These advocates have been perpetrating criminal justice myths that have done a great deal to undermine effective law enforcement. What is at stake here is more than an interesting, and somewhat esoteric, academic debate. The body count has risen—lives have been lost—because pernicious ideas have formed an intellectual template for crime and punishment in America. One of the purposes of this book, then, is to explode some of these myths and help to change the terms of the national debate on crime and drugs.

One concern that we have tried to address is that the reader might get overwhelmed by the statistics, compelling though they are. For while numbers matter, the individual human dramas and tragedies behind them matter far more. The statistics can only provide a context for the human reality. In telling some of the genuine dramas and tragedies, our explicit aim is to convey the reality behind the figures.

As you read *Body Count*, it is important to keep the crime debate in its larger political and social context. There is a growing, justified outrage at what is happening to modern American society. People are frustrated because government is failing to carry out its first and most basic responsibility: to provide for the security of its citizens in order to meet the promise of liberty and justice for all. Indeed, we have an anomalous situation in which the federal government is involved in far more areas of American life than it ought to be, while at the same time it has (in many communities at least) forsworn its obligation to the primary tenet of the social contract. That needs to change. And fast.

We offer our arguments for reform for another, often overlooked reason. To some these reforms will appear harsh, though we would certainly take exception to that characterization. Regardless, they are not nearly as harsh as what might lie just over the horizon. For the American public will not accept widespread lawlessness indefinitely. Our free democratic institutions cannot withstand much more crime without a terrible counterreaction. If violent crime continues to rise; if out-of-wedlock births continue to increase; if more children are thrown into moral poverty; if the human carnage continues to mount; then the public will demand restored order at any cost—including a more-rapid-than-you-think rollback of civil liberties. Social anarchy usually triggers an authoritarian backlash. We need to give citizens another option, rooted in the ideal of justice and the traditions of a civilized society: punishment that recognizes the requirements of lawful order, safe communities, and human dignity—and a system that teaches clear and firm lessons and is itself a good example to children.

A word here on the connection between law and morality. The law is one important way to combat moral poverty because the law *teaches*. As Justice Oliver Wendell Holmes, Jr., once wrote, the law is "the witness and external deposit of our moral life." The law teaches responsibility or irresponsibility; it teaches children that crime doesn't pay or that crime does pay.

Good laws—good laws when they are obeyed—can also help restore order, civility, and beauty to the public square. As we have seen in New York City and other places, cleaning streets and neighborhoods of panhandlers, vandals, graffiti, boom-box cars, public drunkenness, street prostitutes, and squeegee pests can do a lot to reduce violent crime. This is a similar point to the one Plato made in the *Republic* when he wrote that the stamp of baseness on a building will sink deep into the souls of those it surrounds. The point is obvious enough: a good criminal justice system *per se* helps combat moral poverty; it is a necessary though not a sufficient condition.

In the end, the task we face is not an intellectually complicated one. We know what it takes to become a more civilized and decent nation. Previous civilizations have been overthrown from without; our present dissolution is from within—which means it is entirely within our capacity to save ourselves. But the hour is growing late. Very late. Many among us have heard the chimes at midnight. It is time we set to work.

2

THE ROOT CAUSE OF CRIME: MORAL POVERTY

THE DRUG AND CRIME BODY COUNT

Since "We The People" celebrated the bicentennial of the U.S. Constitution in 1987, more than 200,000 people have been murdered. From 1990 to 1994 the body count from murder (119,732) was more than twice the 58,000-person body count from the Vietnam War. In 1994 alone Americans were victimized by criminals more than 42 million times: some 31 million property crimes (thefts, burglaries) and 10.8 million violent victimizations. The violent crime toll in 1994 encompassed 2.5 million aggravated assaults, 1.3 million robberies, and 400,000 rapes and sexual assaults.[1] According to reliable estimates, the rate at which Americans are victimized by violent crime is more than twice the rate at which we are injured in vehicle accidents, and ten times the rate at which we die from heart attacks.[2] The violent crimes committed each year in this country cost victims and society an estimated $426 billion, not counting such crimes as drunk driving.[3] This $400-plus billion "violent crime tax" is more than four times the total amount spent each year by all levels of government on *all* criminal justice agencies and activities ($94 billion).[4]

Except for some advocates of drug legalization, no one seriously doubts that drug abuse kills and injures millions of Americans and their children each year, while contributing mightily to the nation's crime problem. Drug abuse acts as a multiplier of many types of street crime, and drug-addicted parents "threaten the health and safety of large numbers of children," some of them before they are even born. For example, in 1994 "between 30,000 and 65,000 children were exposed to cocaine in utero . . . hundreds of thousands of other children remain in the care of drug-addicted parents, where they are being raised under conditions of troubling inadequacy."[5] Although we know of no scientific study that has put a dollar value on the "drug abuse tax," it no doubt rivals the costs of violent crime.

Of course, if the body count were merely a matter of money, that would be one thing. But the body count is a matter of human misery, family tragedy, and social destruction. And while it is true that the nation's overall crime rate has leveled off in recent years, crime rates today remain far higher than they were when our parents and grandparents were growing up in this country. In 1965, for example, America's 9,850 murders translated into a rate of 5.1 per 100,000 citizens. By 1993 the United States was witness to 24,526 murders, and the nation's murder rate was 9.5 per 100,000 citizens.[6] In 1994, the number of murders fell to 23,305, a one-year decline of 4.98 percent, but still more murders than in all but four (1990–93) of the last thirty years.

Or consider a slightly more complicated but revealing calculation by Professor Alfred Blumstein. Blumstein estimates that if the murder arrest rate in 1991 were the same as it had been on average from 1970 to 1985, then there would have been 19,373 murders in 1991. But there were actually 24,703 murders in 1991—5,330 more than there would have been had the homicide rate in 1991 equaled the 1970–85 average. And note: more than 80 percent of these 5,330 "excess murders" were committed by youth between the ages of 15 and 18.[7]

It is clear that youth violence has reached epidemic proportions that must be addressed. . . . In 1993, law enforcement agencies made almost 2.4 million juvenile arrests; if present trends continue, the violent crime arrest levels alone will double by the year 2010.

—CHIEF DAVID G. WALCHAK
CONCORD, NEW HAMPSHIRE
PRESIDENT, INTERNATIONAL ASSOCIATION OF CHIEFS OF POLICE[8]

Here is the terrible rub in the body count: even as overall crime rates have been stable or declining, violence has been soaring among America's young, as has drug abuse. As Figure 2-1 indicates, the drug problem among high school seniors has been expanding. According to the estimates of policy makers and analysts of both parties in the 104th Congress, the drug problem will not abate anytime soon.[9] Indeed, the nation's drug and crime problem is bound to grow over the next ten years, especially among young urban minority males. For starters,

FIGURE 2-1. TRENDS IN PREVALENCE FOR ANY ILLICIT DRUG USE AMONG HIGH SCHOOL SENIORS, 1981–1994

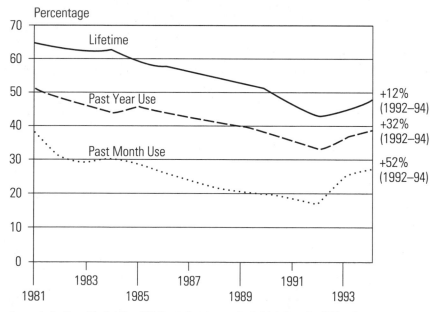

Source: *Losing Ground Against Drugs* (U.S. Senate Committee on the Judiciary, December 1995), p. 3.

however, let's focus on the violent crime problem and the literal center of the body count—deaths due to murder.

THE TICKING CRIME BOMB

To better understand the criminal landscape in America, here are some important facts you need to know: most of the street crimes that concern and frighten us are committed by men under the age of 25. Over the next decade or so, the number of young men in the population will increase substantially. And a large fraction of boys are likely to be raised in circumstances that put them at risk of becoming street predators. In short, America is a ticking crime bomb.

The evidence is overwhelming. First, consider the latest and best numbers on homicides as compiled by Professor James Alan Fox. Take a look at Figure 2-2. It shows that since 1985 the rate of homicide committed by adults age 25 and older has dropped by 25 percent (from 6.3 to 4.7 per 100,000). Over the same period, however, the homicide rate among 18- to 24-year-olds increased by 61 percent (from 15.7 to 25.3 per 100,000). And over the last decade, the rate of homicide

FIGURE 2-2. HOMICIDE OFFENDING RATE BY AGE, 1976–1994

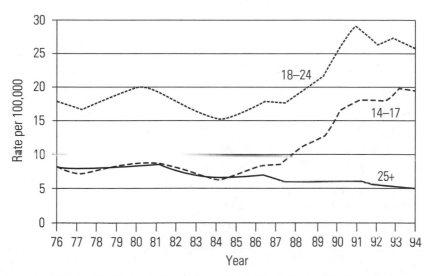

Source: James Alan Fox, *Trends in Juvenile Violence* (Bureau of Justice Statistics, March 1996), p. 7.

committed by teenagers ages 14 to 17 more than doubled (from 7 to 19.1 per 100,000). Thus, as Fox concludes, "although the percentage of 18- to 24-year-olds has declined in recent years, younger teens have become more involved in serious violent crime, including homicide, thereby expanding the limits of the violence-prone group to as young as 14."[10]

Males ages 14 to 24 are now about 8 percent of the population but they constitute 27 percent of all homicide victims and 48 *percent* of all murderers.[11] Between 1985 and 1992 the rate at which males ages 14 to 17 committed murder increased by about 50 percent for whites and over 300 percent for blacks.[12] By the early 1990s the homicide offending rate per 100,000 among black males ages 14 to 17 hovered around 150 (versus 15 for whites), while the homicide offending rate for black males ages 18 to 24 hovered around 200 (versus 20 for whites). Ominously, white males ages 14 to 17 "have diminished in relative size to less than 7 percent [of the population], but have remained 10 percent of homicide victims and 17 percent of the perpetrators. More striking, however, is that over the past decade, black males ages 14–24 have remained just above 1 percent of the population yet have expanded from 9 to 17 percent of the victims and from 17 to 30 percent of the offenders."[13]

The trends are also ominous for nonfatal acts of criminal violence and rates of weapons offenses among young males. For example, between 1973 and 1992, the rate of violent victimizations of black males ages 12 to 24 increased about 25 percent; black males ages 16 to 19 sustained one violent crime for every eleven persons in 1973 versus one for every six in 1992.[14] From 1987 to 1992, the average annual rate of handgun victimization per 1,000 young black males was three to four times higher than for young white males.[15]

As we will explain later in this chapter, black-white differences in rates of criminal offending reflect the fact that, on average, black children are more likely than white children to grow up without two parents or other adults who supervise, nurture, and provide for them. As Professor Glenn Loury has eloquently written, crime is a problem of "sin, not skin."[16] So, as you read these data, do keep in mind that race is, in effect, a proxy for the density of stable, consistent adult supervision in the lives of at-risk children. Give black children, on average, the level of positive adult social support enjoyed by white children, and the rates would reverse themselves.

> A Philadelphia jury convicted three suburban teens of third-degree murder for beating an altar boy to death with baseball bats in front of his church. Eddie Polec, 16, suffered seven skull fractures on the steps of St. Cecilia's Catholic Church. . . . The killing followed a fight between youths in two Philadelphia-area neighborhoods after a rumored rape of a girl, which proved to be untrue. . . . All [the assailants] were from Abington Township, a group of mostly affluent suburbs north of Philadelphia.[17]

To get an idea of what such body count numbers can mean in a particular place, consider the case of Philadelphia. For many years, crime rates in Philadelphia have generally been lower than in other big cities. Still, Philadelphians, as residents of Pennsylvania's largest urban metropolis, experience more murders and other crimes than other citizens of the Keystone State, and young black males experience them at a much higher rate than do young whites. Thus, in 1990 Philadelphia's overall crime rate was about twice that of the four surrounding Pennsylvania counties, and its violent crime rate was three times that of those counties. Forty-two percent of all violent crimes committed in Pennsylvania occurred in Philadelphia, which contained only 14 percent of the state's population.[18]

Gaze at Figure 2-3, a "murder map" produced by two local Philadelphia newspaper reporters, Don Russell and Bob Warner. In 1994, 433 people were murdered in the City of Brotherly Love, 340 of them black. In other words, blacks were less than 40 percent of the city's population but almost 80 percent of its crime victims. While Philadelphians of every race, creed, and zip code experienced violent crime in 1994, the number of murders per 100,000 residents varied greatly from one neighborhood to the next. In one predominantly black and Latino neighborhood known to residents and police as "the Badlands" (part of census tract 176 on the map), the murder rate was over 100, more than four times the citywide average of 23. As Russell and Warner also discovered, almost all of Philadelphia's 89 juvenile murder victims were nonwhite.[19]

FIGURE 2-3. PHILADELPHIA MURDERS IN 1994, BY ZIP CODE

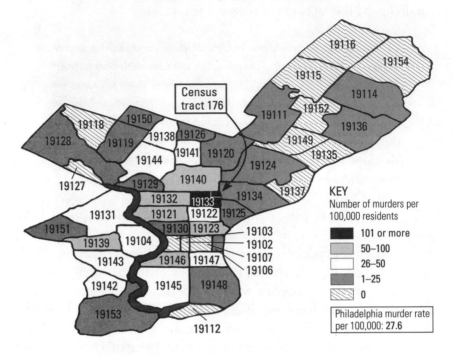

In 1994 the National Research Council, led by Professor Mark H. Moore, issued a conference report on violence in America. The report began: "The violence now occurring within our cities is a national scourge. The fact that minority youth are disproportionately its victims makes it a tragedy and a disgrace as well."[20]

We agree, and we are concerned that the problem is intensifying. For, as bad as America's high-crime "badlands" already are, veteran law enforcement officials, like our colleague on the bipartisan Council on Crime in America, Philadelphia District Attorney Lynne Abraham, are worried—very worried—about things getting worse. Though known for her don't-scare-easily professional demeanor, Abraham uses such revealing phrases as "totally out of control" and "never seen anything like it" to describe the rash of youth violence that has begun to sweep over Philadelphia and other cities. She is not just talking about teenagers or black inner-city teenagers, she stresses. She is talking about boys whose voices have yet to change. She is talking about elementary school youngsters who pack guns instead of lunches. She is talking about kids who have absolutely no respect for human life and no sense of the future.

And she is not alone.

> On October 13, 1994, 5-year-old Eric Morse and his 8-year-old brother, Derrick, ran into two of the toughest bullies their South Side Chicago neighborhood had to offer. The intimidating boys lured the brothers to a vacant 14th floor apartment. Twice, they dangled a terrified and wailing Eric—who had refused to steal candy for them—out the window. When Derrick tried to pull in his brother, the older bully bit his hand so hard he let go. Eric plunged to his death. Derrick ran downstairs, thinking he might catch his brother in time. It was a blood-curdling crime at any age. But these killers, whose names have not been released by officials, were all of 10 and 11. . . . "It's 'Lord of the Flies' on a massive scale," says Cook County State's Attorney Jack O'Malley. "We've become a nation terrorized by our children." O'Malley recently reorganized his juvenile justice division because of the growing number of very young offenders.[21]

> Americans believe something fundamental has changed in our patterns of crime. They are right. We were unhappy about having our property put at risk, but we adapted with the aid of locks, alarms, and security guards. But we are terrified by the prospect of innocent people being gunned down at random, without warning and almost without motive, by youngsters who afterwards show us the blank, unremorseful face of a feral, pre-social being.
>
> —PROFESSOR JAMES Q. WILSON[22]

> America's beleaguered cities are about to be victimized anew by a paradigm-shattering wave of ultra-violent, morally vacuous young people some call "the super-predators."
>
> At least that is the consensus emerging within precinct houses, university think tanks and living rooms across the country. Indeed, some of those who have become experts against their will can testify that in some places the super-predators have already arrived.

The trend should concern all Americans, wherever they live.
Pathologies first sighted in cities rarely stay there for long.
— BOSTON SUNDAY GLOBE,
MAY 19, 1996

THE SUPER-PREDATORS

To reiterate a point we have already made: as high as America's body
count is today, a rising tide of youth crime and violence is about to lift
it even higher. A new generation of street criminals is upon us—the
youngest, biggest, and baddest generation any society has ever known.

How did we come to this conclusion? As Table 2-1 indicates, between now and the year 2010, the number of juveniles in the population will increase substantially. Today, for example, America is home
to roughly 7.5 million boys ages 14 to 17. UCLA Professor James Q.
Wilson has estimated that by the year 2000, "there will be a million
more people" in that age bracket than there were in 1995, half of
them male. Based on well-replicated longitudinal studies, he predicts
that 6 percent of these boys "will become high rate, repeat offenders
—thirty thousand more young muggers, killers, and thieves than we
have now. Get ready," he warns.[23]

The problem, however, is not just that a growing population of boys
means more bad boys. The problem is that today's bad boys are far

TABLE 2-1. U.S. JUVENILE POPULATION, 1990 AND PROJECTED 2010

	Population		Increase	
	1990	2010	Number	Percent
All juveniles	64,185,000	73,617,000	9,432,000	15
Ages 0–4	18,874,000	20,017,000	1,143,000	6
Ages 5–9	18,064,000	19,722,000	1,658,000	9
Ages 10–14	17,191,000	20,724,000	3,533,000	21
Ages 15–17	10,056,000	13,154,000	3,098,000	31
White	51,336,000	55,280,000	3,944,000	8
Black	9,896,000	12,475,000	2,579,000	26
Latino	7,886,000	13,543,000	5,657,000	71

Source: Bureau of the Census, 1993, Office of Juvenile Justice and Delinquency Prevention, 1995.

worse than yesteryear's, and tomorrow's will be even worse than to-day's. As Wilson has observed, there are

> only two restraints on behavior—morality, enforced by individual con-science or social rebuke, and law, enforced by police and courts. . . . As the costs of crime decline or the benefits increase, as drugs and guns become more available, as the glorification of violence becomes more commonplace, as families and neighborhoods lose some of their re-straining power—as all of these things happen, almost all of us will change our behavior to some degree. For the most law-abiding among us, the change will be modest. . . . For the least law-abiding among us, the change will be dramatic. . . .[24]

Based on all that we have witnessed, researched, and heard from people who are close to the action, here is what we believe: America is now home to thickening ranks of juvenile "super-predators"—radi-cally impulsive, brutally remorseless youngsters, including ever more preteenage boys, who murder, assault, rape, rob, burglarize, deal deadly drugs, join gun-toting gangs, and create serious communal disorders. They do not fear the stigma of arrest, the pains of imprisonment, or the pangs of conscience. They perceive hardly any relationship be-tween doing right (or wrong) now and being rewarded (or punished) for it later. To these mean-street youngsters, the words "right" and "wrong" have no fixed moral meaning.

These super-predators regret getting caught, and prefer pleasure and freedom to incarceration and death. Under some conditions, they are affectionate and loyal to fellow gang members or relatives. But not even mothers or grandmothers are sacred to them; as an adult prisoner quipped to one of us regarding today's young urban criminals, "Crack killed everybody's 'mama.'"

The super-predators place no value on the lives of their victims, whom they reflexively dehumanize as just so much worthless "white trash" if white, or by the usual racial or ethnic epithets if black or Latino. They are perfectly capable of committing the most heinous acts of physical violence for the most trivial reasons (for example, a perception of slight disrespect or the accident of being in their path). They live by the meanest code of the meanest streets, a code that reinforces rather than restrains their violent, hair-trigger mentality. In prison or out, the things that super-predators get by their criminal behavior—sex, drugs, money—are their own immediate rewards. *Nothing else matters to them.* So for as long as their youthful energies hold out, they will do what comes "naturally": murder, rape, rob, assault, burglarize, deal deadly drugs, and get high.

In some ways this is not only not surprising, but it is also entirely predictable. Here's why: many of these super-predators grow up in placcs that may best be called criminogenic communities—places where the social forces that create predatory criminals are far more numerous and stronger than the social forces that create decent, law-abiding citizens. In these places, the forces of decomposition over-whelm the forces of composition. At core, the problem is that most inner-city children grow up surrounded by teenagers and adults who are themselves deviant, delinquent, or criminal. At best, these teenag-ers and adults misshape the characters and lives of the young in their midst. At worst, they abuse, neglect, or criminally prey upon the young. The problem is not merely that so many inner-city children grow up insufficiently socialized to the norms and values of a civilized, noncriminal way of life, but that they grow up almost completely unmoralized and develop character traits that are more likely to lead them into a life of illiteracy, illicit drugs, and violent crimes than into a life of literacy, intact families, and steady jobs.

> *Debra Dickerson's brother, Johnny, was almost killed by another young man. In her intensely personal and gripping essay, "Who Shot Johnny?" she recounts how her brother was shot, paralyzed from the waist down, and left for dead. His crime? Waving hello at a car full of boys whom he mistakenly thought he knew. The assail-ant stood over her brother's barely conscious body and said, "Bet-ch'ou won't be doin' nomo' wavin' motha'fucker." The vicious young attacker was never caught.*[25]

Virtually everyone we know who is close to the nation's crime problem, from big-city police officers to inner-city preachers, from juvenile probation officers to public school teachers, agrees that more and more of today's crime-prone kids are sheer terrors. The exceptions are certain crime "experts" and pundits—the same ones who denied or trivialized the crack and crime epidemic of the 1980s until it was too late for anything but eulogies to its victims. We have yet to meet anyone who seriously doubts that today's troubled teens are more troubled than those of the 1950s. Common sense alone should be sufficient to prove that the one-drive-by-shooting-a-night street gangs of the late 1980s and early 1990s represent a far greater physical and moral menace than the one-knife-fight-a-year street gangs of earlier decades.

STATISTICS: PUZZLE BUILDING

Still, it is impossible to know exactly how much worse, on average, today's youth criminals are than those of previous eras. Our best guess-timate is that they are several times as bad, but no one can really quantify the difference with any degree of precision. The reason is that the statistical data, even from the most famous of scientific studies, are full of holes.

For example, the famous study of Professor Marvin E. Wolfgang tracked all 10,000 boys born in 1945 who lived in Philadelphia between their tenth and eighteenth birthdays. Over one-third had at least one recorded arrest by the time they were 18. Most of the arrests occurred when the boys were ages 15 to 17. Half of the boys who were arrested were arrested more than once. Once a boy had been arrested three times, the chances that he would be arrested again were over 70 percent. And—the study's most famous and well-replicated finding— 6 percent of the boys committed five or more crimes before they were 18, accounting for over half of all the serious crimes, and about two-thirds of all the violent crimes, committed by the entire cohort. A subsequent study of boys born in Philadelphia in 1958 found much the same, and a comparison of the two data sets indicated that the boys in the latter cohort were about five times more likely to commit robberies than the boys in the former.[26] According to Professor Wolfgang, the dean of scholars who do such research, each male cohort has been about three times as violent as the one before it.[27] We concur.

Still, as Professor Wolfgang and others acknowledge, there are numerous difficulties with basing generalizations about the criminality of a given birth cohort strictly on the findings of this longitudinal literature. First, a large fraction of juveniles, including the most serious offenders, are never apprehended. For example, as revealed through

follow-up surveys, while 35 percent of the boys in the 1945 Philadelphia cohort had a police contact before age 18, about 60 percent of
the worst offenders did not.[28] Second, the research captures only the
official number and types of crimes done by the fraction of youth
criminals who did see the inside of a police station, plus information
on the apprehended boys' race, income category, and a few other
bare-bones variables.[29] Third, even if police records could be found on
all juvenile offenders in a given city, and even if the records included
meaningful background information on them, many complications
would still remain. For example, about 30 percent of all juvenile cases
are handled within police departments and never referred to court, and
America has no comprehensive national juvenile justice information
system.[30] Police Chief David G. Walchak, president of the International Association of Chiefs of Police, laments that current "juvenile
records (both arrest and adjudication) are inconsistent across the
states, and are usually unavailable to the various programs' staff who
work with youthful offenders. For example, only 26 states even allow
law enforcement access to juvenile records."[31]

Aristotle said it best: "It is the mark of the educated person to look
for precision in each class of things just so far as the nature of the
subject admits."[32] The subject of youth crime and violence quickly
reduces statistics from an exact science to an interpretive art. In the
real world, a good statistician draws inferences about populations from
samples, and finds patterns in numerical puzzles that have missing,
fragmentary, or ill-fitting pieces.

Wearing our best statistician's hat, we find, with the coming of the
super-predators, many pieces of numerical data that fit together. They
suggest to us that today's baddest boys do at least three times as much
serious harm and gratuitous violence as did their crime-prone cousins
and uncles of the 1950s or 1970s. Here are just some of the pieces:

- The number of gun homicides by juveniles has nearly tripled
  since 1983.[33]
- Weapons law violation arrest rates for teenage males ages 15 to
  18 more than doubled between 1983 and 1992.[34]
- The fastest growing murder circumstance is juvenile gang kill-
  ings, which nearly quadrupled from 1980 to 1992.[35]

- Unlike in the past, today most murders are between strangers, and clearance rates for murder dropped from 91 percent in 1965 to an all-time low of 65 percent in 1992, probably as the result of the increase in stranger-stranger murders.[36]
- Victims ages 15 to 17, both black and white, accounted for almost all the increase in juvenile murders from 1976 to 1994; and since the mid-1980s, the increases in both the number and the rate of murder among 15- to 17-year-olds, especially among blacks, have outpaced changes in murder in all other age groups.[37]
- Nationally, juveniles under age 18 were responsible for nearly 30 percent of juvenile murders in 1994.[38]

There are gang death rhymes too. "Chitty Chitty Bang Bang" is a Piru Blood rhyme recited, they say, after killing a Crip. The tale is that Bloods, driving through a Crip neighborhood, stop when they see a Crip. Leaning out the window one says, "Hey cuzz, yo cuzz, come on, cuzz, come here." The Crip, without thinking about the danger, walks over to the car and is shot to death. The Bloods then sing,

> *Chitty Chitty Bang Bang,*
> *It's all about the Crip thang.*
> *Hah, Hah, fooled you.*
> *Undercover Piru!*

Gang members' tags often connote death. I asked Body Count how he got his name. "When da shootin's ova', das what I do, coun' da bodies."

—PROFESSOR MARK S. FLEISHER[39]

Looking at state and local as opposed to national numbers brings the coming of the super-predators into even sharper focus. For example, Professor Anne Morrison Piehl has found that between 1990 and 1994 some 155 persons age 21 or younger were murdered with guns or knives in Boston: 22 (14 percent) were on probation when they were killed, and 95 others (61 percent) had been arraigned in Massachusetts courts prior to their deaths. Likewise, 117 of the 155 young murder victims (75 percent) had criminal histories. And among the 125 known murderers age 21 or younger, 33 (26 percent) were on probation when they killed, and 63 others (50 percent) had been arraigned in Massachusetts courts prior to the murders. Thus, 77 percent of the known killers and three-quarters of the young victims had criminal histories.[40]

All types of adult street predators, not just murderers, normally begin as juvenile street criminals. A recent study confirms this for known, adjudicated adult felons from Milwaukee, Wisconsin. The study reconstructed the complete official adult and juvenile criminal records of a scientifically selected sample of Wisconsin prisoners and probationers from Milwaukee County. The study found that about 91 percent of the offenders had been convicted at some point of a violent crime; under 2 percent of the offenders were mere first-time property offenders or drug offenders. About 62 percent of them had a documented juvenile record, often including serious and violent crime and multiple violations of community supervision rules set by juvenile court judges. For example, an offender classified as a "burglar" and "low-risk" felon was placed on probation. He had compiled four adult arrests and two adult incarcerations, plus a juvenile record that included auto theft, armed robbery, and other crimes. The state's presentencing investigation report noted that the felon "first became involved in the correctional system at the age of 11 [and] has established a very lengthy criminal record. . . . He has substantially ignored the orders of the Court and continued to violate his parole on many occasions."[41]

The problem is that more (and more violent) young street criminals are on the way. Take the case of Florida. Florida's juvenile population as a percentage of total state population actually dropped from 31 percent in 1970 to 23 percent in 1995 (a 26 percent drop). Additionally, between 1982 and 1993 the 15- to 17-year-old age cohort not only declined as a percentage of the state's population (from 4.5 to 3.3 percent), but declined in absolute numbers (from 470,000 to 458,000).[42]

Just the same, proportionately fewer juveniles committed a larger share of all serious crimes. Table 2-2 compares juvenile and adult arrests in Florida for 1971 and 1995. It shows plainly that for all crimes (except larceny and burglary), juveniles became a larger percentage of all arrests for murder, rape, robbery, and aggravated assault.

And now for the bad news. By the year 2010, Florida will have 36.4

TABLE 2-2. JUVENILE AND ADULT ARRESTS IN FLORIDA, 1971, 1995

	Juvenile					Adult				
Offense	1971	1995	% change 1971–1995	1971 % of total	1995 % of total	1971	1995	% change 1971–1995	1971 % of total	1995 % of total
Murder	47	182	287.2	5.3	16.2	838	943	12.5	94.7	83.8
Forcible Sex	—	614	—	—	17.4	—	2,908	—	—	82.6
Rape	88	372	322.7	10.0	16.2	791	1,921	142.9	90.0	83.8
Robbery	743	3,326	347.6	19.0	32.5	3,169	6,904	117.9	81.0	67.5
Aggravated Assault	1,186	7,094	498.1	13.1	15.8	7,845	37,740	381.1	86.9	84.2

Source: *Youth Crime in Florida* (Florida Department of Law Enforcement, April 25, 1996), p. 5.

percent more juveniles, and 43.9 percent more in the 15–17 age bracket, than it did in 1990.[43] Officials in Florida, California, and other states fully expect juvenile arrests to *double* between now and the year 2010.[44] As Figure 2-4 suggests, as go the states, so goes the nation—and here come the super-predators.

FIGURE 2-4. JUVENILE POPULATION AND PROJECTED ARREST RATES, 1980–2010

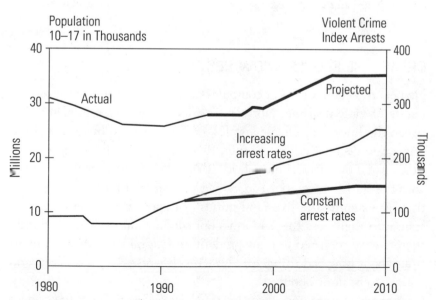

Source: *Combatting Violence and Delinquency* (Coordinating Council on Juvenile Justice and Delinquency Prevention, March 1996), p. 1.

SLAIN TEACHER RECORDED HER PLEAS TO ABDUCTOR
Prosecutor Charges Teen With Murder

*Facing death at the hands of a teenage thief who wanted her new
car to celebrate his 17th birthday, a Tinton Falls teacher left an
extraordinary and chilling legacy: she secretly tape-recorded a conversation with her killer . . . Michael LaSane, a student at Toms
River South who turned 17 on the day after the killing and allegedly
bragged to his friends that he was going to get a "brand new Toyota
Camry" for his birthday. . . . The dramatic 24-minute recording
gave investigators a clear picture of the attempts by Kathleen Stan-
field Weinstein, 45 (a popular teacher, wife, and mother of a
6-year-old son), to not only save her life, but understand her abductor as she helped him empty her car of personal belongings near the
wooded area in Berkeley Township where she was found bound and
smothered with her own clothes. . . . It is clear from the transcript
of the conversation released by the prosecutor that Weinstein tried
to bargain for her life. She is heard saying: "Don't you understand,
though, what kind of trouble you are going to get in? Don't you
think they are going to find you?" and "You haven't done anything
yet. All you have to do is let me go and take my car." . . . LaSane
is heard on the tape asking about the car's service record and lease
arrangement.*[45]

CRIME: THE PEOPLE KNOW BEST

No neat rows of numbers or computer printouts can capture the bloody
reality of violent crime. Nor can one locate the super-predators between the lines of academic articles, or capture them by recalculating
crime rate decimal points. Rather, the crime problem facing this nation can be understood only if, in addition to fiddling as best we can
with the statistics, we look squarely at the deeds of killers, rapists, and
thieves; examine the lives and minds of today's street criminals; and
stare into their eyes the way innocent victims must. Then, and only
then, are we prepared to draw prudent and morally grounded conclusions about how bad things are, how much worse they could get, and
what is to be done about it.

Of course, we are not suggesting that our readers rush out to conduct
interviews at the nearest violent prisoner intake center. But we are

suggesting that you reflect on your own crime-avoidance behavior and expertise; pay attention to the crime reports on local news; read a few books that detail the lives of today's and yesteryear's street criminals; be on the lookout for factual literature and reports by victims' rights organizations; and heed the statistics, ethnographies, and anecdotes offered in this book.

We know how the local news, both print and electronic, sometimes exaggerates or sensationalizes the crime problem to attract customers and advertisers: "If it bleeds, it leads." "Super-predators" itself, a concept that one of us first trotted out in a small-circulation magazine in 1995, unexpectedly proved to be a real headline-grabber, and, within months of its debut, was discussed on several major network news shows and television magazines.

But the fact that violent crime stories make big news—like the fact that cynical politicians often use law and order as a campaign issue, and the fact that most of us are naturally inclined to think things were "better when"—doesn't mean that there's no reality behind the headlines or the campaign slogans, or that things weren't significantly better when. Nor does it mean that average citizens are incapable of judging the relative violent crime risks that they now face. In fact, all of the evidence suggests that the relative intensity of average Americans' concerns about violent crime is more a mirror than a mirage of their respective objective risks of being victimized by violent crime today.

For example, in just about every major public opinion survey since January 1994, crime has been ranked ahead of unemployment, the deficit, pollution, and other issues as the main problem facing the country. But while nearly all Americans now feel more threatened by crime than they did in the past, urban Americans feel more threatened than suburban or rural Americans, and urban blacks feel more threatened than other urban residents. In 1991 about 7.4 percent of all households, 16.5 percent of black households, and 22.7 percent of central-city black households identified crime as a major neighborhood problem. Between 1985 and 1991, the fraction of rural households that identified crime as a major neighborhood problem remained fairly stable, rising from 1.4 to 1.9 percent. But the fraction of black central-city households that did so nearly doubled from 11.8 to 22.7 percent.[46]

A number of surveys, including one conducted by the Black Community Crusade for Children, have found that black urban children, who are far more likely than black urban adults to be murdered or victimized by many types of violent crime, ranked their top four present life concerns as follows: kids carrying guns (70 percent); violence in school (68 percent); living in a dangerous neighborhood (64 percent); and involvement with gangs (63 percent).[47] As Table 2-3 indicates, black teenagers, who are more likely than white teenagers to be murdered or victimized by many types of violent crime, feel more threatened.

Likewise, a recent survey reported that 26 percent of blacks, versus

TABLE 2-3. TEENAGERS AND THE THREAT OF VIOLENT CRIME, 1994

	White Teenagers	Black Teenagers
How much of the time do you worry about being the victim of a crime?		
A lot or some of the time	36%	54%
Hardly ever or never	64	46
What kind of crime do you think is likely to happen to you?		
Robbery/mugging	13	10
Shooting	5	27
Assault	6	7
Rape	7	2
Other	2	3
Who do you think is more likely to commit that crime against you?		
Teenager you know	7	11
Teenager you don't know	18	37
An adult	9	4
Do you know someone who has been shot in the past five years?		
Yes	31	70
What is the biggest problem where you go to school?		
Violence	19	37
Gangs	5	8
Drugs	14	8
Racism	8	6
All other	40	23
Are organized gangs a problem in your school?		
Yes	18	33

Source: *New York Times*, July 10, 1994, p. 16, based on New York Times/CBS News poll.

16 percent of the general population, answered "yes" when asked whether, in the past two years, they or someone close to them had been victimized by a violent crime, and 52 percent of blacks versus 31 percent of whites answered that they would be afraid to walk alone within two or three blocks of their homes at night.[48]

Furthermore, when it comes to the crime menace, Americans have voted with their feet. Between 1985 and 1990, nearly 47 percent of Americans moved from one residence to another, with more than one in five moving across state or county lines.[49] As a number of studies have shown, crime is now a big factor in Americans' decisions about where to live and when and where to move. Crime has helped fuel suburbanization, depress property values in central business districts, and reduce household incomes.

In sum: on crime and other public policy issues, "voters are not fools" and the American people generally comprise a "rational public."[50] Especially, but not only, with regard to youth crime and violence, the facts and figures support the public's fears, and the concerns that have put crime near the top of the domestic policy agenda are reasonable, not reactionary.

> *When first entering law school, Elaine never dreamed she would become a prosecutor. Like many of her peers, she presumed that the "black struggle" could be best pursued as a member of the defense bar. However, a summer in the public defender's office changed that. "I realized that all of our clients were guilty, some of the most heinous offenses." Shaken from her naivete, she applied for an assistant D.A. position upon graduation. . . . "They're just shooting each other, and we're sweeping up the mess," she says. . . . "I just don't know how long I can go on, staring into the vacant eyes of these children who have, without apparent remorse, done the most awful things." In one case, a 14-year-old child used a baseball bat to bludgeon a parent to death. In another, youngsters aged 13 and 14 collaborated in a robbery-cum-murder, masquerading as drug dealers to lure their prey out of his automobile. . . . Elaine constantly laments that "these little gang bangers have no fear, either of jail or of death, it seems."*
>
> —PROFESSOR GLENN LOURY[51]

New Jersey's maverick former Superior Court Judge, Daniel R. Coburn, long ago earned a statewide reputation as a no-nonsense liberal and father of the Garden State's only highly successful adult and juvenile alternative-to-jail and victim restitution programs. Over the last few years, however, his close encounters with young street toughs have given him pause. He now declares: "Unlike post-Vietnam criminals, who feared prison, police and peers, and took care to avoid arrest and notoriety, this new teenage horde from hell kills, maims, and terrorizes merely to become known or even sometimes for no reason at all. These teens have no fear of dying and no concept of living." Whether many other judges share Coburn's acute awareness of the super-predator problem we do not know. But it is interesting to note that in a 1994 survey of judges conducted by a trade paper for lawyers, 93 percent agreed that juveniles should be fingerprinted, 85 percent said that juvenile records should be available to adult authorities, and 40 percent said that the minimum age for facing murder charges should be 14 or 15.[52]

Asked for an alternative to killing another drug dealer, young murderers in Washington, D.C., speculate only that they could have shot their rival once rather than six times, or could have stabbed instead of shot him. Their sole regret is that incarceration "took a lot of my life"; one went to his victims' funerals to assure himself that they were indeed dead. Most chillingly, some seem incapable of seeing the future as potentially different from the past; "when asked, 'what are your thoughts about the future?' several youth asked for an explanation of the question." One cannot be further removed from the ideology of the American dream than to be unable to imagine a future. . . . I know of no study that systematically examines the racial or class composition of unsocialized delinquents, or analyzes whether their number has changed over time. But a few such people, now armed with Uzis, are at the core of what Cornel West calls the "nihilistic threat to . . . [the] very existence" of black America—the "monumental eclipse of hope, the unprecedented collapse of meaning, the incredible disregard for human (especially black) life and property."

—PROFESSOR JENNIFER L. HOCHSCHILD[53]

THE USUAL SUSPECTS: SOME LIBERAL FALLACIES

Whatever the degree of factual consensus about the drug and crime body count and the rise in youth violence, when it comes to explaining why so many Americans are exposed to so much criminal victimization, liberals and conservatives generally part company, often quickly, and sometimes completely.

Some liberals insist that the problem stems from a lack of meaningful programs; some conservatives insist that it stems from a lack of no-frills prisons. Liberals argue that criminals kill because there are too many guns; conservatives respond that criminals kill because there are too few executions. Liberals assert that the justice system is shot through with procedural racism; conservatives assert that the justice system is shot through with technical loopholes. And while both liberals and conservatives may agree that adverse economic conditions breed crime, the former are more inclined to lament the lack of well-paying jobs, the latter to lament the lack of well-motivated job-seekers.

These are the usual explanatory suspects—programs, prisons, guns, executions, racism, loopholes, and economic circumstances. Each of them, we believe, explains a little. But none of them, either alone or in combination with the others, explains crime and disorder, rampaging youth violence, or the ever-deadly drug-crime nexus.

Poor(ly Socialized) Criminals

No one can deny that street criminals have been, and continue to be, concentrated in economically disadvantaged neighborhoods. Many boys who go on to commit serious crimes do start life in relative material deprivation. From this fact, many leading criminologists of the twentieth century have concluded that poverty and joblessness breed crime. For decades now, the experts have prescribed more government programs to cut poverty and thereby—or so they have argued—reduce crime and delinquency. And, since 1980, not a few leading criminologists have blamed big increases in youth crime on small cuts in the rate of growth in federal spending for social programs.

There is a germ of truth in what they say. Whether funded by government or not, and whether run by bureaucrats or community leaders, any programs that *constructively* engage the youthful energies

of disadvantaged juveniles (indeed, of any juveniles) who might otherwise be hanging out on street corners and looking for trouble have
value. Government programs as diverse as Medicaid (half of the recipients of which are children), Head Start (which offers intensive early
learning experiences to low-income children), job training, and, yes,
even the much-maligned "midnight basketball" can help to keep economically disadvantaged children and young adults on the straight
and narrow.

Other things being equal, kids, rich or poor, who get adequate
medical care, learn well (and stay) in school, receive meaningful prep-
aration for available jobs, and keep busy with athletics or other whole-
some activities are under most conditions less likely to become violent
and repeat criminals. For example, one recent study found that some
government-sponsored apprenticeship programs "can succeed in reducing the boredom and frustration of young people, in raising their
self-esteem through actual accomplishment, in giving them the realistic prospect for a rewarding career. . . . In the cost-benefit analysis of
the Job Corps, the social benefits from reduced crime were among the
most significant in making the program look cost effective." [54] By the
same token, Professor Mark A. Cohen—the same Vanderbilt University economist who carefully estimated the annual social costs per year
of violent crime (over $400 billion) that we cited at the start of
this chapter—has found compelling statistical evidence that public
investments in certain types of programs for high-risk youth do pay
social dividends in the form of reduced crime and fewer other social
ills. [55]

But there is a huge difference between recognizing, on the one
hand, the marginal anti-crime reduction value of certain types of
government social programs, and believing, on the other, that poverty
causes crime, that any program is better than no program, or that all
successful programs can be widely and successfully replicated if only
they are perpetually and lavishly funded by the taxpayers.

In a number of books and articles published since 1975, the country's leading criminologist, UCLA's Professor Wilson, has demolished
the conventional expert wisdom about crime, poverty, and the crime-
reduction value of much-touted (but invariably oversold) social programs. As Wilson has explained:

The root cause of crime, in this view, is poverty and deprivation, which can be ended by social programs. There is certainly more crime in most poor neighborhoods than in most well-off ones and most criminals are less prosperous than most law-abiding citizens. . . . [But] it is far from clear that giving more opportunities or higher incomes to offenders will lead them to commit fewer crimes, and it is even less clear that programs designed to make society as a whole better off will lower the crime rate. I make this point not to denigrate social progress, but to clarify our thinking.[56]

For example, despite increased government spending on many types of social programs, and despite overall economic prosperity, in the 1960s crime rates soared. As Wilson insightfully observed, "crime amidst plenty" was the real "paradox of the sixties."[57] Economically, the first waves of baby-boomers to hit the streets were better off than the tens of millions of Americans who suffered lawfully through the Great Depression. Socially, however, many of America's youth were undoubtedly worse off. And because their numbers increased dramatically, so too did their potential for trouble. "During the first *two* years of the decade of the 1960s, we added more young persons (about 2.6 million) to our populations than we had in any preceding *ten* years since 1930."[58] Wilson cited the provocative words of Princeton University demographer Professor Norman B. Ryder:

There is a perennial invasion of barbarians who must somehow be civilized and turned into contributors to the fulfillment of the various functions requisite to societal survival. . . . The increase in the magnitude of the socialization tasks in the United States during the past decades was completely outside the bounds of previous experience.[59]

Thus, in the 1960s, America's primary socializing institutions— families, schools, churches, and others—were swamped by huge increases in the juvenile population. And, as Wilson perceptively argued, these institutions were starting to crumble at the very moment when they were needed to be towers of socializing strength. This is not a happy precedent for predicting how our society, now enervated as it is by record rates of illegitimate birth, divorce, and related social problems, will cope with the next demographic bulge of juveniles. Indeed, Wilson's comprehensive analysis of crime in the 1960s may prove sadly prophetic for the 1990s and the first decade of the next century:

> There is, perhaps, a "critical mass" of young persons such that, when that number is reached, or when an increase is sudden and large, a self-sustaining chain reaction is set off that creates an explosive increase in the amount of crime, addiction, and welfare dependency. What had once been relatively isolated and furtive acts (copping a fix, stealing a TV) became widespread and group-supported activities.[60]

Increasingly, the "widespread and group-supported activities" of today's juvenile criminals include not just using drugs and stealing but assaulting and senselessly killing.

In a masterful work he co-authored with Professor Richard J. Herrnstein of Harvard University, Wilson summarized the best and latest scientific studies on criminal behavior in relation to a wide array of social, biological, and situational factors.[61] As we read it, their review of the literature indicates that while objective material circumstances apparently do play a role under some conditions, each of many different types of criminal behavior has many possible "root causes."

Economic poverty never stands alone as a determinant of crime, and deviant, delinquent, and criminal behavior never occurs in a social vacuum. Among all economic classes, including low-income people and the poor, it is irritable, impulsive, and poorly socialized males who are most likely to commit crimes, and "after all is said and done, the most serious offenders are boys who begin their criminal careers at a very early age."[62] Even early intervention government programs like Head Start, which reach economically disadvantaged children early, actually do little to reduce crime and delinquency, least of all among children whose families have failed them.[63]

> *[There is a] nearly invisible relationship between unemployment and crime rates. Charting homicide since 1900 reveals two peaks. The first is in 1933. This represents the crest of a wave that began in 1905, continued through the prosperous '20s and then began to*

*decline in 1934 as the Great Depression was deepening. Between
1933 and 1940 the murder rate dropped nearly 40%. Property
crimes reveal a similar pattern.*

—DAVID RUBINSTEIN[64]

*From slavery times until present, black families and churches
helped people resist this insidious effect of oppression. How they
did so is one of the most important things we have to think about
here. We know already, from bitter experience, what happens when
these crucial institutions can no longer play their vital role. . . .
The failure to pass on the values that helped black Americans to
survive not decades, but several centuries, of mistreatment is taking an awesome toll, especially among the young. In many urban
neighborhoods today, random murder stalks the streets. The stray
bullets of gang clashes and drug-related executions claim the lives
of infants and passersby. . . . When a people has passed through
hell and survived to curse the devil, why should they suddenly
collapse just as they push aside its open gates? Can the answer be
racism or economic deprivation? If so, how do we explain the fact
that our ancestors endured racial and economic abuse that was
arguably greater and more systematic than we face now, yet managed to resist self-destructive moral disintegration of the type that
is killing our people today?*

—DR. ALAN L. KEYES[65]

RACIAL DISPARITIES

Racism is an even less persuasive explanation for the present-day
crime problem than poverty. Tragically, it is true that until the second
half of this century, America's criminal justice institutions, like many
other American institutions, were guilty of discrimination based on
race. Fortunately, however, the justice system, like the rest of American society, has come a long way.

As a National Research Council study, published by the National
Academy of Sciences, concluded, "Few criminologists would argue
that the current gap between black and white levels of imprisonment
is mainly due to discrimination in sentencing or in any of the other
decision-making processes in the criminal justice system."[66] Once one

controls for such characteristics as the offender's criminal history or whether an eyewitness to the crime was present, racial disparities melt away. To cite a typical example, a 1991 RAND Corporation study of adult robbery and burglary defendants in fourteen large urban jurisdictions across the country found that a defendant's race or ethnic group bore almost no relation to conviction rates, disposition times, or other key outcome measures.[67]

In 1980, 46.6 percent of state prisoners and 34.4 percent of federal prisoners were black. As the prison population increased during the 1980s, the percentage of it that consisted of blacks changed little. By 1990, 48.9 percent of state prisoners and 31.4 percent of federal prisoners were black. Compared to white prisoners of the same age, black prisoners were more likely to have committed crimes of violence. In 1988 the median time served in confinement by black violent offenders was 25 months, versus 24 months for white violent offenders. For crimes of violence, the mean sentence length for whites was 110 months versus 116 months for blacks, while the mean time served in confinement differed by only 4 months (33 months for whites versus 37 months for blacks).[68]

At the federal level, a 1993 study showed that the imposition between 1986 and 1990 of stiffer penalties for drug offenders, especially crack cocaine traffickers, did not result in racially disparate sentences. The amount of the drug sold, the seriousness of the offenders' prior criminal records, whether or not weapons were involved, and other characteristics of offenses and offenders that federal law and sentencing guidelines establish as valid considerations in sentencing decisions accounted for all of the observed variations in imprisonment sentences.[69]

Similarly, a recent analysis of data representing 42,500 defendants in the nation's 75 largest counties finds "no evidence that, in the places where blacks in the United States have most of their contacts with the justice system, the system treats them more harshly than whites."[70] The same species of conclusion holds firmly for the death penalty. As a recent review of the scientific literature demonstrated beyond a reasonable doubt, once one controls for all relevant legal and other variables, there is simply no systematic evidence of racial disparities in post-1972 capital sentencing.[71]

In short, the best available research indicates that race is not a significant variable in determining whether a convicted adult offender is sentenced to probation or prison, the length of the term imposed, or how prisoners are disciplined.[72]

What, then, is one to make of the widely reported reality that a third of black men in their twenties are under some form of correctional supervision today (about one-third of them in prison or jail, the rest on probation or parole)? The same, we think, that one should make of the fact that blacks are about 50 times more likely to commit violent crimes against whites than whites are to commit violent crimes against blacks.[73] Both sad statistics originate largely in the fact that young black males commit crime at higher rates than do young white males. For example, "although blacks have constituted approximately 12 percent of the nation's population, they have accumulated 50 to 60 percent of the arrests for criminal homicide, about 50 percent of the arrests for forcible rape, close to 60 percent of the arrests for robbery, and between 40 and 50 percent of the arrests for aggravated assault."[74] Blacks have been "responsible for a disproportionate amount of serious violent crime."[75]

As our colleague on the Council on Crime in America John W. Gillis has stressed, the rap sheets of convicted black drug dealers and violent felons are punctuated with crimes reported by and committed against other blacks. Gillis, a black veteran police officer and parole chief, is right. He does not argue—nor do we—that there is absolutely no racism in America or inside the justice system. That would be ridiculous. The point is not that "there's no racism." The point is that racism does not even begin to explain racial disproportionalities in the system; real differences in crime rates do.

Here's a suggestive calculation.[76] In 1991, 372,200 black men were in prison, along with 363,600 white men. About 60 percent of all prisoners in 1991 had committed one or more violent crimes in the past. Suppose that we released 40 percent of the black prisoners—the 40 percent, say, with either no official history of violence or the least severe records of it. That would leave 223,320 black men behind bars. Then, because slightly more than half of the violent crimes committed by blacks are committed against whites, let's release, say, 55 percent of the remaining black violent male offenders. That would leave 100,494

black males in prison, 27 percent of 1991's actual total. They would
be doing time with 3.6 times as many white males. But since whites in
the general population still would outnumber blacks by roughly eight
to one, the racial "disproportionality" would persist. To make it disap-
pear completely—to get an eight-to-one white-black ratio in prison
—we would have to release all but 45,450 of the 372,200 black men
in prison in 1991.

Similarly, 605,062 black adults were on probation in 1993, compared with 1,132,092 white adults, and 240,767 black adults were on
parole, compared with 236,083 white adults. Thus, the total black
adult community-based corrections population (probation plus parole)
numbered 845,829, compared with 1.37 million whites. Let's say we
believed that fully 70 percent of all black probationers and parolees,
but none of the white ones, were innocent victims of a racist "war on
drugs" and should never have been arrested. That would leave 253,749
black adults on probation and parole. We would still have only 5.3,
not eight, times as many white adults as blacks "in custody" in the
community. To eliminate entirely the racial "disproportionalities" in
probation and parole, all but about 170,000 of the more than 800,000
black adults under community-based supervision in 1993 would have
to be expunged from the rolls.

Nonetheless, it would be odd if black Americans were not ambiva-
lent about the justice system. After all, blacks have been, and continue
to be, singled out and treated unfairly for such "crimes" as "DWB"
(driving while black).[77] We all know this happens, and, as Americans,
we all must feel deeply ashamed and work to see that it stops, here
and now, once and for all.

By the same token, it is again worth stressing that differences in
crime rates reflect differences in social circumstances and socializing
influences. As we will discuss a bit later in this chapter, the disproportionate number of black children who commit crimes is largely trace-
able to the disproportionate number of black children who grow up
without two parents, and who suffer abuse and neglect.

As we will document in the next two chapters, if the system is racist
in any true sense of the word, it is racist in that it permits the black
body count to mount so high by allowing known, adjudicated violent
and repeat criminals to find fresh victims as they circulate in and out

of custody, and by doing so little to combat drug trafficking. For no Americans suffer more from revolving-door justice and anemic anti-drug policies than do black Americans, solid majorities of whom strongly oppose legalizing drugs and favor incarcerating violent and chronic criminals, adult and juvenile.

> *Henry's mother swears she has not used cocaine in three weeks, but her good pink suit cannot hide the shaking in her voice and the twitches in her body as she begs juvenile court Judge Cheryl Allen Craig for her children's return. Her 13-year-old son, slumped in a chair between his younger brother and his lawyer, has his own troubles. "Henry" (not his real name) has helped adult friends commit a burglary, regularly ditches his after-school probation program and has been shot twice, the last time at Christmas. Craig keeps Henry in a cousin's care and orders Pittsburgh police to take him to the juvenile jail if he misses curfew. "I'd rather have you be an angry, alive child than a dead child," she says. . . . Three days a week, children come to answer charges that they have committed a crime. On the other two days, the court hears cases of child abuse and neglect and of parents needing help controlling their children. . . . Police accustomed to picking up 16- and 17-year-olds are now arresting 12- and 13-year-olds.*[78]

THE USUAL SUSPECTS: SOME CONSERVATIVE FALLACIES

The usual liberal explanations relating to poverty and racism fall far short of explaining the body count. But that does not mean the body count explanations of some conservatives—relating to prisons (make them tougher), executions (make them more certain for capital crimes), guns (make them more widely available to law-abiding citizens), and legal loopholes (close them)—are correct, complete, or realistic.

1. More "No-Frills" Prisons: Less Crime and Delinquency?
For most of American history, prisons were hellholes. In the twentieth century, prisons became more humane. Today, prisoners enjoy a wide variety of constitutional and legal rights. While some federal and state prisons have been terribly "overcrowded," at the end of 1994

thirteen states had more prison beds than prisoners.[79] The relationship between "overcrowding" and inmate violence, illness, and other problems is by no means as simple as it might seem.[80] Many dedicated and competent prison managers have run overcrowded prisons without any increases in such problems.[81] Moreover, as the nation's prison stock has grown, an ever larger fraction of all prisoners has been housed in new, well-designed minimum- and medium-security facilities, not old, dungeon-like maximum-security structures. In many states half or more of every prison dollar is now spent not on custody or security basics but on prisoner medical services, education, "treatment programs," and other functions.[82] Over 90 percent of prisoners enjoy some type of training, program activity, or work assignment.[83]

Some conservatives believe that prisons coddle criminals, and that toughening prison conditions is a key to cutting crime. We would certainly agree that some prisons are virtual resorts.[84] And while we are persuaded that certain types of no-nonsense prison-based programs are definitely worthwhile (if only as prison management tools or intrinsic aspects of humane confinement), we would also agree that the empirical evidence in support of the rehabilitative value of most prison-based programs remains mixed, anemic, or nonexistent.[85]

There are, to be sure, good moral and cost-effectiveness arguments for scaling back prisoner amenities and services. After all, why in the world should violent and repeat criminals enjoy at taxpayer expense educational programs, health plans, recreational equipment, and other benefits that many law-abiding citizens can hardly afford for themselves and their children?

But it is, we believe, a mistake to think that "no-frills" prisons are the answer to crime and delinquency. Remember: most criminals don't expect to get caught, convicted, and locked away in the first place. Many felons think little about the risks of going to prison, and even less about likely conditions of confinement should they prove so "unlucky." One study, for example, found that half of state prisoners convicted of a crime that carried a mandatory prison term did not know the penalty structure at the time they did the crime; half of those who didn't know said they would have done the crime even if they had.[86] Likewise, a recent ethnography of "persistent thieves" by Professor Neal Shover reveals that "young offenders know little and care less about the schedule of penalties. . . . Juveniles and young adults often have little awareness or appreciation of the legal and personal repercussions of their criminality."[87] As one subject said, when he was young he "just didn't give a fuck, you know. I was young, simple, man. . . . Doing time to me was nothing, you know."[88]

It is, therefore, a bit fanciful to suppose that many violent and career criminals, least of all the young ones, would respond to the threat of more spartan prison conditions by ceasing to behave like street gladiators. Few street criminals would forgo the immediate pleasures of crime (sex, drugs, money) in order to avoid the future deprivations of a "no-frills" prison life—no cable television, no barbells, no Pell education grants.

Of course, forcing those who do end up behind bars to do long, hard time would undoubtedly avert crimes and increase the marginal deterrence value of prisons. But we know of no evidence to suggest that doing so would deter the young, impulsive army of youth predators about whom we are most concerned. As we will explain in the next chapter, despite recent "get tough" policy changes, only a tiny fraction of all criminal victimizations results in a prison term.

Thus, whatever the moral or cost-effectiveness rationales for taking excessive amenities and services away from incarcerated felons (and we sympathize with these rationales), eliminating prison "frills" ought not to be viewed as a practical or moral substitute for ending revolving-door justice. And to those who insist that a return to such practices as chain gangs and the rock pile are our only hopes, we commend a prison library full of books on the racially polarizing legacy of such obsolete and discredited approaches.

2. Death Penalty: Symbolism vs. Substance[89]

Between 1977 and 1993 a third of a million Americans were murdered. Now take this multiple-choice test and guess what happened to their killers:

1. How many people were on death row in 1993 for all those lives stolen since 1977?
   (a) 58,590
   (b) 14,152
   (c) 2,716

2. How many of the thousands of individuals on death row in 1993
   were actually put to death that year?
   (a) 491
   (b) 164
   (c) 38
3. Between 1977 and 1993, how many murderers do you suppose
   were executed in America in total?
   (a) 22,600
   (b) 2,260
   (c) 226
4. What is the average sentence these days of someone in state
   prison for murder?
   (a) 40 years
   (b) 30 years
   (c) 20 years
5. How much time does the average murderer actually spend in
   lockup before being released?
   (a) 21 years
   (b) 14.7 years
   (c) 8.5 years

The correct answer to each question is "c." Which means that our
justice system's message to anyone who believes murder should be
punished by the death penalty is currently something like: "Get lost!"

In recent years, no state has executed more murderers than Texas.
In 1993 Texas carried out 17 capital punishments; Virginia was a
distant second with five. But Texas, like other states, had commuted
all death sentences to life imprisonment after the Supreme Court
abolished the death penalty in 1972, and a recent study by Professor
James W. Marquart tells us what happened to those death row inmates
when Texas stopped executing them.[90] It reveals that since 1974 about
three times as many Texas prisoners have been released from death
row by commutation or judicial reversals or dismissals as have been
executed. After being released into the general prison population, 12
of 47 commuted prisoners were responsible for 21 serious violent offenses against other inmates and prison staff. One commuted death
row inmate killed another prisoner. And within a year of his release
on parole, another commuted death row prisoner killed a girl.

This is not to say that every murderer on death row would murder again if released. But these individuals do tend to be repeat criminals. Over 40 percent of the persons on death row in 1992 were on probation, parole, or pretrial release at the time they murdered.

One of the things that has obstructed and delayed the carrying out of death sentences most is fear that they might be handed out in racially unfair ways. There are scores of studies that test this by weighing racial factors in capital sentencing. As noted earlier in this chapter, those studies that control for all relevant factors including crucial legal variables (eyewitnesses present, aggravating circumstances) find absolutely no evidence of racial bias in contemporary capital sentencing. Of those persons under sentence of death in 1993, about 58 percent were white. This is actually much higher than the proportion of all murderers who are white.

No matter what type of realistic reforms might be adopted to reduce the endless legal appeals that currently block most death sentences from being completed, America is never going to make it easy or inexpensive to execute convicted killers. Besides, the real bottleneck discouraging use of the death penalty today is not at the back end, it's at the front end: prosecutors wary of controversy don't seek the death penalty if they can help it, least of all in racially charged cases. When the Supreme Court terminated the death penalty in 1972, murder cases fell into the plea-bargaining pit along with other violent crimes. When the Court reinstated the death penalty in 1976, prosecutors were not eager to pull it out. Today, the bureaucratic, mass-assembly culture of most big-city district attorney's offices favors doing a little deterrence on the cheap, and frankly, not a lot of justice at great effort and financial cost.

Every major opinion survey of the last decade shows that majorities of Americans—whites, blacks, young and old alike—support the execution of murderers. Americans value the death penalty not just for its utility as a crime-reduction tool but also as a way of doing justice. Only a tiny fraction of even the most vicious killers ever get executed. Neither deterrence nor justice can possibly be achieved in this way.

In our view, there is a moral case for the death penalty, and for preventing duly-convicted killers from seeking one appeal after another. But there is not a chance that the death penalty in America can be retrieved from symbolism and made into a substantive tool of crime control. Conservatives who hope to reduce the body count by increasing or speeding executions are bound to be mightily disappointed.

3. Guns: Straight Shooters? [91]

As the nation's big-city police know all too well, much inner-city crime, especially the murderous violence wrought by drug-financed street gangs, involves guns. In the 1980s the Fraternal Order of Police became a principal voice in support of strict gun control measures. Between 1981 and 1994, such proposals as a weeklong waiting period for the purchase of handguns sparked intense constitutional arguments in Congress and frantic lobbying efforts behind the scenes by groups opposing and favoring gun control. Unfortunately, however, there is little empirical knowledge about the crime reduction effects of such measures. Police and other proponents of gun control measures were unable to muster much systematic evidence in support of their position because such evidence simply did not exist.

In 1981 the Attorney General's Task Force on Violent Crime recommended measures that would tighten controls on gun ownership and require states to adopt a mandatory waiting period to allow for a records check to see whether a prospective handgun buyer had a criminal history.[92] This Reagan administration proposal, and the gun control bills that have since been debated in Congress, were common-sense responses to the fact that many crimes, including about 60 percent of all murders, involve firearms. Moreover, in every year since 1972, at least 70 percent of the general public has favored some gun control measures. The movement in favor of gun control that grew up around the efforts of former White House spokesman James Brady, who was shot in the 1981 attempt on President Reagan's life, put the nation's most powerful opposing group, the National Rifle Association, on the defensive.

The question, however, is how efficacious such measures are likely to be in reducing gun-related crime. Nobody knows the number of guns held privately in this country. Some have estimated at least one-fifth of American homes have guns.[93] Numerous federal, state, and local laws already regulate the manufacture, sale, and use of most firearms. What, if anything, additional federal laws add to the crime reduction effects of the existing battery of state and local laws remains unclear.

Despite the paucity of meaningful evidence, both liberals who favor gun control and conservatives who oppose it continue to make sweeping generalizations about what works and what doesn't. For example, some pro-gun-control advocates have already pronounced the Brady Bill a major success. Never mind that the information systems needed to implement the law have been slow to develop. Meanwhile, some anti-gun-control advocates have already applauded the success of "shall issue" concealed-weapons laws that extend gun permits to any of-age applicant who's not a convicted felon or mental outpatient. Never mind that there has yet to be a systematic study of the effects of these laws in the twenty-eight states that had adopted them as of early 1996.

To be frank, neither side in the gun control debate has been shooting entirely straight with the facts and figures. There are important truths on both sides. For example, we fail to see any argument for permitting easy access to assault weapons. By the same token, however, we accept the evidence, amassed mainly by Professor Gary Kleck, which indicates that the vast majority of citizens who possess guns do no harm to themselves or others, and often succeed in using their weapons to foil criminal mischief against their persons and property.[94]

If more (or fewer) guns is the answer, then precisely what is the question? More (or fewer) guns in whose hands under what conditions? Conservatives who insist that a libertarian approach to guns is best needed to explain how putting more guns in the hands of more juvenile super-predators won't further increase the body count. Of course, they can't, because putting more guns in those hot, hair-trigger hands would only bring more death.

We agree with Professors Mark H. Moore and Philip J. Cook when they write that the "goal of gun control policy over the next decade should be to develop and evaluate specific gun control measures that can reduce gun crimes, suicides, and accidents, while preserving as much legitimate use of guns as possible . . . a portfolio of policies that reflects the full array of gun 'problems' . . . [and] differ[s] according to local circumstances and values."[95]

Our view, then, is that gun control cannot reverse crime trends; those who argue that gun control legislation is the most important step we can take to reduce crime—and hence ought to be the center-piece of anti-crime legislation—are simply deluding themselves. At the same time, we believe that some gun control laws can make a small positive difference—and so we believe they are well worth doing. Specifically, we support the eminently reasonable provisions of the Brady bill. Laws that succeed in restricting the circulation of guns to criminals are bound to have a positive effect—and in fact, they do.

4. Blame It on Miranda?

The last in our lineup of usual suspects are the legal loopholes that conservatives love to hate—exclusionary rules that prohibit illegally seized evidence from being used in criminal trials; unlimited appeals by felons who have been tried and convicted many times; and procedural requirements such as the Miranda rule, which makes even a voluntary, uncoerced confession by a suspect who hasn't been read his rights inadmissible in court.

The United States Supreme Court issued its Miranda decision on June 13, 1966. The court held that under the Fifth Amendment ("No person . . . shall be compelled in any criminal case to be a witness against himself"), the police must inform a suspect that he has the right to remain silent, warn him that anything he says might be used against him in court, and tell him that he has the immediate right to a lawyer (a defender provided at public expense if he can't afford one). As one thoughtful conservative critic of Miranda, Robert James Bidinotto, has noted, should "the police make the slightest omission or error in this ritual, any evidence they get can be thrown out, and the suspect can 'walk.' "[96]

There can be no question that in a number of cases justice is delayed or denied because of Miranda and Miranda-style legal loopholes. But how many cases, and with what overall impact on crime? The highest estimates have been made in two recent articles by Professor Paul G. Cassell. He finds that about "3.8 percent of cases are lost due to Miranda," a total which includes about "28,000 arrests for serious crimes of violence and 79,000 arrests for property crimes . . . and al-most the same number of cases are disposed of on terms favorable for defendants."[97]

Even if one took these estimates at face value, it would be hard to know what they mean. As Cassell himself explains, "We have little knowledge about what police interrogation looked like shortly after Miranda, much less what it looks like today. How many suspects waive their Miranda rights? How many confess? How important are confessions to the outcome of prosecutions? Even the most informed observers can offer little beyond speculation on these fundamental subjects." [98]

No one can say for sure how, if at all, police might perform better if they did not have to "Mirandize" suspects. Likewise, while relaxing exclusionary rules on evidence and curtailing prisoner appeals are desirable for the sake of justice, just how much lower would the body count be if illegally obtained evidence were routinely admitted in court and the appeals process was short-circuited?

That counterfactual question will never be answered. We can trim the pro-criminal, pro-prisoner excesses of the present-day system, but we will quickly discover that only minor changes are possible lest we wish to tinker with the Bill of Rights. As UCLA's Wilson has reminded us, Americans "have preserved and even extended the most comprehensive array of civil liberties found in any nation on earth despite rising crime rates and (in the 1960s) massive civil disorder." The price of our "wide-ranging bill of rights" includes "a willingness both to accept a somewhat higher rate of crime and disorder than we might otherwise have and to invest a greater amount of resources in those institutions (the police, the prosecutors, the courts, the prisons) needed to cope with those who violate our law while claiming its protections." [99]

Thus, even if we enacted such reasonable measures to close legal loopholes as are politically feasible—and we think we should—the body count would still mount.

Participation in East Jersey State Prison's "Lifers' Group" doesn't shorten any inmate's sentence. . . . What it does, and has done for 20 years, is give inmates who have essentially thrown away the bulk of their lives the chance to make a difference in the lives of complete strangers, a chance to keep some kid from making the same mistakes the Lifers themselves have made. . . . The Lifers' confrontational, almost brutal, method of bringing home the reality

*of prison life quickly gained notoriety around the country. The
program was captured on the Oscar-winning 1978 documentary
film, "Scared Straight." . . . And the kids are getting harder and
harder to "scare straight." Lt. Randall Sandkuhl, a corrections
officer who works with the Lifers, said some of the young men and
women who come in are already so hardened and tough they end
up scaring the inmates. "You stand next to a kid in court and hear
the judge sentence them to 40 years in prison without parole and
they turn to you and say, 'What's for lunch, officer?' " Sandkuhl
said. "They just don't care."* [100]

THE TRUE CULPRIT

So, if it's not the handicaps we've imposed on cops and prosecutors,
and it's not institutionalized racism, and it's not material want, then
what *is* the fundamental cause of predatory street crime?

Moral poverty.

Moral poverty mocks well-intentioned programs and fills no-frills
prisons. Moral poverty makes some young men pull triggers the way
some old men fire off angry letters. Moral poverty unleashes more
murderers in a single year than America has executed in this century.
Moral poverty makes both racism and legal loopholes mere backdrops
in a crime drama featuring family disintegration, child abuse, and child
neglect. And moral poverty, not economic poverty, is what marks
some disadvantaged youngsters for a life of drugs and crime while
passing over others in equal or greater material distress.

To repeat what we mentioned in Chapter 1: moral poverty is the
poverty of being without loving, capable, responsible adults who teach
you right from wrong; the poverty of being without parents and other
authorities who habituate you to feel joy at others' joy, pain at others'
pain, satisfaction when you do right, remorse when you do wrong; the
poverty of growing up in the virtual absence of people who teach
morality by their own everyday example and who insist that you
follow suit. In the extreme, moral poverty is the poverty of growing up
severely abused and neglected at the hands of deviant, delinquent, or
criminal adults.

Whatever their material circumstances, kids of whatever creed, color, demographic description, socioeconomic status, region, or zip code are far more likely to become (pace West Side Story) criminally depraved when they are morally deprived. The abject moral poverty that produces super-predators most often begins very early in life in settings where deep and abiding love is nowhere but unmerciful abuse is the norm. An extremely morally impoverished beginning early in life makes children vicious who are by nature merely aggressive, makes children remorseless who are disposed to be uncaring, and makes children radically impulsive who have difficulty sitting still, concentrating, and thinking ahead. In general, we believe, today's juvenile super-predators are children who, in order to be civilized and socialized into adulthood, would have needed a maximum dosage of moral tutelage from parents, teachers, coaches, clergy, and other responsible adults, but instead received either no such moral education, or were persistently exposed to its opposite by adults who severely abused and neglected them, encouraged them to act out, and rewarded their antisocial words and deeds.

The twin character scars left by moral poverty—lack of impulse control and lack of empathy—reinforce each other and make it far more likely that the individual will succumb to either the temptations of crime, or the blandishments of drugs, or, as so often happens, both. Once a morally impoverished individual has mixed crime with drugs, he is far more likely to go right on mixing them, and, in turn, pursuing whatever instant gratifications he desires (sex, money, laughs, "respect"), and at whatever human and financial cost to others (up to and including the sudden loss of their lives) it may entail.

Below we will flesh out some of the empirical evidence that we believe supports our theory of moral poverty, and justifies our confidence that its explanatory reach far exceeds the explanatory grasp of any and all of the usual suspects.

The flip side of moral poverty is moral health. Being born healthy to or raised by loving biological or adoptive parents or guardians of whatever race, creed, color, socioeconomic status, or demographic description is perhaps the luckiest fate that can befall a human being. To be born into or raised by such a family, and to grow up surrounded by loving, caring, responsible adults—parents or guardians, neighbors, teachers, coaches, clergy—is to be raised in moral wealth.

Children need the love, attention, and guiding discipline of loving, caring, responsible adults who are there to hug and scold, encourage and restrain, reward and punish in accordance with basic social norms governing how people should relate to one another—speak respectfully to peers and authorities; use physical force against others only in self-defense; never simply to express anger for "the fun" of it; and so on. To become civilized and socialized, let alone to be made cooperative and good-natured, all children need to be taught right from wrong by adults who, most if not all of the time, teach it by their own, everyday example.

As every parent of more than one child knows, children differ in their personalities, temperaments, and sociability. Before they're out of diapers, some children seem to listen and cooperate almost without being told; others seem naturally disposed to go their own way; and a few behave like "untamed terrors." Generally speaking, and other things being equal, boys are a harder-to-tame, harder-to-socialize lot than girls, and some boys are naturally more irritable, more impulsive, and harder to control than others.

Thus, some children require more, and more persistent, adult guidance and supervision than others if they are to become good adults (at the outside) and refrain from wantonly harming other people or stealing their property (at a minimum). In any functional society, even most "untamed terrors" and "troubled teens" become good people. Most never even come close to being totally self-centered liars, thieves, domestic abusers, or violent predators. The reason is that along the way—in homes, in schools, on playing fields, in churches, and elsewhere—most receive the necessary doses of loving, caring, responsible adult guidance and supervision they need.

Of course, growing up nestled in a loving, stable, economically solvent two-parent family in a relatively drug-and-crime-free community is best, but it is by no means the only way for a child to accumulate the moral capital needed for a successful journey to adulthood.

For example, a recent study by Public/Private Ventures, the country's premier youth and community development research organization, examined 959 10- to 16-year-olds who applied to Big Brothers/ Big Sisters (BB/BS) of America. Just over 60 percent were boys, and more than half were minority group members (of those, about 70 percent were black). Almost all lived with one parent (the mother, in most cases), the rest with a guardian or relatives. Many were from low-income households, and a significant number came from households with a prior history of either family violence or substance abuse (in some cases both). Just the same, compared to otherwise comparable children not in the BB/BS program, Little Brothers and Little Sisters who met with their "Bigs" regularly for about a year were 46 percent less likely than their peers to start using illegal drugs, and 32 percent less likely than their peers to assault someone, not to mention less likely than their peers to skip school, get poor grades, or start drinking.[101]

The BB/BS example is but one of many powerful illustrations of the fact that, even among children who are well out of diapers, and even where the positive adult-child relationship happens as it does in BB/BS for only three to four hours three times a month, *positive nonparental adult influences can make a positive difference in the lives of even the most at-risk youth.*

The single most important body count, super-predator reality with which we are dealing, therefore, is that millions of children in America today are neither born into the bosom of loving, caring, responsible adults, nor given much in the way of positive adult supervision and guidance outside the home. More and more children in this country are growing up not in moral wealth but in abject moral poverty.

> *We assume that for a man to become good he must first be trained and habituated properly, and then go on to spend his time, in the spirit thus engendered, on worthy occupations, doing nothing base or mean, either willingly or unwillingly.*
>
> —ARISTOTLE,
> THE ETHICS[102]

> *His home on the southwest side of Detroit was a crack house. His father used to beat his mother. Jacob saw his sister shot in the face when he was 4 or 5. His father was shot to death in a bar fight about the same time. . . . He has seen family members pull guns on one another. . . . He was 9 when he took his first drag of mari-*

juana. An older sister gave it to him. . . . Court records show that
[Jacob's mother] drank heavily, used crack and once even sold her
children's clothes for drug money. She failed to show up at Jacob's
first court hearings on the armed-robbery charge. She was drunk
when she finally came to testify. . . . She did not even know her
son's birthday.[103]

The empirical evidence to support our moral poverty theory of
crime and delinquency is diverse, pervasive, and, we think, commonsensical. Our theory is that, *ceteris paribus*, the probability that a child
will become a super-predator or adult career criminal varies inversely
with the number and quality of positive and persistent adult influences
in a child's life (parents, teachers, coaches, clergy, and others). Moral
wealth breeds social health; moral poverty breeds crime and social
decay.

For starters, consider the findings of several recent and sophisticated
studies:

- In a major re-analysis of data from a classic study of crime and
  delinquency, Robert J. Sampson and John H. Laub confirmed the
  primacy of family factors: "Despite controlling for these individual difference constructs, all family effects retained their significant predictive power. And once again mother's supervision had
  the largest of all effects on delinquency, whether official or unof-
  ficial. A major finding of our analysis is that family process variables are strongly and directly related to delinquency . . . family
  processes of informal social control still explain the largest share
  of variance in adolescent delinquency."[104]
- A study by Professor Daniel S. Nagin and others explored the
  relationship between adolescent motherhood and the criminality
  of her offspring. The study revealed a birds-of-a-feather phenomenon. About "25 percent of boys with criminal fathers also have
  a criminal mother, compared to 4 percent in the case of non-
  criminal fathers. Similarly, 67 percent of boys with criminal
  mothers also have a criminal father, compared to just 19 percent
  when the mother is not convicted. . . . Our results suggest that
  the children latest in the birth order of women who begin

childbearing early are at greatest risk of criminality. This finding appears to reflect the coming together of the deleterious impacts of poor parenting and role modeling and diminished resources per child." [105]

- A study of "resilient youth"—the half of all high-risk children who do not engage in delinquency or drug use—by Professor Carolyn Smith and others indicates that child "maltreatment itself has for a long time been associated with problematic outcomes for children. . . . Considerable research in both criminology and child development suggests that family deviance, including criminality and substance abuse of family members, affects developing children because such parents are likely to tolerate and model deviance for children." [106]

- A National Institute of Justice statistical analysis found that maltreatment of children increased their chances of future delinquency and criminality by 40 percent. [107]

- In the most significant ethnography of urban street criminals published in over a decade, Professor Mark S. Fleisher concludes: "An abundance of scholarly research shows that anti-social and delinquent tendencies emerge early in the lives of neglected, abused, and unloved youngsters, often by age nine. My ethnographic data support these findings and show that, once these youngsters leave home and go on the street, they are at best difficult to extricate from street culture. . . . In 1991, 50 percent of an estimated 6.4 million nonfatal acts of violent crime were committed by these adolescents and young-adult street criminals." [108]

At age nine, Willie Bosket was in a state reformatory, the same reformatory that his father, Butch—a man he never met—had entered at age nine. There Willie assaulted, stole, and choked a nurse in the "Quiet Room." Lesser delinquents praised him: "Man, you real bad." At one point, he fought one of the men who kept company with his mother. His mother rarely visited him. Butch had been beaten by his father, James, who also sexually abused his grandson Willie. By age 15, Willie was shooting and robbing New York subway passengers. He killed two men in cold blood. Released after five years because he was technically still a juvenile, he did more crime, and in 1988 attempted to murder a prison guard. By then, he had done some 2,000 crimes, including 200 armed robberies, 25 stabbings, numerous for-fun-and-profit shootings, and the two murders. "Boiled down to its core," summarizes Willie's biographer, Fox Butterfield of the New York Times, the best research reveals "that most adolescents who become delinquents, and the overwhelming majority of adults who commit violent crimes, started very young. . . . They were the impulsive, aggressive, irritable children. . . . If children know someone is watching them and they may get caught, they are less likely to get into trouble." Nobody tended to Willie. Now, however, someone is watching him—watching him do three 25-years-to-life sentences in a prison isolation cell, that is.[109]

Additional evidence of the dire criminogenic consequences of moral poverty in America—if any is needed—is easy to come by.[110] For example, a National Research Council study of adolescents in high-risk settings concluded that adults "in poor neighborhoods differ in important ways from those in more affluent areas." These neighborhoods lack "good role models for adolescents" and have a "far higher percentage of adults who are involved in illegal markets. The poorest of neighborhoods seem increasingly unable to restrain criminal or deviant behaviors."[111]

That is a polite and politic way of saying that some fraction of children who grow up in inner-city neighborhoods today grow up amidst deviant, delinquent, and crime-prone teenagers and elders, many of them felons, ex-felons, and drug addicts. Indeed, as almost every seasoned prison official knows, virtually all prisoners begin their criminal careers early in life, and a large fraction of them come from families where fathers, mothers, or siblings have also been in trouble with the law.

Studies show that more than half of young persons in long-term state juvenile institutions have one or more immediate family members (father, mother, sibling) who have also been incarcerated. A study that compared the family experiences of more violent and less violent incarcerated juveniles found that 75 percent of the former group had suffered serious abuse by a family member, while "only" 33 percent of the latter group had been abused. Likewise, 78 percent of the more violent group had been witnesses to extreme violence, while 20 percent of the less violent group had been witnesses.[112]

Most prisoners come from single-parent families, more than one-quarter have parents who have abused drugs or alcohol, and nearly one-third have a brother with a jail or prison record. Many produce the same sad experience for their own children. In 1991 male and female prisoners were parents to more than 825,000 children under age 18.[113] The facts about women in state prisons are particularly revealing and disturbing. Women in state prisons in 1991 were most likely to be between the ages of 25 and 34 (50 percent). Between 1986 and 1991 the number of women in state prisons rose by 75 percent. More than 70 percent of female prisoners had served a previous sentence. About 58 percent of them grew up in a household without both parents present; more than half had used drugs, including crack cocaine, in the month before the current offense; 47 percent had at least one immediate family member who had also been incarcerated; 43 percent had been physically or sexually abused; and 34 percent had parents or guardians who abused alcohol or drugs.[114]

There are countless analyses of how best to help inner-city children resist the blandishments of alcohol and drugs, remain in school, and avoid criminal involvement and victimization. For example, a 1993 report by the Office of Juvenile Justice and Delinquency Prevention concluded that the "behavioral factors that contribute to serious, violent, and chronic juvenile crime" are delinquent peer groups, poor school performance, high-crime neighborhoods, weak family attachments, lack of consistent discipline, and physical or sexual abuse. The first of the OJJDP's "key principles for preventing and reducing juvenile delinquency" is "strengthen families."[115]

The punch line to the old joke about the economist marooned on a desert island with unopened cans of food is, "Assume a can opener!" The punch line of virtually all juvenile delinquency prevention research is, "Assume a good family!" or "Assume a better neighborhood!" The problem is that so many children who go on to become serious juvenile offenders and predatory adult criminals begin life in homes and neighborhoods where the teenagers and adults in their midst are hardly more likely to nurture, teach, and care for them than they are to expose them to neglect, abuse, and violence.

As a study of delinquent and high-risk young people in California concluded, we "know from a number of well-designed studies that chronic delinquency usually has its origins in early childhood experiences."[116] Very bad boys do come disproportionately from very bad homes in very bad neighborhoods. As a survey of the literature on the need for intensive interventions into the lives of high-risk youths concluded, most juveniles who "engaged in frequent criminal acts against persons and property . . . come from family settings characterized by high levels of violence, chaos, and dysfunction."[117]

As is commonly believed, a good deal of the violence, chaos, and dysfunction in these crime-infested settings is related to drug and alcohol abuse. Studies show that alcohol abuse is a major public health problem in inner-city black neighborhoods. Nearly one-quarter of state prisoners initially became involved in crime to get money for drugs. Children who are exposed regularly to substance-abusing adults are far more likely to develop substance abuse and related problems of their own later in life than otherwise comparable children who are not so exposed.

LIQUOR, DISORDER, AND CRIME

Following the L.A. riots of 1992, two reporters for U.S. News & World Report, *David Whitman and David Bowermaster, perceptively challenged their readers to imagine the life of a typical inner-city child who lives near the flash point of the riot: to middle-class African-Americans and whites, liquor stores are generally a remote presence, located far from where adults pray and children play. But to John, Tom's Liquor is a short walk from his house, school and storefront church in the same shopping strip. A slew of transactions take John to Tom's. He tags along with his mom when she goes to cash her welfare checks free of charge. With no supermarket nearby, John goes to Tom's when he wants a candy bar. Even when his mother takes him to the adjoining neighborhoods, John rarely sees a bank or supermarket. . . . Many neighborhood traits convey disorder but unchecked public drinking is a particularly potent affirmation that "no one cares." That is the message John gains by observing Tom's Liquor, where winos and crack addicts congregate at night in the parking lot. . . . In fact, eight times in the 14 months preceding the riot, LAPD dispatchers sent squad cars to the store to investigate robberies, assaults, and a shooting.*[118]

In Chapter 4, we shall diagram the relationship between drug abuse, crime, and moral poverty. But make no mistake: liquor is as much a part of the problem as drugs, perhaps a bigger part. Scientific research on alcohol-related crime and other social ills has been somewhat crowded out by studies of the social consequences of drug abuse. Still, a number of significant findings have emerged from the literature on the epidemiology of alcohol-related crime and other problems. Perhaps the single best summary of the evidence in relation to crime is as follows:

> Alcohol use has been associated with assaultive and sex-related crimes, serious youth crime, family violence toward both spouses and children, being both a homicide victim and a perpetrator, and persistent aggression as an adult. Alcohol "problems" occur disproportionately among both juveniles and adults who report violent behaviors.[119]

Of course, the fact remains that most crime is not related to drinking, and most drinking never results in crime. But some people are far more prone to crime and violence when they are drinking or drunk than when they are clean and sober. For example,

> while under the influence of alcohol, a parent may strike a child, a college student may force [his] date to have sex, friends may escalate an argument into a fist fight, a robbery victim may attempt to resist an armed mugger, and soccer fans may turn disappointment over an unsatisfactory game into a riot.[120]

Still, all scientific studies of the subject stress that the relationships among excessive drinking, social disorders, and violent crimes are complex, changeful, and contingent on a wide variety of circumstances. As one study pointed out, much of "the connection between drinking and violence is attributable to the fact that intoxication is often coincident with situations in which the probability of aggression would be elevated regardless of the presence of alcohol."[121] Moreover, "conceptions of how drinking affects social behavior are largely a product of social learning, shaped more by powerful cultural, economic, and political forces than by scientific evidence regarding the direct effects of alcohol."[122]

But exactly the same species of cautions can be made—indeed, have been made—in reference to the relationships among drug abuse, crime, and other social problems. The empirical evidence that "drug abuse causes crime" is of the same kind and quality as the evidence that "alcohol abuse causes crime"—namely, plentiful but inferential, generally persuasive but not scientifically precise.

What the literature suggests is that alcohol, like drugs, acts as a "multiplier" of crime. Aggressive behavior or criminality often occur prior to involvement with drugs or alcohol, but the onset of use (especially, but not exclusively, in cases where use leads to abuse and addiction) results in higher levels of aggressive behavior or criminal activity.

An estimated 10.5 million Americans are alcoholics and 73 million Americans have been directly affected by alcoholism in some form.[123] Each year, the nation suffers some 45,000 alcohol-related traffic fatalities.[124] Cirrhosis of the liver ranks among the top ten leading causes of death in America.[125] Half of black men ages 30 to 39 drink heavily.[126] Black males are at extremely high risk for acute and chronic alcohol-related diseases, such as cirrhosis of the liver, hepatitis, heart disease, and cancers of the mouth, larynx, tongue, esophagus, and lung.[127] And alcohol figures prominently in disorder and crime—especially in poor, minority, inner-city neighborhoods, where liquor outlets cast their shadows everywhere.

Neighborhood disorder takes many forms—public drinking, prostitution, catcalling, aggressive panhandling, rowdy teenagers, battling spouses, graffiti, vandalism, abandoned buildings, trash-filled lots, alleys strewn with bottles and garbage.[128] But no social disorder is at once so disruptive in its own right and so conducive to other disorders and crime as public drinking. It's clear that "increased alcohol consumption is associated with increased violent crime" and there's little doubt that "interventions that reduce drinking may also reduce violent crime" and related disorders.[129]

Some of the solitary statistics that can be teased from the last few decades of research on liquor, disorder, and crime are simply striking.

- Sixty percent of convicted homicide offenders drank just before committing the offense.[130]
- Sixty-three percent of adult jail inmates incarcerated for homicide had been drinking before the offense, versus about 27 percent of juvenile corrections inmates incarcerated for homicide.[131]
- Sixty percent of prison inmates drank heavily just prior to committing the violent offense for which they were incarcerated, and 40 percent "of all persons convicted of rape, assault, or burglary had been heavy drinkers in the year before they went to prison."[132]
- Between 1973 and 1992, the rate of violent victimization among young black males (ages 12 to 24) increased by 25 percent,[133] and between 1985 and 1992, the black male homicide rate increased by 300 percent.[134] Most of these violent crimes—including homicides—are committed by poor, inner-city black males against other poor, inner-city black males. Other things being equal, however, the relationship between poverty and homicide is stronger in neighborhoods with high rates of alcohol consumption than it is in neighborhoods with average or below-average rates of alcohol consumption.[135]
- Numerous studies report a strong association between sexual violence and alcohol, finding that "anywhere between 30 and 90 percent of convicted rapists are drunk at the time of the offense."[136]
- Numerous studies indicate that, while aggressive and criminal behavior among youths often begins well before the onset of alcohol use, juveniles (especially young males) who drink to the point of drunkenness are more likely than juveniles who do not drink to get into fights, get arrested, commit violent crimes, and recidivate later in life.[137]
- Alcohol-dependent male factory workers are over three times as likely to physically abuse their wives as otherwise comparable non-alcohol-dependent male factory workers are to physically abuse theirs.[138]

It is important, however, not to be swept away by the seemingly self-evident power or suggestiveness of such findings. For example, the high incidence of drinking among convicted criminals does not necessarily "prove" that drinking stimulates crime; it may be nearer to being evidence that criminals who drink are more likely to get caught and convicted than criminals who do not drink or do not drink a lot. The fact remains that alcohol consumption "has no uniform behavioral effects," and it is often difficult or "impossible to judge whether alcohol is a genuine or a spurious correlate of violence or under what circumstances alcohol may contribute to the occurrence of violence."[139] Overinterpreting disturbing aggregate statistics is a mistake that has plagued much of the applied research and policy-relevant commentary on the drugs-disorder-crime nexus; it ought not to be repeated here.

At the same time, however, it is equally important not to discount or deny the probable—and, in some cases, patently obvious—connections among liquor, disorder, and crime. Where these connections are concerned, researchers will probably never be able to untie or cut through every last causal knot, at least not in ways that meet every last test of scientific validity. But common sense supposes that the connections are real and important. Some research may challenge or complicate the suppositions of common sense. Generally speaking, however, the more sophisticated the model and methods, the more it happens that research reinforces rather than rebuts the counsels of common sense.

So it is with the scientific literature on alcohol availability, alcohol consumption, and alcohol-related crime and social problems: *ceteris paribus*, easy availability increases consumption, and consumption increases the incidence of disorder, crime, and other problems.[140]

RESTRICTING ALCOHOL, CUTTING CRIME

The practical question is how best to cut disordered crime by restricting (without prohibiting) alcohol availability and consumption among those citizens who are most at risk. The scientific research literature that addresses this question is in its infancy. Still, already a number of fascinating, well-documented, and important findings have emerged. The main finding is that both changes in the price of alcohol and changes in liquor law regulations can succeed in reducing alcohol availability, alcohol consumption, and alcohol-related problems, including violent crime among at-risk youths and adults.

First, it is clear that alcohol price and alcohol consumption tend to vary inversely: the more it costs, the less people buy; the less they buy, the less they consume; the less they consume, the fewer social problems that result. Alcohol taxes influence per capita alcohol consumption, and per capita alcohol consumption is closely linked to violent crime rates.[141]

- On average, a 10 percent increase in alcohol consumption can mean an estimated 9.13 percent increase in robberies, a 6.8 percent increase in rapes, a 5.8 percent increase in assaults, and a .87 percent increase in homicides. A 10 percent increase in a state beer tax can mean an estimated .48 percent reduction in per capita alcohol consumption, and, in turn, a 1.32 percent drop in rapes, a .87 percent drop in robberies, a .32 percent drop in homicides, and a .26 percent drop in assaults.[142]
- A 10 percent increase in the price of alcohol can mean an estimated 3 percent reduction in beer consumption and a 10 percent reduction in wine consumption.[143]

One aspect of the drinking-disorder-violent-crime nexus that must be considered is its apparently age-specific character. Most violent crime is committed by young males. Drinking in males normally begins around adolescence and rises until the late teens or mid-twenties. Longitudinal research suggests that the relationship between drinking and serious crime is strongest before young males reach age 31.[144] The "good news," however, is that youths (including the high fraction of youths who drink only beer) tend to be highly price-sensitive. As one of the most comprehensive studies concluded, increasing beer taxes to their real (inflation-adjusted) 1951 levels in 1990 "would have reduced the number of heavy drinkers among youth" by "almost 20 percent."[145] Such a reduction in youth drinking would spell fewer adult alcoholics, fewer traffic fatalities, and fewer violent deaths.[146]

The economics of figuring out precisely what types of taxing or other fiscal strategies work best in discouraging alcohol consumption can be extremely complicated (to put it mildly). Under the user-fee conception of what constitutes a socially optimal tax rate, the challenge is to set alcohol taxes "high enough so that the total revenues from these taxes are equal to the total external costs resulting from alcohol abuse."[147] But that is far easier said than done. Even as an exercise in advanced econometrics or public finance economics, things can get very difficult very quickly. For one thing, no one really has a reliable estimate of just what the annual "total external costs" of alcohol abuse are. One 1985 study, for example, estimated that the total economic costs of alcohol abuse were (in constant 1983 dollars) $116 billion in 1983, $136 billion in 1990, and would rise to $150 billion by 1995. The same study estimated that about 60 percent of the costs of alcoholism consisted of lost employment and reduced economic productivity, while about 13 percent was due to health care costs and treatment.[148] But various drug legalization advocates have come in with estimates many times that amount, and it is an inherently difficult task to estimate the total costs to society of so complicated a phenomenon as alcoholism.[149]

There is no doubt that price changes can have some effect on alcohol consumption and alcohol-related problems. There is, however, a second approach—namely, laws and regulations that directly reduce the physical availability of alcohol. For "independent of the effects of beverage prices . . . physical availability of alcohol" is "directly related to sales of spirits and wine."[150]

A number of first-rate studies have already found "statistically significant relationships between per capita outlet densities and consumption and alcohol problem rates."[151] Policies that reduce the geographic density of liquor outlets have been found to work in a wide variety of settings. "Fewer outlets per square kilometer and/or lower per capita outlet densities would result in reductions in both consumption and problems."[152]

The fact, however, is that most states do not have strong liquor law regulations and procedures. Even states that do have strong liquor laws and regulations tend to underfund the agencies that are responsible for enforcing them. Naturally, "anemic funding" often leads to "inadequate enforcement."[153] And whether related to funding levels or other variables, loose enforcement opens up the possibility of socially harmful concentrations of liquor outlets and other regulatory failures that can lead, willy-nilly, to a hornet's nest of alcohol-related social problems, including disorder and crime.

- Liquor outlet densities have been found to be "related in important ways to the alcohol problem" and felony arrest rates.[154]
- A detailed study of 44 alcohol beverage control (ABC) jurisdictions in the United States found that the strict enforcement of formal laws restricting access to alcoholic beverages, including laws that effectively regulate densities of alcohol outlets, can succeed in reducing alcohol consumption and alcohol-related problems.[155] But in "the absence of increased enforcement, it is unlikely that any formal alcohol beverage control law would have any effect upon the distribution and sales" of alcohol.[156]
- A study of all 25 California ABC offices and 167 ABC investigators found that the state's liquor laws were loosely enforced. Community concerns and considerations of community welfare generally received short shrift in decisions governing the granting of retail liquor licenses. The ABC investigators were "less concerned with public health and welfare than with the rights of applicants."[157] The study concluded that "the selling of alcohol in California is treated more as a right than a privilege."[158]

BROKEN BOTTLES

But should one leap to the conclusion that if distressed urban neighborhoods had fewer liquor outlets, they would also have less alcohol consumption and less crime? The answer is that while one should *not* leap to that conclusion, anyone who cares about reducing community breakdown and crime in the inner city should begin moving in the direction of policies that restrict alcohol availability and reduce the density of liquor outlets.

Think about it. Most American citizens would not tolerate for one second laws that permitted any such concentration of liquor (let alone beer-to-go) stores in or around the places where they and their loved ones live, work, shop, go to school, or recreate. It makes no sense to insist that it is all merely a matter of free markets, as if liquor stores simply go where the people want what they sell and sell to whomever they want. As a nation, Americans have embraced laws that raise the drinking age to 21, punish drunken drivers, and educate the young about the dangers of alcohol and drug use. At various times, California and other states have attempted to limit the density of liquor outlets around college campuses; indeed, California once had a statute that prohibited liquor stores and bars within a one-mile radius of a college campus.[159]

Nor, for that matter, can one hide behind a fog of empirical uncertainties about the connections among liquor, disorder, and crime. The liquor-disorder-crime nexus is increasingly well substantiated: let any researcher who doubts it relocate his or her working office to a flat above any inner-city malt-liquor-to-go outlet.

Following a famous article by Professors James Q. Wilson and George L. Kelling, criminologists as well as many journalists refer to the realities of such inner-city neighborhoods as evidence of the "broken windows" syndrome—that when a broken window in a building goes unfixed, soon all of its windows will be broken.[160] The broken window is an invitation to incivility, disorder, and crime:

> Where disorder problems are frequent and no one takes responsibility for unruly behavior in public places, the sense of "territoriality" among residents shrinks to include only their own households; meanwhile, untended property is fair game for plunder or destruction . . . [and] a concentration of supposedly "victimless" disorders can soon flood an area with serious, victimizing crimes.[161]

But as the evidence summarized above makes plain, broken bottles have an even worse effect on community order and safety than broken windows. The fact that government itself licenses the entire mess by letting the liquor stores proliferate and the broken bottles pile up so high in poor, inner-city neighborhoods is the single most compelling symbol that nobody cares, the ultimate invitation to disorder and crime, the sharp-edged evidence of moral poverty.

Without adopting either the most sinister or the most cynical perspective on the subject, it seems clear that the high concentrations of liquor outlets in these urban neighborhoods reflects

> the relative power of alcohol producers and wholesalers, who supply liquor outlets, banks who loan money to store owners, and state regulators whose activities are more oriented towards the interests of alcohol industry lobbying than the regulation of that industry, and the relative powerlessness of the poor and unemployed individuals and groups who live in greater concentration in these areas of high outlet density.[162]

Reduce Alcohol Availability

The time has come to experiment with policies aimed at cutting crime by cutting alcohol availability and consumption. The place to begin the experiment is in those poor, minority, high-crime neighborhoods where the density of liquor outlets far exceeds citywide averages. The theory behind this policy experiment should be guided by the large and methodologically sophisticated body of research which documents that in inner-city neighborhoods the relationship between poverty on the one side and crime and disorder on the other is mediated by community norms and the extent of citizens' attachments to traditional institutions like home, school, and church.[163]

As a rule, the stronger the community norms and traditional institutional attachments, the weaker is the link between poverty and crime and the lower are the chances that children growing up in disadvantaged settings will become deviant, delinquent, or predatory (assault, rape, rob, burglarize, deal deadly drugs, murder). Studies have shown that "religious affiliation fosters less drinking."[164] Indeed, one major study finds that, even after controlling for all relevant individual characteristics (race, gender, education, parental education, family structure, religious involvement, and so on), youths whose neighbors attend church are more likely to find a job, less likely to use drugs, and less likely to be involved in criminal activities whether or not the youths themselves attend church or have other attachments to traditional institutions.[165]

But in poor neighborhoods where alcohol is readily available and liquor outlets dot every intersection, informal and indirect social controls on deviant, delinquent, and criminal behavior are diluted. Where broken bottles fill the gutters, social bonds are weakened and social capital goes down the drain. In economic terms, high rates of alcohol consumption and high densities of liquor outlets create negative "externalities" that compete against, cancel out, or overwhelm the positive "externalities" associated with traditional institutions and behaviors like church going. Whether or not they themselves drink to excess, hang out at bars, or engage directly in related behaviors, it is probable that poor, inner-city youths who grow up in places where drinking is common and liquor outlets are everywhere are more likely than otherwise comparable youths to have diminished life prospects that include joblessness, substance abuse, and getting into serious trouble with the law. Indeed, as one recent study speculates, this is probably true even with respect to homicides:

> Social bonds that tie individuals to each other and to larger social collectivities have played a key role in the understanding of how crime and violence come about. . . . [But social bonds] break down in the presence of high rates of alcohol consumption. . . . [T]he basic form of this relationship may be one in which higher alcohol consumption reduces the effectiveness of attachment to institutions, thus leading to higher rates of homicide.[166]

There are at least three specific types of policy experiments that should be considered as a means of deepening our understanding of the alcohol-disorder-crime nexus and confronting the apparent reality that "drinking does indeed cause violence: Interventions that reduce drinking can also tend to reduce violent crime."[167] And there is one specific policy change that should be avoided at all costs—namely, lowering the drinking age.

First, *conduct systematic empirical research* to determine whether there is "a significant relationship behind the fact that parts of cities where the alcohol outlet density is extremely high are also places that frequently come to the attention of law enforcement and community residents as the location of violent crimes."[168] As a preliminary step, it would be necessary to develop a rich database that includes detailed information about the precise degrees of spatial overlap among liquor outlets, the incidence of communal disorders (public fighting, child and spousal abuse, aggressive panhandling, rowdy teenagers), rates of criminal activity (assault, rape, robbery, homicide), and the frequency of police responses (911 calls, arrests). To build such data sets would require the concerted efforts and cooperation of a number of different state and local agencies. The data would then need to be analyzed in relation to a complete list of relevant socioeconomic and demographic variables in order to determine whether the links among alcohol availability, consumption, disorder, and crime are truly causal.

Second, *impose stricter zoning ordinances for liquor stores.* In essence, the new zoning laws would increase the distance between liquor stores, reduce the total number of bars and/or liquor stores in the city, and ban the sale of malt liquor to go. Other jurisdictions around the country have experimented with such zoning laws, but in each case states and cities have faced a unique set of political, legal, and administrative hurdles.[169] The possible menu of such limitations includes stricter laws and enforcement procedures governing "population-based and geographically-based limits on permissible densities of alcohol outlets; limitations on types of outlets; limitations on service of alcohol; requirements for architectural features of outlets; and special spacing arrangements for distances between outlets of the same type."[170]

Third, make strong efforts to *limit alcoholic beverage advertising*. There have been few systematic, scientifically rigorous studies of the relationship between alcohol ads on the one side and the incidence of excessive drinking, disorder, crime, and related social problems on the other. But it seems clear that the alcohol industry believes that these ads make a positive difference in their sales. Liquor manufacturers have not been the least bit reluctant to invest in bombarding urban neighborhoods with messages like the one contained in the lyrics of a malt liquor commercial:

> Get a grip, take a sip,
> And you'll be picking up models
> And it ain't no puzzle my cousin
> 'Cause I'm more a man
> I'm downin' a forty [a 40-ounce bottle]
> Be a man and get a can of St. Ides.[171]

Indeed, the alcohol industry seems perfectly well aware of the relationship among alcohol, disorder, and crime—and in some infamous cases, it has been quick to exploit it for commercial gain. In the early 1990s, for example, one of the billboarded spokesmen for St. Ides malt liquor was Ice Cube, a "gangsta" rapper whose hits include the song "Black Korea." The song includes "lyrics such as, 'Pay respect to the black fist or we'll burn your store right down to a crisp' and 'Don't follow me up and down your market, or your little chop-suey ass will be a target.'"[172] Ice Cube appeared "in a poster holding a can of St. Ides flashing a gang sign" and claimed in a televised ad, "I gotta 40 [ounce bottle] every 'hood that you see me in."[173] Only after a vigorous protest and retaliatory boycott of the product by Korean merchants did the company that produces St. Ides pull the ads.

In many big cities, "religious leaders in black communities have taken to the streets to whitewash old billboards, thereby ridding their communities of the destructive advertisements."[174] But city officials ought to take the lead in enforcing zoning limitations on alcohol billboard advertising, banning such ads from the horizons of schools, churches, and public housing centers.

Finally, *under no circumstances should states lower the legal drinking age* or enact other measures that would increase alcohol consumption, disorder, crime, and other social problems. For starters, there is a tremendous stock of research showing that lowering the legal drinking age increases alcohol-related auto fatalities.[175] And unless one simply refuses to accept the overwhelming weight of the evidence on the relationship among drinking, disorder, and crime, then one must believe that reducing the minimum drinking age or any other measure that would increase, rather than further limit, the availability of alcohol would have socially undesirable, even disastrous, consequences— most especially in neighborhoods where the crime and body count is already way above the national average.

> *Homicide for children under the age of 4 has reached a forty-year high. It is now the leading cause of death among this age group. . . . Most of these deaths were perpetrated by parents or caretakers. . . . It is estimated that about 22 percent of children with learning disabilities acquired their disability as a result of severe child abuse and neglect. . . . [The National Institute of Justice has reported that] being abused or neglected as a child increases the likelihood of arrest as a juvenile by 53 percent, as an adult by 38 percent, and for a violent crime by 38 percent.*
>
> —J. TOM MORGAN,
> METROPOLITAN DISTRICT ATTORNEY[176]

> *Many caretakers were criminals; most had violent tempers; most physically abused their children; most had addictions to drugs and alcohol; most had little affection for each other or their children.*

There was no family intimacy; the parents had no commitment to each other or to their children's emotional, physical, or educational well-being. Most addicted parents were more attentive to drug and alcohol addictions than to their children. Children cared for themselves as if they were orphans. . . . Years of neglect by parents are followed by rejection outside the family too, when primary and secondary school teachers and peers can't cope with these children. My informants, even before their teenage years, were driven away from homes and schools. . . . Once they began to commit delinquent acts and were arrested and imprisoned in juvenile detention facilities, social isolation heightened, and opportunities to acquire the social skills and daily experiences that lead "normal" children into adulthood were gone.

—PROFESSOR MARK S. FLEISHER [177]

She wants to be called Charlette. She lives in a New York shelter for teenagers who've had babies. Her story is not unusual. The guy's name was Mickey. He was older, in his mid-20s. Charlette was going through a bad time: her stepfather had come home from prison, was beating her mother, was beating on her. "I lived in the streets for a while, starting when I was 14," she said. "I was young and vulnerable, I had problems. He was going to protect me, teach me things, discipline my mind. But when I told him I was pregnant, he was gone. I began to ask around. I asked his cousin. I found he had six other children, mostly with younger girls. I was naive, and he took advantage of me." This is what we're learning about teen pregnancy: it is, too often, a form of child abuse.

—JOE KLEIN [178]

MORAL POVERTY AND OUR CHILDREN

In our view, it is hardly surprising that the rise in serious youth violence has coincided with a rise in instances of child abuse and neglect. As Table 2-4 indicates, the number of reported instances more than quadrupled between 1976 and 1993. Part of the increase is explained by the fact that over the past thirty years "professionals and laypersons have become more likely to report apparently abusive and neglectful

TABLE 2-4. INSTANCES OF CHILD ABUSE AND NEGLECT REPORTED, 1976–1993

Year	Number of children reported	Year	Number of children reported
1976	669,000	1985	1,919,000
1977	838,000	1986	2,086,000
1978	836,000	1987	2,157,000
1979	988,000	1988	2,265,000
1980	1,154,000	1989	2,435,000
1981	1,225,000	1990	2,557,000
1982	1,262,000	1991	2,690,000
1983	1,477,000	1992	2,916,000
1984	1,727,000	1993	2,989,000

Source: Douglas J. Besharov, "Child Abuse Reporting," in Irwin Garfinkel et al., eds., *Social Policies for Children*, p. 259.

situations."[179] Even so, tens of thousands of cases still go unreported each year, and child maltreatment is now the sixth leading cause of death for children under fourteen.[180]

If we are even half-right about how moral poverty breeds crime, child abuse and neglect are leading causes of youth homicide and violence. But child abuse and neglect are not the only sources of moral poverty. Children who are born out of wedlock and placed in substitute care also are thereby placed at risk. Thus, as Tables 2-5 through 2-7 suggest, black-white differences in crime rates have their mirror images in black-white differences in child abuse and neglect, out-of-wedlock births, and other factors which reduce the likelihood that a child will grow up under the guiding, restraining, civilizing influence of decent, nurturing, loving, and law-abiding adults.

The simple truth is that children of whatever race, creed, color, or socioeconomic status cannot be socialized by abusive, neglectful adults who are themselves unsocialized (or worse), families that exist in name only, and neighborhoods in which violent and repeat criminals circulate. The moral poverty that has bred so much crime and drug abuse in our society, and that threatens us with so much more to come, must be recognized as the deeply rooted problem it is.

We must wage a war on moral poverty, enlisting the support of revitalized civil institutions and the cooperation of the media and other channels of influence over our young. We must attack the moral poverty problem root and branch, up to and including enforcing the laws against child abuse and neglect with a seriousness of purpose that

TABLE 2-5. BIRTHS TO UNMARRIED WOMEN, BY RACE OF CHILD AND AGE OF MOTHER, 1970–1992

Race of Child and Age of Mother	1970	1980	1985	1990	1992	Race of Child and Age of Mother	1970	1980	1985	1990	1992
NUMBER (1,000)						20 to 24 years	31.8	35.6	36.3	34.7	35.6
Total live births¹	**399**	**666**	**828**	**1,165**	**1,225**	25 to 29 years	10.2	15.0	18.4	19.7	19.1
White	175	320	433	647	722	30 to 34 years	4.8	6.2	8.1	10.1	10.4
Black	215	326	366	473	459	35 years and over	3.1	2.4	3.4	4.5	5.1
Under 15 years old	10	9	9	11	11	AS PERCENT OF ALL BIRTHS IN RACIAL GROUPS					
15 to 19 years old	190	263	271	350	354	**Total**¹	**10.7**	**18.4**	**22.0**	**28.0**	**30.1**
20 to 24 years old	127	237	300	404	436	**White**	**5.7**	**11.0**	**14.5**	**20.1**	**22.6**
25 to 29 years old	41	100	152	230	233	**Black**	**37.6**	**55.2**	**60.1**	**65.2**	**68.1**
30 to 34 years old	19	41	67	118	128	BIRTH RATE²					
35 years old and over	12	16	28	53	63	**Total**¹	**26.4**	**29.4**	**32.8**	**43.8**	**45.2**
PERCENT DISTRIBUTION						White³	13.9	17.6	21.8	31.8	35.2
Total¹	**100.0**	**100.0**	**100.0**	**100.0**	**100.0**	Black³	95.5	82.9	79.0	93.9	86.5
White	43.9	48.1	52.3	55.6	58.9	15 to 19 years	22.4	27.6	31.4	42.5	44.6
Black	54.0	48.9	44.1	40.6	37.5	20 to 24 years	38.4	40.9	46.5	65.1	68.5
Under 15 years	2.4	1.4	1.1	0.9	0.9	25 to 29 years	37.0	34.0	39.9	56.0	56.5
15 to 19 years	47.8	39.5	32.7	30.0	28.9	30 to 34 years	27.1	21.1	25.2	37.6	37.9

¹ Includes other races not shown separately.
² Rate per 1,000 unmarried women (never-married, widowed, and divorced) estimated as of July 1.
³ Covers women aged 15 to 44 years.
Source: *Statistical Abstract of the United States—1995,* The National Data Book (U.S. Department of Commerce, Economics and Statistics Administration, Bureau of the Census. 115th ed., Washington, D.C., 1995), p. 77.

has never characterized "child protective services" agencies. We must put saving the children ahead of "family preservation" fantasies. And we must think broadly and boldly about how best to increase adoptions and assist the inner-city churches that are struggling to resurrect civil society, provide real moral leadership, and give fatherless, Godless, and jobless children faith and hope.

In the concluding chapter, we sketch out our plan for winning the war—or, more properly, starting the battle—against moral poverty. But in the next two chapters we first explain and critique how the war is now being waged on two fronts—restraining violent and repeat criminals, adult and juvenile, and containing the drug abuse dilemma.

TABLE 2-6. CHILD ABUSE AND NEGLECT CASES SUBSTANTIATED AND INDICATED—
VICTIM CHARACTERISTICS, 1990–1993

ITEM	1990		1991		1992		1993	
	Number	Percent	Number	Percent	Number	Percent	Number	Percent
TYPES OF SUBSTANTIATED MALTREATMENT								
Victims, total [1]	801,143	(X)	819,922	(X)	1,044,480	(X)	1,057,255	(X)
Neglect	358,846	44.8	366,462	44.7	474,871	51.7	492,211	48.8
Physical abuse	205,057	25.6	206,235	25.2	212,300	23.1	232,061	23.0
Sexual abuse	127,853	16.0	129,425	15.8	130,248	14.2	139,326	13.8
Emotional maltreatment	47,673	6.0	46,334	5.7	48,898	5.3	47,659	4.7
Other and unknown	61,714	7.7	71,466	8.7	178,163	19.4	145,998	14.5
RACE/ETHNIC GROUP OF VICTIM [2]								
Victims, total	775,409	100.0	818,527	99.9	956,248	100.0	916,185	100.0
White	424,470	54.7	454,059	55.5	509,111	53.2	497,913	54.3
Black	197,400	25.5	218,044	26.6	242,357	25.3	229,596	25.1
Asian and Pacific Islander	6,408	0.8	6,585	0.8	7,139	0.7	7,775	0.8
American Indian, Eskimo, and Aleut	10,283	1.3	10,873	1.3	12,782	1.3	13,657	1.5
Other races	11,749	1.5	12,982	1.6	15,094	1.6	13,659	1.5
Hispanic origin	73,132	9.4	77,985	9.5	89,426	9.4	85,026	9.3
Unknown	51,967	6.7	37,999	4.6	80,339	8.4	68,559	7.5

X Not applicable.

[1] More than one type of maltreatment may be substantiated per child.

[2] Some states were unable to report on the number of Hispanic victims, thus it is probable that nationwide the percentage of Hispanic victims is higher.

Source: *Statistical Abstract of the United States—1995*, The National Data Book (U.S. Department of Commerce, Economics and Statistics Administration, Bureau of the Census. 115th ed., Washington, D.C., 1995), p. 215.

As presently constituted, the government's response to the moral poverty crisis on both fronts is profoundly misguided and counterproductive.

Imagine that you are an at-risk, inner-city kid struggling against the odds, playing by the rules, and suffering the horrors of abuse and neglect without taking it out on others. What do you witness all around you? You witness drug dealers who repeatedly beat the system. You see violent thugs respected as conquering heroes and law-abiding adults cowering behind locked doors in fear. You live in a place where the drug and crime culture is not a renegade culture but a dominant one. And you watch as public authorities seem paralyzed to rescue

TABLE 2-7. RACE/ETHNICITY OF CHILDREN IN FOSTER CARE, 1980–1993

| | Race/Ethnicity | | | | | | |
Fiscal Year	White	Black	Hispanic	Others	Unknown	Number of States Included[1]	Percent Total Substitute Care Population
1993	35.8%	43.7%	13.1%	2.6%	4.8%	20	57.8%
1992	35.6%	44.1%	12.5%	2.6%	5.2%	20	57.3%
1991	36.3%	42.4%	12.8%	2.8%	5.7%	20	55.4%
1990	39.3%	40.4%	11.8%	4.3%	4.2%	31	75.4%
1989	48.1%	34.3%	9.7%	7.2%	0.7%	32	63.7%
1988	45.5%	36.5%	10.1%	4.2%	3.7%	34	82.9%
1987	46.1%	37.1%	10.2%	4.4%	2.2%	31	72.3%
1986	50.7%	34.9%	8.2%	4.6%	1.6%	42	89.4%
1985	51.9%	33.4%	8.6%	5.1%	1.0%	38	81.7%
1984	52.5%	32.9%	8.2%	5.4%	1.0%	41	77.9%
1983	52.7%	33.9%	7.3%	4.8%	1.3%	40	81.6%
1982	52.7%	34.2%	6.7%	4.6%	1.8%	38	81.0%

[1] Eight states were able to provide data for all twelve fiscal years included in this table.

Source: American Public Welfare Association, Voluntary Cooperative Information System.

abused children, punish predators, and protect the good people from the bad.

Where moral poverty is concerned, we owe the abused, neglected, rejected child who is confronted with the choice about how to respond to the living hell our deepest sympathy, our best help, our most fervent prayers. But we owe it to other children who are similarly situated, to our fellow citizens, and to ourselves, to restrain violent and repeat criminals—whatever their life histories—from preying upon the life, liberty, and property of innocent others. We owe it to them and to ourselves to take the drug abuse problem seriously, offer a morally consistent anti-drug message, and support those whose job it is to enforce our anti-drug laws.

In far too many ways, however, the failure of parental authority is reinforced by the absence of public authority; the immoral lessons of the streets are not rebutted by the practical example of public officials who succeed in punishing violent criminals and stigmatizing drug merchants. Where the drug and crime body count is concerned, the first two steps in the war on moral poverty—the immediate short-range effort—must be to stop revolving-door justice and to reinvest in anti-drug efforts.

3

RESTRAINING AND PUNISHING STREET CRIMINALS

As we will document below, today and every day the "justice" system permits known, convicted, violent, and repeat criminals, adult and juvenile, to get away with murder and mayhem on the streets. Criminals who have repeatedly violated the life, liberty, and property of others are routinely set free to do it all over again.

But the revolving-door justice system is not just a public safety disaster; it is a moral disaster, a virtual no-fault system that completes, perfects, and excuses the selfish, impulsive, predatory propensities of morally impoverished street criminals. It does this by in effect saying to them, "Do the crime and you *won't* do the time. And why should you? Getting caught means you're unlucky, not bad. We authorities are just as eager to abandon you to your own deviant, delinquent, and criminal devices as were virtually all the other adults you have known. And we are doubly eager to abdicate any real responsibility for guiding, disciplining, or protecting you."

Our aim in this chapter, therefore, is not only to document the facts and figures that support the American public's crime fears, but to suggest how better incarceration and policing policies can help not only to cut crime and disorder but also to send the morally right socializing, civilizing message to would-be juvenile super-predators and other street criminals.

In the course of our discussion, we hope to furnish the information and perspective necessary to demolish five myths about the justice system in relation to crime, drugs, and moral poverty. The myths are these:

- Revolving-door justice isn't for real.
- Prisons are full of "first-time, nonviolent" offenders.
- Incarceration does not cut crime and costs "too much."
- Police can do little or nothing to cut crime rates.
- It doesn't pay to punish those who criminally violate the life, liberty, and property of others.

By rebutting these myths, we hope to rebut the biggest and most pernicious myth of them all—that the justice system neither can nor should serve as an effective moral tutor that restrains dangerous criminals, condemns their actions, backs up the positive socializing influences of families, churches, and communities, and mitigates, not mirrors, the moral depravity of its charges. If we hope to restore order to our streets, the no-fault, revolving-door system must be replaced by a morally centered, effective-punishment system.

We want to make it clear, however, that tough anti-crime policies for our most affected communities require support from those communities themselves. Residents must be willing to convict criminals. They must be prepared to be witnesses in child abuse cases. They must be prepared to testify against drug dealers and violent criminals. And they must be allies and not enemies of the police. These things cannot simply be imposed from on high. Nor should they. Those of us who believe in the principle of subsidiarity and empowerment believe that the best place to resolve these matters is within the community itself. We recognize, too, that there is a good deal of ambivalence—sometimes even outright hostility—among some members of inner-city communities to some of the positions we advocate. There are also many inner-city residents who support imprisoning more criminals and deploying more police. In the end, the concentrated will of the latter must prevail if these policies and what derives from these policies—the chance for real security and the equal protection of the law —ever hope to see the light of day. We hope that will happen; indeed, we hope this book may contribute to that day.

> *Four young Milwaukee men charged in a recent crime spree that included gunshot murders at a Blockbuster Video store and a liquor store had 92 prior arrests for armed robbery, burglary, battery, arson, weapons violations, theft and other alleged violations, according to Milwaukee police records. One of the defendants, 24-year-old Willie Dortch, had 51 arrests alone, records show. The four defendants slipped through the cracks of the justice system— through plea bargains, early release from prison on parole, luck and brazen arrogance—leaving them free to allegedly carry out numerous violent crimes outlined in criminal complaints, a check of police and criminal records showed.* [1]

CRIME WITHOUT PUNISHMENT

As Table 3-1 indicates, there is a tremendous gap between how much time average citizens think convicted criminals should serve in prison (generally lots) and how much time the criminals actually serve (often little). But for over a decade now, the justice system has been overloading the streets faster than it has been "overcrowding" the prisons.

As Figure 3-1 and Table 3-2 both indicate, about 70 percent of the over 5 million people under correctional supervision on any given day are not incarcerated. Nationally, in 1994 about 3 million persons were on probation and 690,000 were on parole. Between 1980 and 1994, the parole population and the prison population both grew by 213 percent.

TABLE 3-1. ACTUAL VS. RECOMMENDED SENTENCES

Offense	Actual average time served, released in 1992	Average recommended time in prison, 1987
Rape	4 years, 11 months	
with no other injury		15 years, 5 months
with forced oral sex, no other injury		16 years, 10 months
Robbery	3 years, 3 months	
no weapon, threat of force, no injury, $10		3 years, 8 months
threat of force with weapon, no injury, $10		5 years, 8 months
shot victim with gun, hospitalization, $1,000		10 years, 3 months
Assault	2 years	
intentional injury, treatment by doctor, no hospitalization		5 years, 7 months
intentional injury, treatment by doctor, and hospitalization		7 years, 9 months
Burglary	1 year, 10 months	
burglary of a home with loss of $1,000		4 years, 5 months
Drug trafficking	1 year, 6 months	
cocaine sold to others for resale		10 years, 6 months

Note: This table compares the actual time served for selected serious offenses by those released from prison in 1992 with the prison sentences recommended by a representative sample of Americans in 1987.

Source: Joseph M. Bessette, "Crime, Justice, and Punishment," *Jobs and Capital*, Winter 1995, p. 22.

Indeed, in 1992 over 10.3 million *violent* crimes were committed, but barely 165,000 led to convictions, and only 100,000 or so to state prison sentences, which on average ended before the convict had served even half his time behind bars.[2]

THE REAL IMPRISONMENT RATE

In 1992 the country's "imprisonment rate" was about 500, meaning that there were 500 persons incarcerated (about 170 in jail awaiting trial or serving a short sentence and 330 in state and federal prisons) per 100,000 adult Americans. By the same mode of calculation, we note, in 1992 the nation's "Medicare rate" was about 14,000, meaning that there were 14,000 persons insured by Medicare per 100,000 adult Americans.

Stop and think about this. Knowing that the "imprisonment rate" is 500, the "Medicare rate" is 14,000, and that the latter rate is 28 times the former rate is fine. But the crucial and relevant information

TABLE 3-2. NUMBER OF ADULTS ON PROBATION, IN JAIL OR PRISON, OR ON
PAROLE, 1980–1994

Year	Total estimated correctional population	Probation	Jail[a]	Prison	Parole
1980[b]	1,840,400	1,118,097	182,288	319,598	220,438
1985	3,011,500	1,968,712	254,986	487,583	300,203
1990	4,348,000	2,670,234	403,019	743,382	531,407
1991	4,536,200	2,729,322	424,129	792,535	590,198
1992	4,763,200	2,811,611	441,781	851,205	658,601
1993	4,943,900	2,903,160	455,500	909,186	678,100
1994	5,135,900	2,962,166	483,717	999,808	690,159
Percent change,					
1993–94	4%	2%	6%	10%	2%
1980–94	179%	165%	165%	213%	213%

Note: Every year some states update their counts. Counts for probation, prisons, and parole population are for December 31 each year. Jail population counts are for June 30 each year. Prisoner counts are for those in custody only. Because some persons may have multiple statuses, the sum of the number of persons incarcerated or under community supervision overestimates the total correctional population.

[a] Includes convicted and unconvicted adult inmates.

[b] Jail count is based on estimates.

Source: Bureau of Justice Statistics, 1995.

FIGURE 3-1. ADULTS IN JAIL, ON PROBATION, IN PRISON, OR ON PAROLE IN THE
UNITED STATES, 1980–1993

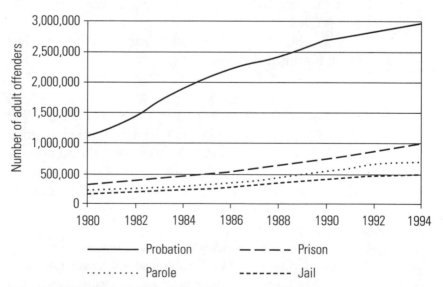

Source: *Correctional Populations in the United States, 1993* (Bureau of Justice Statistics, October 1995); *Sourcebook of Criminal Justice Statistics, 1994* (Bureau of Justice Statistics, 1995).

we need to know is the size of each population vis-à-vis the relevant characteristics of individuals—violent and repeat criminals duly tried and convicted of felony crimes in the case of prisoners, senior citizens and other Americans (certain disabled citizens and persons with life-threatening kidney disease) who qualify for federal health insurance in the case of Medicare. The pertinent public policy question in the former case is "How many street predators who commit serious crimes can and should be punished for how long by imprisonment?" while the pertinent question in the latter case is "How many eligible citizens who fall ill can and should be helped by Medicare?"

Clearly, there are less crude ways of calculating the imprisonment rate than simply dividing the total number of people in prison by the total U.S. population. One is to calculate the rate relative to the number of criminal victimizations for which convicted criminals are sent to prison.

For example, in 1992 nearly 43 million crimes were committed, for which about 400,000 convicted criminals went to prison. Thus, the overall imprisonment rate (total number of crimes divided by the number of convicted felons who went to prison, in this case 400,000 divided by 43 million) was .009—fewer than one convicted criminal was sent to prison for every 100 crimes. Likewise, in 1992 there were some 10 million violent crime victimizations, but only about 100,000 persons convicted of a violent crime went to state prison. Thus, the violent crime imprisonment rate in 1992 (100,000 divided by 10 million) was roughly .01—only 1 criminal convicted of a violent crime went to prison for every 100 violent crimes committed.[3]

Of course, some violent criminals commit more than one violent crime, and some violent crimes are less serious than others. But even if we eliminated 75 percent of all violent crimes from the foregoing calculation, we would still be left with 2.5 million violent crimes, only 100,000 convicted violent criminals sent to prison, and an imprisonment rate of .04—only four criminals convicted of a violent crime for every 100 violent crimes committed.

Another good way to calculate the real imprisonment rate is to multiply the probability of imprisonment by the length of time served. Professor Morgan O. Reynolds, an economist, and a few other scholars have calculated year-to-year changes in the imprisonment rate measured in terms of a criminal's "expected punishment," that is, his

FIGURE 3-2. REVOLVING-DOOR JUSTICE

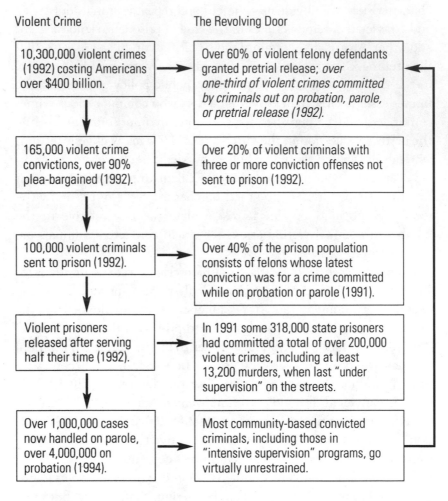

Violent Crime   The Revolving Door

10,300,000 violent crimes (1992) costing Americans over $400 billion.	Over 60% of violent felony defendants granted pretrial release; *over one-third of violent crimes committed by criminals out on probation, parole, or pretrial release (1992).*
165,000 violent crime convictions, over 90% plea-bargained (1992).	Over 20% of violent criminals with three or more conviction offenses not sent to prison (1992).
100,000 violent criminals sent to prison (1992).	Over 40% of the prison population consists of felons whose latest conviction was for a crime committed while on probation or parole (1991).
Violent prisoners released after serving half their time (1992).	In 1991 some 318,000 state prisoners had committed a total of over 200,000 violent crimes, including at least 13,200 murders, when last "under supervision" on the streets.
Over 1,000,000 cases now handled on parole, over 4,000,000 on probation (1994).	Most community-based convicted criminals, including those in "intensive supervision" programs, go virtually unrestrained.

chances of getting caught multiplied by his chances of getting convicted, sent to prison, and actually serving most of the sentence behind bars. Thus measured, the imprisonment rate fell from a high of 93 days of expected punishment in 1959 to 14 days of expected punishment in 1975. From 1975 through 1986, it inched up to 19 days—barely a fifth of its 1959 level.[4]

Although imprisonment rates are by no means the sole or most significant factor in determining crime rates, there is a definite inverse relationship between expected punishment and criminal activity. As

Professor Reynolds has demonstrated clearly in studies of Texas and other states, as expected punishment fell in the 1960s and 1970s, the crime rate soared. When expected punishment rose between 1975 and 1980, the crime rate moderated. Then expected punishment fell again in the early '80s and crime rates picked up once more. The reverse occurred beginning in 1988 when the crime rate dipped partly in response to increased expected punishment supported by increased prison capacity.[5]

But isn't it still true that America is the "most punitive" nation in the world? In the 1980s the United States had the highest "imprisonment rate" in the world, together with the totalitarian Soviet Union and the racially repressive South African regime. The most obvious flaw with this comparison is that it doesn't tell you anything about *who* was being imprisoned. Violent criminals? Or poets and writers? In addition, when you measure the imprisonment rate sensibly and control for differences in rates of serious crime and other relevant factors (for example, plea bargaining), the differences between the United States and other democratic countries narrow considerably.

For example, as Professor Wilson has documented, even if one eliminates all homicides committed by blacks from the equation, the "estimated number of homicides committed by whites in the U.S. is at least twice as great as the total homicide rate" in France, Germany, the Netherlands, Spain, Sweden, and the United Kingdom.[6] Likewise, in 1992, 13 percent of all crimes reported to the police in the United States were violent, while only 5 percent of all crimes reported to the police in England and Wales were violent.[7] Nonetheless, in each country about one in three prisoners was in custody for a violent offense such as murder, rape, robbery, or assault; in each country 3 percent or less of all prisoners were charged merely with petty property crimes; and in each country a majority of convicted inmates had been in custody before.[8] While U.S. prisoners, on average, receive longer sentences for comparable crimes of conviction than inmates in England and Wales, on average, inmates in the latter countries actually serve about half of the imposed sentence; inmates in America a third of it.[9]

Likewise, after factoring in differences in crime rates and adjusting for differences in charge reduction between arrest and imprisonment, the United States in the early 1980s had an imprisonment rate virtually identical to that of Canada and England for theft, fell between those two countries in the case of burglary, and lagged well behind each of the others in imprisonments for robbery.[10]

Just the same, no one can seriously doubt that differences of culture matter to how people from one country to the next, or from one region of a given country to the next, view crime and punishment. And no one can seriously doubt that such differences in outlook influence crime policies and law enforcement practices. Thus, for example, we note that compared to the people of Great Britain, Germany, Italy, and France, Americans are far more likely to profess a belief in God, view prayer as an important part of daily life, and insist that there are clear guidelines about what is morally right and wrong.[11] It would be amazing if such differences in belief among democratic peoples did not translate into policy-relevant differences in decisions about who ought to be punished by law, for what, how, and under what conditions, up to and including differences on capital punishment (which most Americans, unlike most Europeans, have tended to favor).

So, while it is true that the United States has more duly tried and convicted criminals behind bars relative to its total population than do countries as diverse as Singapore and Spain, Mexico and Japan, we reject the usual anti-incarceration spin on this fact, and its use as an excuse for depreciating law-and-order and imprisonment policies that most Americans favor. Besides, many countries, including democratic ones, with lower per capita imprisonment rates than the United States, follow law enforcement and prison disciplinary practices that would send a dozen American Civil Liberties Union criminals' rights lawyers screaming into the night. Even the Sentencing Project, a Washington-based group that advocates alternatives to prison and has released several reports on "the international use of incarceration," has conceded that "a nation's rate of incarceration in itself only describes one aspect of its criminal justice or social policies."[12] We doubt, therefore, that the Sentencing Project, the ACLU, the National Council on Crime and Delinquency, the National Center on Alternatives and Institutions, their like-minded funders, their university-based criminology supporters, and those in the media who insist that America incarcerates too many convicted criminals, including too many prisoners who are ostensibly "petty," "first-time," or "nonviolent," would want to trade the American system for that of countries with lower rates of imprisonment but fewer real protections of the rights of the accused and convicted. We most certainly would not.

The truth, which we now turn to document, and which no amount of crude international comparisons or unthinking assertions about "too many" people behind bars can mask forever, is that virtually all of those in prison in this country are just what most average Americans suppose them to be—not victims of unfettered capitalism, rampant racism, a reactionary citizenry, or Reagan-era budget cuts, but duly tried and convicted violent and repeat criminals who are either dangerous enough, or deserving enough (or both), to merit secure confinement. To repeat, the problem is that they too often escape justice entirely, get released early, commit more crimes, and manufacture more misery for victims, their families, and society.

> On June 29, 1992, Kimber Reynolds pulled up outside Fresno, California's popular Daily Planet Restaurant. She and a friend went into the restaurant and ordered dessert. At about 10:30 p.m. they headed back to Kimber's car. Her friend let himself in on the passenger side. Kimber checked the one-way street for traffic and started to get in.
>
> She never made it. Two men on a stolen motorcycle appeared, pinned her against the door, and grabbed her purse. She resisted. One assailant put a .357 magnum in her ear and shot her in cold blood. Her parents' phone rang with the news at 2:30 a.m. They rushed to the hospital. Twenty-six hours after she was shot, and four months shy of her nineteenth birthday, Kimber Reynolds was dead.
>
> Kimber's killers were violent and repeat offenders with long drug-and-crime offense records. The shooter, Joe Davis, had been on a major crime spree since his most recent release from prison. When the police tracked him down and surrounded his house, he vowed to his mother, "I'm gonna take some cops out with me." He wounded one officer, but his gun jammed. The officers fired every round they had at him. He was hit by ten rounds of pistol fire and four gunshot blasts in 52 seconds. His mother chose to have his body viewed without hiding the wounds. She told a local newspa-

per, "I wanted to let others know what happens when you abuse drugs, when you get involved in crime." [13]

In 1990, the National Council on Crime and Delinquency (NCCD) published a study based on interviews with 154 incoming inmates in three states. The NCCD claimed in its summary that "the vast majority of inmates are sentenced for petty crimes." Writing in the New York Times, columnist Tom Wicker asked, "Why does our nation spend such an exorbitant amount of money each year to warehouse petty criminals?" He summarized the NCCD study as finding that "80 percent of those going to prison are not serious or violent criminals but guilty of low-level offenses: minor parole violations, property, drug and public disorder crimes." Others made similar claims, and the NCCD study is cited to this day. But when Professor Charles H. Logan, a University of Connecticut criminologist and fellow at the U.S. Department of Justice, scrutinized the NCCD study, he discovered that 25.4 percent of the inmates whose conviction offense was categorized as "petty" had revealed to the interviewers that they were high-rate offenders committed to a criminal lifestyle. By Logan's count, nearly three-quarters of the new admissions were either serious or high-rate offenders, not even counting the 21 percent of the sample who, while not identified as high-rate offenders, were described as having been on a "crime spree" at the time of their commitment offense. Logan's sobering analysis of who really goes to prison, however, wasn't touted in the New York Times, which had labeled Wicker's column on the NCCD report "The Punitive Society." [14]

WHO REALLY GOES TO PRISON?

How have we reached the day when our justice system imprisons barely one criminal for every 100 violent crimes? How is it that millions of convicted criminals with a history of violence end up on probation or parole rather than behind bars? Who really goes to prison, for how long, and under what conditions? What really happens on probation and parole? And how much violent crime is actually done by repeat violent criminals, including those who are legally "under supervision" at the very moment they find their latest victims?

The revolving door starts to spin when 65 percent of all felony defendants, and 63 percent of all violent felony defendants, are released prior to the disposition of their case. As Table 3-3 indicates, in 1990 in the nation's 75 largest counties, 44 percent of all released defendants, and 11 percent of all released violent felony defendants, had a history of prior convictions, and 5 percent had 10 or more prior convictions. About 19 percent of released violent felony defendants simply fail to appear in court. About 16 percent of released violent felony defendants are arrested again within the year, a quarter of them for another violent crime.[15] And in 1992, 71 percent of the defendants charged with felony weapons offenses were released prior to trial.[16]

TABLE 3-3. NUMBER OF PRIOR CONVICTIONS OF FELONY DEFENDANTS, BY WHETHER RELEASED OR DETAINED AND THE MOST SERIOUS CURRENT ARREST CHARGE, 1990

| | Percent of felony defendants in the 75 largest counties | | | | | | | |
| | | | Total with | | Number of prior convictions | | | |
Detention/release outcome and the most serious current arrest charge	Number of defendants	Total	No prior convictions	Prior convictions	10 or more	5–9	2–4	1
Released defendants								
All offenses	33,085	100%	56%	44%	5%	9%	17%	13%
Violent offenses	8,452	26	15	11	1	2	4	4
Property offenses	11,481	35	20	15	2	3	5	4
Drug offenses	10,474	32	17	15	1	3	6	5
Public-order offenses	2,678	8	4	4	—	1	2	1
Detained defendants								
All offenses	18,348	100%	29%	71%	11%	20%	27%	13%
Violent offenses	4,933	27	9	18	2	5	7	4
Property offenses	6,143	33	10	24	4	7	8	4
Drug offenses	6,027	33	9	24	4	6	10	4
Public-order offenses	1,245	7	1	6	1	2	2	1

Source: *Pretrial Release of Felony Defendants, 1990* (Bureau of Justice Statistics, November 1992).

But it is at the point of sentencing that the revolving door for violent felons *really* begins to rotate wildly. As Table 3-4 shows, in 1992 fully 47 percent of state felons convicted of one violent crime were not sentenced to prison, and nearly a quarter of those convicted

TABLE 3-4. CONVICTED VIOLENT FELONS NOT SENTENCED TO PRISON, BY NUMBER OF CONVICTION OFFENSES, 1992

Most serious conviction offense	Percent of convicted felons *not* sentenced to prison for 1, 2, or 3 or more felony conviction offenses		
	One	Two	Three or more
All violent offenses	47	31	23
Murder	9	5	3
Rape	39	23	20
Robbery	30	21	14
Aggravated assault	61	45	38
Other violent[a]	65	51	36

Note: This chart reflects prison nonsentencing rates for felons based on their most serious offense. For example, if a felon is convicted of murder, larceny, and drug possession, and not sentenced to prison, he would be represented in this chart under murder (the most serious offense) with three or more offenses.

[a] Includes offenses such as negligent manslaughter, sexual assault, and kidnapping.

Source: *Felony Sentences in State Courts* (Bureau of Justice Statistics, January 1995), p. 6.

of three or more felony crimes, one or more of which was a violent crime, were not sentenced to prison.

Here, then, is the important point that we think ought to be underscored: *Virtually all convicted criminals who do go to prison are violent offenders, repeat offenders, or violent repeat offenders.* It is simply a (deadly) myth that our prison cells are filled with people who don't belong there, or that we would somehow be safer if fewer people were in prison. The widespread circulation of that myth is the result of ideology masquerading as analysis.

In fact, as depicted in Figure 3-3, based on a scientific survey representing 711,000 state prisoners in 1991, a former director of the U.S. Bureau of Justice Statistics, Lawrence A. Greenfeld, found that fully 62 percent of the prison population had a history of violence, and that 94 percent of state prisoners had committed one or more violent crimes or served a previous sentence of incarceration or probation.

THE PRISONER CGPA—CRIMINAL GRADE POINT AVERAGE

In effect, this 94 percent statistic is a measure of the prison population's "criminal grade point average," accounting for the totality of prisoners' adult and juvenile criminal acts against life, liberty, and property. Performing the same analysis on other large state prisoner data sets yields virtually the same results: since 1974 over 90 percent of all state prisoners have been violent offenders or recidivists.

FIGURE 3-3. PROFILE OF PRISON INMATES, 1991

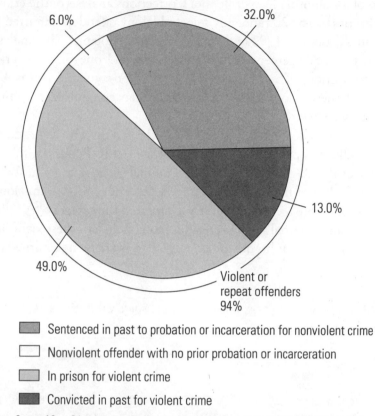

6.0%   32.0%

13.0%

49.0%

Violent or
repeat offenders
94%

◼ Sentenced in past to probation or incarceration for nonviolent crime

☐ Nonviolent offender with no prior probation or incarceration

◼ In prison for violent crime

◼ Convicted in past for violent crime

Source: *Survey of State Prison Inmates, 1991* (Bureau of Justice Statistics, 1992). Statistics based on a sample representing 711,000 adults in state prisons.

Indeed, between 1980 and 1993 the growth in the number of state inmates was greatest among offenders whose most recent and serious conviction offense was violent. During that period, the number of violent offenders behind bars grew by 221,000, representing 42 percent of the total growth in state prison populations.[17] The closer one looks into the criminal and conviction histories of prisoners, the clearer it becomes that there are precious few petty, nonviolent, or first-time felons behind bars who pose no real threat to public safety and who simply do not deserve to be incarcerated.

For example, in 1994 California's prison population rose to over 125,000 inmates. Since the mid-1980s, numerous experts and journalists have insisted that the state's prisons were overflowing with first-time offenders and harmless parole violators. Table 3-5 summarizes the results of a California Department of Corrections analysis of the criminal histories of 16,520 randomly selected felony offenders admitted to the state's prisons in 1992 and classified as "nonviolent." The analysis reveals that 88.5 percent of these offenders had one or more prior adult convictions. The average number of prior convictions was 4.7. A fifth of these "nonviolent" felons had been committed to prison once or twice before.

Likewise, in a detailed portrait of the 84,197 adults who were admitted to California prisons in 1991, Professor Joan R. Petersilia, former director of the RAND Corporation's criminal justice program, found that only 3,116 of the prisoners (under 4 percent of total admissions) were, in fact, mere technical parole violators (in the category "Administrative, non-criminal"). As Petersilia has concluded, these data disprove the notion that hordes of "parole violators are being returned for

TABLE 3-5. FELONY OFFENDERS ADMITTED TO CALIFORNIA PRISONS IN 1992 AND CLASSIFIED AS NONVIOLENT, BY CRIMINAL HISTORIES

	Percent
Prior convictions	
Juvenile (one or more)	18.2
Adult (one or more)	88.5
Adult—Average number	4.7
Adult—Violent (PC 667.5[c]) (one or more)	1.4
Prior probations	
Prior probation (one or more)	82.0
Current probation resulting in:	
Probation revocation with additional conviction(s)	24.2
Probation revocation without additional conviction(s)	21.7
Prior juvenile hall incarcerations (one or more)	5.8
Prior jail—adult incarcerations	
One or more	65.9
Three or more	32.8
Prior California youth authority commitments	10.5
Prior prison commitments	
One or more	20.6
Three or more	1.8

Source: Department of Corrections, State of California, March 1, 1994. Based on an analysis of 16,520 admissions.

strictly technical violations. . . . The bottom line is that true technical violators do not currently represent a large portion of incoming inmates, nor do they serve very long prison terms."[18]

The vast majority of all persons admitted to California's prisons were violent or repeat criminals, together responsible for literally tens of thousands of serious crimes. They accounted for more than 2,000 murder convictions.

Have you heard the one about the "pizza thief," the 29-year-old California man who was sentenced under California's three-strikes-and-you're-out law for stealing a slice of pizza from children in a shopping mall? Although much of the national press spun this story as a self-evident example of the folly of three-strikes (and other "get-tough" legislation), the facts paint a different picture. The offender's adult criminal history dated back to 1985. He had been convicted of five serious felonies inside of a decade. He was granted probation five times in five years for convictions on two misdemeanor charges and three felony charges. Between 1985 and 1990, he had five suspended sentences. At one point he moved to Washington State—and was arrested there on additional charges. During his criminal career, he used eight aliases, three different dates of birth, four different Social Security numbers, and marijuana, cocaine, alcohol, and PCP. Standing six feet four inches, his "third strike" occurred when he and another man frightened and intimidated four children (ages 7, 10, 12, and 14), stole their pizza, and then walked away laughing. He was not sentenced to life; he could be eligible for parole in the year 2014. As one California official quipped, this repeat felon was already "doing life on the installment plan. Three strikes simply reduced the number of future installments and the number of future victims." Indeed, a 1996 series in the Sacramento Bee reported that 84 percent of the 1,477 felons thus far convicted under three-strikes were violent offenders who averaged five felony convictions. And a 1996 survey by the Joint Centers for Political and Economic Studies found that 82 percent of all Americans, including 73 percent of black Americans, favored three-strikes laws.[19]

◆ ◆ ◆

After Three Strikes passed, the supporters expected not only to sentence people with three separate convictions for serious crimes but also four-time and even five-time violent criminals. These four- and five-strike crimes would have been prevented if Washington State had enacted Three Strikes sooner.

Charles Ben Finch has always been a violent predator. Strike one occurred in 1970 when he was convicted of assault and battery with a deadly weapon in Oklahoma. He was also convicted of two non-strike burglaries that same year. He was sentenced to three years but was paroled in 1971.

Strike two was for a first-degree manslaughter conviction in 1976, also in Oklahoma. This time he was sentenced to four years in prison. Again, he did not serve his complete sentence since Finch arrived in Seattle in June 1979.

Finch committed strike three that same year for the first-degree rape of an elderly widow during a burglary. Angry and intoxicated, Finch broke into a home-furnishing store and started breaking lamps, cabinets, tables, and other items. The widow who lived above the store investigated the noise and was dragged into an elevator and raped at least twice.

If Three Strikes had been the law back then, his violent crime sprees would have ended there. Unfortunately, Finch was released on parole just nine years later.

The consequences were deadly. In the summer of 1994, Finch committed strike four when he walked into a mobile home occupied by his estranged wife and fatally shot a visiting blind man in the head. He then threatened his wife and her eighty-one-year-old mother with the gun.

Charles Finch eventually called the police and opened fire when they responded to his 911 call. A Snohomish county deputy sheriff was murdered by one of the six shots fired by Finch.

Finch has now been sentenced to death for the cold, calculated murders of two men. These two murders would have been prevented if Three Strikes had been enacted sooner.

—DAVE LaCOURSE,
"HOW THREE STRIKES HAS FARED IN WASHINGTON STATE,"
WASHINGTON INSTITUTE FOR POLICY STUDIES, FORTHCOMING FALL 1996

The results of a study of Wisconsin prisoners from Milwaukee are very revealing.[20] The study, the first of its kind, was designed to test the validity of such typical "expert" statements about who really goes to prison as the following:

A large number of [Wisconsin prisoners] are not violent or assaultive [and] pose little risk of harm to others. . . . Forty-two percent of Wisconsin prison admissions have been identified on the "low-risk sentence track."

—WISCONSIN CORRECTIONAL SYSTEM REVIEW PANEL,
FINAL REPORT, JUNE 1991

Over half the offenders sent to prison in Wisconsin each year have committed a property offense. . . . About ninety percent have not committed any assaultive offense. . . . While there are certainly some assaultive, dangerous, sophisticated offenders in Wisconsin's prisons, most do not fit this profile.

—ROBERT M. LAFOLLETTE INSTITUTE OF PUBLIC AFFAIRS,
DOLLARS AND SENSE, POLICY CHOICES AND THE WISCONSIN BUDGET, 1994

The Wisconsin study was based on a scientific sample of the prison population. It involved a review of more than 3,500 pages from official inmate files, including information on prisoners' criminal activity as adults and juveniles. Among the findings on the CGPAs—the criminal grade point averages—of those imprisoned in Wisconsin were the following:

- About 91 percent of prisoners had a current or prior adult or juvenile conviction for a *violent* crime.
- About 7 percent of prisoners were in prison for drug trafficking. None were sentenced solely for possession or as drug users. Fewer than 2 percent were first-time drug or property offenders.
- About 90 percent of prisoners had a prior adult or juvenile conviction, 77 percent had violated terms of a prior probation or parole commitment, and 41 percent committed their latest crime while on probation or parole.
- Inmates sentenced to intensive community-based supervision did not fit the "low-risk" profile identified for the program when it

was sold to the legislature in 1991. They were far more dangerous and had longer criminal histories. Not surprisingly, therefore, escapes from "intensive supervision" have been common.

- Prisoners served less than half their sentenced time behind bars; 82 percent were eligible for discretionary parole within a few years.

So much for such misleading labels for prisoners as "nonviolent offender," "low-risk inmate," "first-time offender," "mere drug offender," "petty property offender," and so on. Once we know their CGPAs, the only general terms that apply to over 90 percent of all prisoners are *violent offender, repeat offender, or violent repeat offender.*

READING RAP SHEETS

Try calculating prisoners' CGPAs yourself. Read the CGPA Appendix at the end of the book. You'll be looking at a random sample of 40 individual profiles of "property offenders," "drug offenders," and "low-risk" community-based offenders drawn from the Wisconsin study—the *least* serious offenders. (This is as close as you may ever get to looking at a real rap sheet.) Start counting. Eleven of the 15 "property offenders" and 9 of the 12 "drug offenders" had committed one or more violent crimes. Together they averaged 9.2 adult arrests. About 87 percent of the "property offenders" and 75 percent of the "drug offenders" had violated probation or parole once or more.

Even more important, read what's behind the prisoners' CGPAs. Take a moment and take a close look at the "other background" sections of the profiles. Let's look at some real-life typical cases, two who went to prison with their latest conviction for a drug offense, the other incarcerated for a property crime. The first "drug offender," sentenced to five years for possession of illegal drugs with intent to distribute while armed, had, as an adult, scored three prior arrests and one incarceration (including at least one for a violent crime) as well as parole and probation violations—this following on a juvenile record that included armed robbery as well as unarmed robbery and auto thefts. The state's presentence investigation reported that the subject did not "express any remorse or emotion for being involved in criminal activity [and] totally lacks self control. . . . [P]robation was of minimum significance to him." Another, sentenced to 1.8 years for delivery of cocaine, had been arrested five times (and incarcerated twice) as an adult for burglary and robbery as well as drug possession and, as a juvenile, for third-degree sexual assault and theft.

The "property offenders" had similarly checkered careers. One, having already earned 17 arrests and five prison terms for forgery, burglary, and theft as an adult, had most recently distinguished himself by severely assaulting an elderly priest while robbing him. "Subject admitted he had been consuming alcohol and smoking cocaine prior to the offense," according to the prison intake report when he began serving his three-year sentence.

And that is just what is on their official records. Swept entirely under the rug are all of the more serious crimes that imprisoned drug offenders have plea-bargained away—not to mention all of the wholly undetected, unprosecuted, and unpunished crimes they may have done.

As several studies have estimated, on average, each prisoner commits a dozen or more crimes a year when free, most of which are neither detected nor punished in any way.[21]

So, to return to a question posed earlier: who really goes to prison? The answer is, for the most part, really bad guys. They are career criminals with almost uniformly high CGPAs. They are felons who are very dangerous. That's who.

At the same time, we believe that some nonviolent, first-time offenders do belong in prison. White collar criminals, those who commit fraud, those who extort or embezzle, and those who conspire or cover up can be just as deserving of punishment as any street predator. And we suspect that most Americans—most people who believe in equal justice under the law—agree with us.

Whenever you hear about "nonviolent," "property," or "drug" offenders behind bars, ask, "Is that the whole story—the complete criminal grade point average—or just the felon's latest or best grade in 'Plea Bargaining 101'?" To stop revolving-door justice, we must stop being fooled by so-called experts who claim that prisons are full of misplaced angels who deserve no punishment.

How Much Time Do Violent Prisoners Really Serve?

The unvarnished truth, therefore, is that America's prisons hold few petty, first-time, nonviolent criminals. Moreover, even violent prisoners spend relatively little time behind bars before being released.

As Table 3-6 indicates, violent offenders released from prison in 1992 served an average of 48 percent of their time behind bars (both jail credit and prison time)—in other words, only 43 months of time behind bars on sentences of 89 months. Between 1988 and 1992 the percent of time served in prisons by released violent offenders rose from 43 percent to 48 percent. But over the same period the average sentence *dropped* from 95 months to 89 months, meaning that the actual average time served increased only from 41 months to 43 months. Overall, therefore, between 1988 and 1992, there was little change in the amount of time or in the percentage of sentence served for different types of violent crimes.[22] Among those violent offenders released in 1992, even murderers served only 5.9 years of 12.4-year terms.

TABLE 3-6. TIME SERVED IN CONFINEMENT BY VIOLENT OFFENDERS RELEASED IN 1992

Type of offense	Average sentence (months)	Average time served[a] (months)	Percent of sentence served
All violent	89	43	48
Homicide	149	71	48
Rape	117	65	56
Kidnapping	104	52	50
Robbery	95	44	46
Sexual assault	72	35	49
Assault	61	29	48
Other	60	28	47

[a] Includes jail credit and prison time.

Source: *Prison Sentences and Time Served for Violence* (Bureau of Justice Statistics, April 1995), p. 1.

Much the same picture holds when the data on how much time violent felons actually serve in prison are broken down on a state-by-state basis. For example, Figure 3-4 displays the percent of various categories of convicted violent felons in Virginia in 1992 who had at

FIGURE 3-4. PERCENT OF CONVICTED VIOLENT FELONS IN VIRGINIA WITH PRIOR CONVICTIONS, 1992

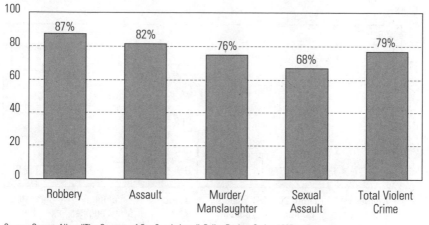

Source: George Allen, "The Courage of Our Convictions," *Policy Review*, Spring 1995, p. 5.

least one prior conviction. More than three-quarters of all violent criminals in Virginia prisons in 1992–93 had prior convictions. Figure 3-5 displays the average time served by Virginia felons released in 1993. Together, these two sets of data confirm that even most violent recidivists imprisoned for murder, rape, and robbery serve less than half of their sentenced time in confinement.[23]

It is possible, however, that truth-in-sentencing and related laws will succeed in increasing the amount of prison time actually served by violent offenders in Virginia and the rest of the nation. For example, the studies estimate that state prisoners admitted in 1992 could serve an average of 62 months (versus 43 months for violent offenders released in 1992) and 60 percent of their sentences (versus 48 percent).[24]

While such increases in the amount of time actually served by violent felons would constitute welcome steps in the right sentencing policy direction, there is reason to be cautious. For one thing, sentencing laws can change, and many states have yet to tighten their grip on convicted violent felons. Despite the universal use of mandatory sentencing laws for murder and many other crimes, state sentencing regimes vary widely.[25] Relatively few states have enacted and implemented strict truth-in-sentencing laws or related measures that keep violent felons behind bars for all or most of their terms.

FIGURE 3-5. AVERAGE SENTENCES VS. ACTUAL TIME SERVED BY VIOLENT
FELONS IN VIRGINIA, 1993, BY OFFENSE AT CONVICTION

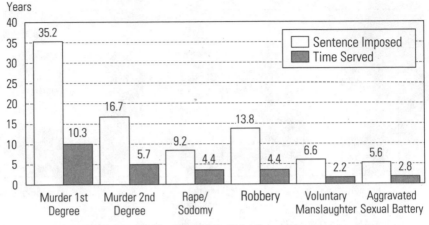

Source: George Allen, "The Courage of Our Convictions," *Policy Review,* Spring 1995, p. 6.

*David Shotkoski had always wanted to become a Major League
pitcher. One day in 1995, he kissed his wife and young daughter
good-bye and left North Aurora, Illinois, for spring training with
the Atlanta Braves in West Palm Beach, Florida. There, the 30-
year-old Shotkoski was taking an evening walk when a gunman
demanded his money. Shot twice, he managed to stagger some 300
feet to a busy street before collapsing near the curb.*

*Indicted for his murder was Neal Douglas Evans, a career crimi-
nal who, despite 13 previous convictions for drug crimes, theft,
burglaries, and robberies, had slip-slided past forgiving judges for
years. Because of a judicial order to relieve alleged overcrowding in
Florida prisons, Evans was on his fourth so-called conditional release when he was charged with killing David.*

*"I just don't understand," Felicia Shotkoski said when she
learned that a habitual felon had been charged with her husband's
murder. How could she understand? For the man who killed her
beloved husband, the man who stole a young girl's father away from
her for life, was a known felon released repeatedly by a justice
system that all the experts agree imprisons mainly first-time, nonviolent, petty drug criminals for long periods.*[26]

CRIME BY COMMUNITY-BASED VIOLENT CONVICTS

It is clear that violent convicted offenders do not do much hard time behind bars. And it is equally clear that they do tremendous numbers of serious crimes when loose on the streets, including a frightening fraction of all murders. For starters, a recent analysis reveals the following:[27]

- In 1991, 45 percent of state prisoners were persons who, at the very time they committed their latest conviction offenses, were on probation or parole.
- Based only on the latest conviction offenses that brought them to prison, the 162,000 probation violators committed at least 6,400 murders, 7,400 rapes, 10,400 assaults, and 17,000 robberies while "under supervision" in the community an average of 17 months.
- Based only on the latest conviction offenses that brought them back to prison, the 156,000 parole violators committed at least 6,800 murders, 5,500 rapes, 8,800 assaults, and 22,500 robberies while "under supervision" in the community an average of 13 months.
- The prior conviction offense was violent for half of parole violators returned to prison for a violent offense. The prior conviction offense was violent for 43 percent of probation violators sent to prison for a violent offense.
- Together, probation and parole violators committed 90,639 violent crimes while "under supervision" in the community.
- Over half of the 13,200 murder victims were strangers.
- Over a quarter of the 11,600 rape victims were under the age of 12, and over 55 percent of them were under 18.
- Of all arrested murderers adjudicated in 1992 in urban courts, 38 percent were on probation, parole, pretrial release, or in some other criminal justice status at the time of the murder.
- A fifth of all persons who were arrested for the murder of a law enforcement officer from 1988 to 1992 were on probation or parole at the time of the killing.

These numbers represent only the crimes done by probation and parole violators who were actually convicted of new crimes and sent to prison. They do not even begin to measure the total amount of murder and mayhem wrought by community-based violent criminals whom the system has had in custody one or more times but failed to restrain.

The number of persons who are on probation or parole in a given year exceeds the number who are on probation or parole on any given day. As Table 3-7 indicates, while 690,000 convicted criminals were on parole at the end of 1994, over 1 million cases were handled on parole in the course of the year. Likewise, while 2.96 million convicted offenders were on probation at the end of 1994, over 4.2 million cases were handled on probation in the course of the year.

TABLE 3-7. ADULTS ON PAROLE AND PROBATION, 1994

	1/1/94	Entries	Exits	12/31/94	Year
Parole	676,000	411,000	396,000	690,000	1,101,000
Probation	2,900,000	1,360,000	1,300,000	2,960,000	4,260,000

Note: Because of nonresponse or incomplete data, the population on 1/1/94 minus exits is not exactly equal to the 12/31/94 population. Also, both the yearly figures and the entry and exit counts may involve a small fraction of double counting because an undetermined number of adults on probation and parole enter and exit the system more than once a year.

Source: Calculated from *Probation and Parole, 1994* (Bureau of Justice Statistics, 1994), pp. 5, 6.

Large numbers of convicted violent criminals are on probation and parole—more, in fact, than are in prison. For example, as Joan R. Petersilia has found:

On any given day in the U.S. in 1991, there were an estimated 435,000 probationers and 155,000 parolees residing in local communities who have been convicted of violent crime—or over a half million offenders. If we compare that to the number of violent offenders residing in prison during the same year, we see that there were approximately 372,500 offenders convicted of violent crime in prison, and approximately 590,000 *outside* in the community on probation and parole![28]

The revolving-door numbers do not become any less disturbing when broken down by violent offense categories. If anything, the reverse is true. For example, 42 percent of felony weapons defendants in 1992 had a criminal status at the time of the offense—17 percent on probation, 10 percent on parole, and 14 percent on pretrial release. And of those felony-weapons defendants with a history of felony convictions, more than half had two or more such convictions.[29]

Nor do the numbers look any more comforting when examined on a state-by-state basis. For example, Table 3-8 tallies the crimes known to have been committed by prisoners released early from Florida prisons between January 1987 and October 1991—crimes committed during the period that the offenders would have been incarcerated had their prison sentences not been reduced. It shows that prisoners released early were responsible for 25,819 crimes, including 4,654 violent crimes. Among the violent crimes that would have been averted had these offenders remained behind bars rather than being released early were 346 murders and 185 sexual assaults.

TABLE 3-8. CRIMES KNOWN TO HAVE BEEN COMMITTED BY CONVICTED OFFENDERS RELEASED EARLY FROM FLORIDA PRISONS, 1/87 TO 10/91

	Number	Percent
Violent crimes	4,654	18.0
Property crimes	11,834	45.9
Drugs	9,331	36.1
Total	25,819	100

Source: *SAC Notes* (Florida Statistical Analysis Center, July 1993), p. 3.

Likewise, Table 3-9 summarizes the data on how many persons convicted of murder in Virginia from 1990 through 1993 were on parole, probation, pretrial release, or had some other form of community-based legal status at the very moment they murdered. It shows that fully a third of the 1,411 convicted murderers were "in custody" at the time they killed—91 on parole, 156 on probation, 81 on pretrial release, and 146 on electronic monitoring, with suspended sentences, or other forms of supervision.

Robert "Mudman" Simon, a violent and repeat offender, was in Pennsylvania's Graterford prison. He was serving a 10-to-20-year sentence for third-degree murder. He was paroled from Graterford in 1995 after serving 12.5 years—longer and a higher percentage of the sentence than most prisoners ever complete. But "Mudman" had a criminal history that involved outlaw motorcycle gangs, and a poor overall prison disciplinary record to boot. During his last two years at Graterford, however, he had no official infractions, so the staff recommended him for parole. A Pennsylvania parole board member spent only a few minutes reviewing the recommendation and "Mudman's" criminal history before authorizing a release date. One condition of "Mudman's" parole was to stay away from criminal associates and bikers. But, like so many parolees, he received no close supervision. Within three months of his release, he fatally shot a New Jersey police officer. As a result of the public furor over the case, Pennsylvania has begun to tighten its parole practices. But, as in most states, there's a long way to go before early-release practices and failures to supervise dangerous criminals released to the streets become things of the past. As a Graterford official described the state's usual, pre-"Mudman" parole process, "We didn't look at the crime." [30]

TABLE 3-9. CONVICTED MURDERERS IN VIRGINIA, LEGAL STATUS AT THE TIME THEY MURDERED, 1990–1993

Year	Probation	Parole	Pretrial Release	Other	None
1990	39	19	18	21	263
1991	36	21	17	40	231
1992	38	26	26	46	235
1993	43	25	20	39	208
1990–93	156	91	81	146	937

Note: Other includes unsupervised probation, community diversion, electronic monitoring, and suspended sentences.
Source: Virginia Department of Corrections, Virginia Department of Criminal Justice Services, 1995.

The closer one examines the facts and figures about how much violent crime is done because of revolving-door justice, the plainer it becomes that the failure to restrain known criminals accounts for much of the predatory street crime that plagues our cities. For example, in 1994 a series of investigative reports by a local newspaper turned up plenty of facts about revolving-door justice in Dade County, Florida, which encompasses Miami. Only 671 of 4,615 identified local career criminals (average of 20 prior felony arrests and six convictions) were behind bars. From January 1992 to March 1994, 5,284 people were arrested twice or more and charged with violent or other serious felony crimes, including murders. Some 2,298 of them (43 percent) were rearrested for crimes worse than their first arrests. Only 9 percent (about 500) were convicted and sentenced to prison.[31]

Similarly, a 1994 local newspaper investigation into crime and punishment in New Jersey revealed that in 1993, 217,347 cases entered the state's criminal justice pipeline. Four out of 10 cases were reduced or screened out of the system. Only 24 percent of those arrested and indicted wound up behind bars. About 40 percent got probation. Of those convicted, under 30 percent saw the inside of a prison for six months or more.[32]

In fact, many local newspapers around the country have done such investigative reports on the reality of revolving-door justice. But such reports are virtually unheard of in the national press, which spills incomparably more ink about how many convicted criminals are in prison rather than how many are not, and focuses little on how many released felons commit more crimes.

By the same token, it speaks volumes that while one can easily find detailed information on such things as the number and kind of treatment programs afforded to convicted rapists,[33] most states compile no data on such things as the ages of rapists' victims,[34] or on how many convicted murderers were on probation, parole, or pretrial release at the time that they killed.[35] Some state probation and parole agencies do not even keep data on how many of their charges are returned to prison during the term of their supervision.[36] Undoubtedly, most Americans would be more interested in knowing whether sex offenders are being punished and incapacitated, whether children are being raped, and whether convicted felons are being set free to murder, than in knowing whether notoriously hard-to-rehabilitate felons are enjoying a certain treatment regimen.

To stop revolving-door justice at the back end, we must do at least four things: (1) demand to know the total CGPAs (criminal grade point averages) of all felons released to the streets, (2) base incarceration decisions on considerations of the offender's dangerousness and deservingness of punishment, (3) keep violent and repeat criminals restrained for as long as is needed, and (4) beef up probation and parole so that community-based criminals are kept on a short leash.

REINVENTING PROBATION AND PAROLE

Similarly, most citizens want to know just why it is that probation and parole are failing to restrain so many violent criminals, and what, if anything, can be done to restrain them. It is all too obvious that hundreds of thousands of convicted criminals now on probation and parole need to be incarcerated.

But adopting either blanket no-parole or no-probation policies would be unwise, unworkable, and impossibly expensive. Remember: even though millions of crimes are committed by community-based felons who relapse, not everyone on probation or parole commits new crimes. For example, we know that within three years of sentencing, nearly half of all probationers and parolees commit a new crime or abscond.[37] But we also thereby know something else of equal importance, namely, that half of these community-based convicts do *not* enter (or flee) through the revolving door.

But how, if at all, can the justice system do a much better job of determining which half is which *before* it is too late—that is, before released community-based felons commit more murder and mayhem on the streets? How can it sort offenders more intelligently so that those who need to be restrained in prison remain behind bars, those who need to be restrained by hands-on supervision on the streets are effectively supervised, and those who are highly unlikely to violate the terms of their community-based sentences are monitored accordingly?

Those who in the 1960s made the initial push for the widespread use of "alternatives to incarceration" stressed that caseloads must be kept within manageable limits. A 1967 presidential commission on crime recommended "an average ratio of 35 offenders per officer."[38] But in many jurisdictions today, officers "supervise" hundreds of "cases" at once. Those who in recent years have attempted to salvage the wreck of probation and parole have claimed that, by returning to intensive supervision, convicted criminals can be handled on the streets in ways that protect the public and its purse better than either routine probation or parole.

Unfortunately, however, more intensive programs have done little to remedy the problems of probationer and parolee noncompliance and recidivism. For example, a recent study found that over 90 percent of all probationers were already part of the very graduated punishment system called for by advocates of "intermediate sanctions"—substance abuse counseling, house arrest, community service, victim restitution programs, and so on. But about half of all probationers still did not comply with the terms of their probation, and only one-fifth of the violators ever went to jail for their noncompliance. As the study concluded, "Intermediate sanctions are not rigorously enforced."[39]

Even the most intensive forms of intermediate sanctions have not proven highly effective. For example, the most comprehensive experimental study of intensive supervision programs for high-risk probationers concluded that these programs "are not effective for high-risk offenders" and are "more expensive than routine probation and apparently provide no greater guarantees for public safety." Similarly, the best experimental study of intensive supervision programs for high-risk parolees found that the "results were the opposite of what was intended," as the programs were not associated with fewer crimes or lower costs than routine parole.[40]

But it is important to note that even the "intensive" programs that failed were not all that intensive. For example, Joan R. Petersilia has recently found that most probationers get almost no supervision, while even probationers who are categorized as high-risk offenders and slated for intensive monitoring receive little direct, face-to-face oversight. As she writes, if "probationers are growing in numbers and are increasingly more serious offenders, then they are in need of more supervision, not less. But less is exactly what they have been getting over the past decade."[41]

And note: this is *not* the fault of America's probation and parole officers, most of whom do the virtually impossible job of "caseload management" as well as it can be done given the legal, budgetary, and other constraints under which they presently operate.

Rather, if Americans want to slow or stop revolving-door justice, then we must be ready and willing to invest not only in keeping more violent and repeat criminals behind bars longer, but in keeping more community-based offenders under strict supervision. We can afford neither to leave probation and parole to business as usual nor to abandon them. Community-based corrections departments must be reinvented administratively as law enforcement agencies dedicated first and foremost to restraining violent and repeat criminals. Reinventing probation and parole will inevitably mean reinvesting in them. As Petersilia has estimated, we "currently spend about $200 per year per probationer for supervision. It is no wonder that recidivism rates are so high."[42] In short, there can be no denying the reality of revolving-door justice, and hence no escape from the need to restrain and punish more violent and repeat criminals more effectively both behind bars and on the streets.[43]

DOES PRISON PAY?

How should we decide whether it's worth the money to imprison a convicted criminal? Imprisonment offers at least four types of social benefits. The first is retribution: imprisoning Peter punishes him and expresses society's desire to do justice. Second is deterrence: imprisoning Peter may deter either him or Paul or both from committing crimes in the future. Third is rehabilitation: while behind bars, Peter may participate in drug treatment or other programs which reduce the chances that he will return to crime when free. Fourth is incapacitation: from his cell, Peter can't commit crimes against anyone save other prisoners, staff, or visitors.

At present, it is harder to measure the retribution, deterrence, or rehabilitation value of imprisonment to society than it is to measure its incapacitation value. The types of opinion surveys and data sets that would enable one to arrive at meaningful estimates of the first three social benefits of imprisonment simply do not yet exist.

As columnist Ben Wattenberg so vividly put it and everyone grasps, "A thug in prison can't shoot your sister." Few criminologists (and even fewer average citizens) doubt that if we emptied the prisons tonight we would have more crime tomorrow. But how much serious crime is averted each year by keeping those convicted criminals who are sentenced to prison behind bars, as opposed to alternative sentences? Do the social benefits of imprisonment, measured only as an incapacitation tool, exceed the social costs? In short, for what types of offenders under what conditions do "prisons pay"? A first step—and only a first step—in answering this question is to estimate how many crimes prisoners commit when free.

Whether or not imprisoning Peter keeps Paul honest, imprisoning Peter for all or most of his term saves society from the human and financial toll he would have inflicted if free. It costs society as much as $25,000 to keep a convicted violent or repeat criminal locked up for a year. Every social expenditure imposes opportunity costs (a tax dollar spent on a prison is a tax dollar not spent on a preschool, and vice versa). But what does it cost crime victims, their families, friends, employers, and the rest of society to let a convicted criminal roam the streets in search of victims?

A recent study of the cost of crimes to victims found that in 1992 a total of 33.6 million criminal victimizations occurred. Economic loss of some kind occurred in 71 percent of all personal crimes (rape, robbery, assault, personal theft) and 23 percent of all violent crimes (rape, robbery, assault). The study estimated that in 1992 crime victims lost $17.6 billion in direct costs (losses from property theft or damage, cash losses, medical expenses, lost pay from lost work). This estimate, however, did not include direct costs to victims that occurred six months or more after the crime (for example, medical costs). Nor did it include decreased work productivity, less tangible costs of pain and suffering, increases to insurance premiums as a result of filing claims, moving costs incurred as a result of victimization, and other indirect costs.[44]

Another recent study took a somewhat more comprehensive view of the direct costs of crime and included some indirect costs as well. The study estimated the costs and monetary value of lost quality of life in 1987 due to death and nonfatal physical and psychological injury resulting from violent crime. Using various measures, the study estimated that each murder costs $2.4 million, each rape $60,000, each arson almost $50,000, each assault $22,000, and each robbery $25,000. It estimated that lifetime costs for all violent crimes totaled $178 billion during 1987 to 1990.[45] And, as noted earlier, the violent crimes committed in America each year cost over $400 billion.[46]

Even these numbers, however, omit the sort of detailed cost accounting that is reflected in site-specific, crime-specific studies. For example, a survey of admissions to Wisconsin hospitals over a 41-month period found that 1,035 patients were admitted for gunshot wounds caused by assaults. Gunshot wound victims admitted during this period accumulated more than $16 million in hospital bills, about $6.8 million of it paid by taxes. Long-term costs rise far higher. For example, just one shotgun assault victim in this survey was likely to cost more than $5 million in lost income and medical expenses over the next 35 years.[47]

How much of the human and financial toll of crime could be avoided by incarcerating violent and repeat criminals for all or most of their terms? All studies that have attempted to analyze the social costs and benefits of imprisonment have employed much cruder and far lower estimates of the social costs of crime than were employed in the studies summarized above. Even so, all have found that, at the margin, the social benefits of imprisonment exceed the social costs. One such study, commissioned by the National Institute of Justice, found that the "lowest estimate of the benefit of operating an additional prison cell for a year ($172,000) is more than twice as high as the most extreme high estimate of the cost of operating such a cell ($70,000)." Another such study, one based on data from the aforementioned Wisconsin prisoner self-report survey, found that imprisoning 100 typical felons "costs $2.5 million, but leaving these criminals on the streets costs $4.6 million." A third such study, based on data from the New Jersey prisoner self-report survey, found that it costs society more than twice as much to let the typical prisoner out as it does to keep him in.[48]

In the 1980s rates of imprisonment rose and crime rates fell. From 1980 to 1992 the 10 states that had the highest increase in their prison populations relative to total FBI index crime experienced, on average, a decline in their crime rates of more than 20 percent, while the 10 states with the smallest increases in incarceration rates averaged nearly a 9 percent increase in crime rates.[49] A 1986 study by the National Academy of Sciences estimated that doubling the prison population between 1973 and 1982 probably reduced the number of burglaries and robberies in the country by 10 to 20 percent.[50] A 1994 review of the statistical literature on the relationship between imprisonment rates and crime rates concluded that a 10 percent increase in the likelihood of being imprisoned after conviction for a violent crime would reduce violent crime by about 7 percent.[51]

It is one thing to say that a person cannot commit a crime while incarcerated and quite another to say that the overall crime rate will go down by the increased use of imprisonment. One recent study suggests that the simple incapacitation effects of imprisonment (how many crimes are averted by keeping known, convicted offenders behind bars or, conversely, the increase in the level of crime caused by an increase in the use of probation or parole) may be socially significant without even being detected in crime rates (rates that can fluctuate for demographic and other reasons having little or nothing to do with sentencing policies or the justice system more generally).[52]

For example, in 1989 there were an estimated 66,000 fewer rapes, 323,000 fewer robberies, 380,000 fewer assaults, and 3.3 million fewer burglaries attributable to the difference between the crime rates of 1973 versus those of 1989 (that is, applying 1973 crime rates to the 1989 population). If only one-half or one-quarter of the reductions were the result of rising incarceration rates, "that would still leave prisons responsible for sizable reductions in crime." Tripling the prison population from 1975 to 1989 "potentially reduced reported and unreported violent crime by 10 to 15 percent below what it would have been, thereby potentially preventing a conservatively estimated 390,000 murders, rapes, robberies, and aggravated assaults in 1989 alone."[53]

The more sophisticated and sound the study, the stronger are the findings that incarceration cuts crime. For example, a prisoner self-report survey conducted in Wisconsin in 1990 and representing a random sample of 6 percent of the state's prisoner population found that in the year before imprisonment, prisoners committed a median of 12 property or violent crimes and a mean of 141 such crimes, excluding all drug crimes. A prisoner self-report survey conducted in New Jersey in 1993 and representing a random sample of 4 percent of the state's prisoner population found that in the year before imprisonment, prisoners committed a median of 12 property or violent crimes and a mean of 220 such crimes, excluding drug crimes.[54] Another study found that "in the 1970s and 1980s [imprisonment of] each additional state prisoner averted at least 17 index crimes on average. . . . For several reasons, the real impact may be much greater, and for recent years a better estimate may be 21 crimes averted per additional prisoner." Strikingly similar findings were reported in a 1995 study produced via the National Bureau of Economic Research and other recent studies.[55]

Still, a great deal of research remains to be done on the social costs and benefits of imprisonment and other sentencing options. For example, the hidden costs of incarceration include losses in worker productivity and employability. Likewise, long-term imprisonment means geriatric inmates and their associated health care costs. But many incarcerated persons enter prison with anemic work records, a history of welfare dependence, and a fair probability of having to rely on government to pay for their health care whether or not they are incarcerated. By the same token, while going to prison undoubtedly lowers the overall life prospects of some, it unquestionably raises the future well-being of others.

Also, we note that per capita corrections spending varies greatly from one jurisdiction to the next. For example, prison operating costs in Texas grew from $91 million in 1980 to $1.84 billion in 1994, about a tenfold increase in real terms, while the state's prison population barely doubled. In Pennsylvania and other big states, corrections spending has grown much more slowly. Before we can get a real policy-relevant handle on the social costs and benefits of incarceration versus other sentencing options, researchers will need to dig much deeper than criminologists have dug into the basic public finance questions related to crime and punishment.

> *One of the youthful criminals whose story is told in Edward Humes'*
> *finely etched, powerfully upsetting portrait of a gloomy corner of*
> *American life is one George Trevino, sentenced to 10 years of*
> *detention for participating in a bungled armed-robbery attempt*
> *when he was 16. George is a remarkable young man, and this*
> *judgment is not made in the spirit of "society is always to blame"*
> *liberalism. George, like the youth in Francois Truffaut's "400*
> *Blows," had been abandoned by almost every adult responsible for*

*his welfare. He was ditched first by his single mother, when he was
5, and thereafter by overburdened social workers for the state of
California who managed his life as though it were a bureaucratic
abstraction. They removed him from places where he was doing
well, for example, and sent him to live with dysfunctional, crack-
smoking relatives. When George (a pseudonym, like those given to
some of the book's other young offenders) started getting arrested
for fights and hanging out with gang members, the probation system
ignored him. "The state made George what he is today," Humes
declares. "No one blamed the nameless bureaucrats who took an
A-B student and sent him to a home troubled by drugs," he writes.
"There is no accountability in the system." Later, after his sentencing, George tells Humes: "That's how the system programs
you. They let you go and they know that just encourages you, and
then they can get you on something worse later on. It's like they set
you up. Of course I'm to blame, too, for going along with it. I didn't
have to do those things, I know that."* [56]

THE FIRST REVOLVING DOOR

The "first revolving door"—the juvenile justice system—is the place
where the need to incarcerate certain types of violent and repeat
offenders, and to structure no-nonsense but treatment-oriented community-based sanctions for less serious youth offenders, is even more
acute and pressing.

As we argued earlier, the fundamental problem is moral poverty—
and not just on the part of the offender. Due to a different sort of moral
poverty—let's call it moral bankruptcy—the violence and mayhem
wrought by moral poverty, the violent and vicious behavior of juvenile
super-predators, are strongly *reinforced* rather than restrained by the
way the justice system responds to kids who kill, rape, rob, steal, and
deal deadly drugs.

As countless studies have shown, adult repeat offenders often begin
as juvenile repeat offenders. For example, a study of juvenile courts in
Maricopa County, Arizona, and the state of Utah revealed that significant fractions of youths returned to juvenile court after a first
referral for the following offenses: burglary (58 percent), motor vehicle

theft (51 percent), robbery (51 percent), forcible rape (45 percent), and aggravated assault (44 percent).[57]

Likewise, take a look at the data on juvenile crime in Virginia presented in Figure 3-6. Only three in ten youths charged with a violent crime are transferred to adult courts or locked up in secure detention facilities. Kids convicted of first-degree murder serve an average of under six years, and cannot be held beyond age 21.

Virginia is not unique. In 1994 all but two states had some statutory provision for sealing or expunging of a juvenile record. And as Table 3-10 shows, while virtually every state permits juvenile delinquency cases to be waived to criminal court, juvenile court judges transferred to criminal court less than 2 percent of juvenile delinquency cases that were filed between 1988 and 1992.[58]

Not surprisingly, most Americans have been calling for changes in the juvenile justice system that would enable law enforcement officials to get a firm grip on youth criminals. As Tables 3-12 to 3-15 indicate, attitudes toward treatment of juveniles who commit crimes have solidified around the idea that kids who do serious crimes should face certain punishments.

But, despite many legislative efforts aimed at trying more juvenile criminals as adults, not much has happened. In 1991 about 58,000

FIGURE 3-6. JUVENILE CRIME IN VIRGINIA

Time Served by Minors Convicted of Violent Crimes

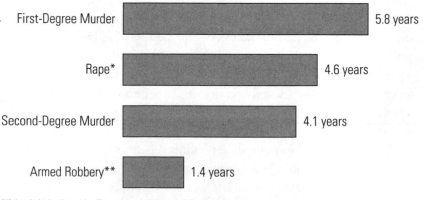

*If the victim is 13 or older. The average is 2.9 years if the victim is younger.
**Robbery of a person; the average is 0.7 years for robbery of a business.
Source: *Washington Post*, January 16, 1996, p. B5

Minors Charged with Violent Crimes
The rate has increased 91 percent in the last decade.

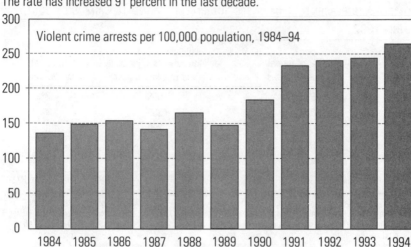

Violent crime arrests per 100,000 population, 1984–94

What Happens to Minors Charged with Violent Crimes

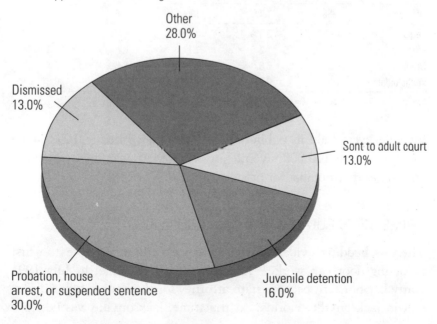

TABLE 3-10. NUMBER OF FORMAL DELINQUENCY CASES NATIONWIDE AND THE NUMBER AND PERCENTAGE OF CASES JUDICIALLY WAIVED TO CRIMINAL COURT, 1988–1992

Year	Number of formal delinquency cases	Number of formal delinquency cases judicially waived to criminal court	Judicial waiver rate[a]
1988	569,596	7,005	1.2%
1989	608,593	8,350	1.4
1990	654,742	8,708	1.3
1991	689,328	10,933	1.6
1992	743,673	11,748	1.6

Note: The broad offense categories used in our analysis included person, property, drugs, and public order as defined by the Office of Juvenile Justice and Delinquency Prevention. The person category includes criminal homicide, forcible rape, robbery, aggravated assault, simple assault, and other person offenses—such as kidnapping and harassment. The property category includes burglary, larceny, motor vehicle theft, arson, vandalism, stolen property offenses, trespassing, and other property offenses—such as fraud, counterfeiting, and embezzlement. The drug category includes unlawful sale, purchase, distribution, manufacture, cultivation, transport, possession, or use of a controlled or prohibited substance or drug. The public order category includes weapons offenses, nonviolent sex offenses, and liquor law violations.

[a] The waiver rate is the ratio of the number of waived cases to the number of formal delinquency cases. The percentage of all delinquency cases that were handled formally varied across states.

Source: *GAO/GGD-95-170 Juvenile Case Dispositions* (developed by GAO using NJCDA data), p. 10.

TABLE 3-11. JUDICIAL WAIVER RATE BY OFFENSE

Offense	1988	1989	1990	1991	1992
Person	1.9%	2.0%	2.1%	2.4%	2.4%
Property	1.2	1.2	1.1	1.2	1.3
Drugs	1.5	2.8	2.7	4.4	3.1
Public order	0.5	0.5	0.6	0.7	0.8

Source: *GAO/GGD-95-170 Juvenile Case Dispositions* (developed by GAO using NJCDA data), p. 11.

juveniles were held in public juvenile facilities.[59] But in 1992 alone there were over 110,000 juvenile arrests for violent crimes, and about 16.5 times that number for property and other crimes.[60]

CRIME *WITH* PUNISHMENT: JACKSONVILLE

There is budding evidence that concerted efforts to close the first revolving door can work.[61] To cite just one example, in July 1991 Harry L. Shorstein became state attorney for the Fourth Judicial Circuit in Jacksonville, Florida. At that time, Jacksonville was besieged

TABLE 3-12. ATTITUDES TOWARD TREATMENT OF JUVENILES WHO COMMIT VIOLENT CRIMES

By race, ethnicity, community, and whether respondent is a crime victim, United States, 1994[a]

Question: "In your view, should juveniles who commit violent crimes be treated the same as adults, or should they be given more lenient treatment in a juvenile court?"

	Treated the same as adults	Given more lenient treatment	Treated tougher[b]	Depends[b]	Don't know
National	68%	13%	c	16%	3%
Race, ethnicity					
White	69	12	c	16	3
Black	71	17	c	11	1
Hispanic	64	15	c	19	2
Community					
City	70	7	1	17	5
Suburb	68	15	c	16	1
Small town	66	17	c	16	1
Rural area	69	14	c	15	2
Victim of crime	71	8	1	15	5

[a] Percents may not add to 100 because of rounding.

[b] Response volunteered.

[c] Less than 0.5 percent.

Source: *Sourcebook of Criminal Justice Statistics 1994* (Bureau of Justice Statistics, 1994), p. 179.

by violent crime, much of it committed by juvenile offenders. In the year before Shorstein arrived, juvenile arrests had risen by 27 percent, but most young habitual criminals were released quickly. Jacksonville's finest were doing their best to remove serious young criminals from the streets, but the rest of the system was not following suit.

Then, in March 1992 Shorstein instituted an unprecedented program to prosecute and incarcerate dangerous juvenile offenders as adults. In most parts of the country, juvenile criminals for whom the law mandates adult treatment are not actually eligible for state prison sentences and are routinely placed on probation without serving any jail time. But Shorstein's program was for real. He assigned 10 veteran attorneys to a new juvenile-prosecution unit. Another attorney, funded by the Jacksonville Sheriff's Office, was assigned to prosecute repeat juvenile auto thieves.

TABLE 3-13. ATTITUDES TOWARD SUCCESS OF TREATING JUVENILE OFFENDERS
DIFFERENTLY THAN ADULT OFFENDERS WHO COMMIT THE SAME CRIMES
By demographic characteristics, United States, 1994

Question: "In most places, there are criminal justice programs that treat juveniles differently than adults who commit the same crimes. These programs emphasize protecting and rehabilitating juveniles rather than punishing them. How successful would you say these programs have been at controlling juvenile crime?"

	Very successful	Moderately successful	Not very successful	Not successful at all
National	1%	24%	49%	23%
Sex				
Male	1	24	46	27
Female	1	23	51	20
Race				
White	1	23	49	23
Nonwhite[a]	6	24	45	23
Black	8	24	40	26
Age				
18 to 29 years	1	32	45	18
30 to 49 years	1	22	51	24
50 to 64 years	4	21	48	24
65 years and older	2	18	47	28
Education				
College post-graduate	1	22	53	19
College graduate	1	24	51	20
Some college	b	27	43	26
No college	2	21	50	24
Income				
$75,000 and over	0	21	54	24
$50,000 and over[c]	b	21	49	27
$30,000 to $49,999	1	24	50	22
$20,000 to $29,999	2	17	54	25
Under $20,000	2	27	46	20

TABLE 3-13, *cont'd*

	Very successful	Moderately successful	Not very successful	Not successful at all
Community				
Urban area	2	25	41	28
Suburban area	1	24	51	22
Rural area	1	23	56	17
Region				
East	1	29	41	24
Midwest	1	20	53	23
South	2	19	52	25
West	1	27	47	21
Politics				
Republican	1	23	55	17
Democrat	2	25	44	26
Independent	1	22	47	27

Note: The "don't know/refused" category has been omitted; therefore percents may not sum to 100.
[a] Includes black respondents.
[b] Less than 1 percent.
[c] Includes $75,000 and over category.
Source: *Sourcebook of Criminal Justice Statistics 1994* (Bureau of Justice Statistics, 1994), p. 179.

By the end of 1994 the program had sent hundreds of juvenile offenders to Jacksonville's jails and scores more to serve a year or more in Florida's prisons. Jacksonville's would-be street predators got the message, and the effect of deterrence soon appeared in the arrest statistics. From 1992 to 1994, total arrests of juveniles dropped from 7,184 to 5,475. From 1993 to 1994, juvenile arrests increased nationwide and by over 20 percent in Florida. But Jacksonville had a 30 percent decrease in all juvenile arrests, including a 41 percent decrease in juveniles arrested for weapons offenses, a 45 percent decrease for auto theft, and a 50 percent decrease for residential burglary. Although Jacksonville still has a serious violent crime problem, the number of people murdered there during the first half of this year *declined* by 25 percent compared with the same period a year ago.

But Shorstein's approach has not been all punishment, no prevention. He has attacked the moral poverty problem as it relates to crime and drugs from both ends. As he has stated, "I believe we need a two-pronged approach to dealing with the epidemic of juvenile crime.

TABLE 3-14. ATTITUDES TOWARD TREATMENT OF JUVENILE FIRST-TIME OFFENDERS COMPARED TO ADULT FIRST-TIME OFFENDERS

By demographic characteristics, United States, 1994

Question: "Do you think that juveniles convicted of their first crime should be given the same punishment as adults convicted of their first crime, or should juveniles be treated less harshly?"

	Treated the same	Treated less harshly	Depends on the circumstances[a]
National	50%	40%	9%
Sex			
Male	50	41	9
Female	50	40	8
Race			
White	50	40	9
Nonwhite[b]	50	44	4
Black	41	50	5
Age			
18 to 29 years	53	41	6
30 to 49 years	48	43	9
50 to 64 years	53	38	7
65 years and older	50	37	10
Education			
College post-graduate	41	51	8
College graduate	41	51	8
Some college	48	43	9
No college	56	34	8
Income			
$75,000 and over	40	55	5
$50,000 and over[c]	39	54	7
$30,000 to $49,999	52	39	8
$20,000 to $29,999	51	37	12
Under $20,000	56	34	7
Community			
Urban area	47	45	7
Suburban area	53	39	8
Rural area	52	35	11
Region			
East	43	42	14
Midwest	50	45	5
South	53	37	7
West	53	39	8

TABLE 3-14, *cont'd*

	Treated the same	Treated less harshly	Depends on the circumstances[a]
Politics			
Republican	51	41	7
Democrat	51	39	9
Independent	50	40	9

Note: The "don't know/refused" category has been omitted; therefore percents may not sum to 100.
[a] Response volunteered.
[b] Includes black respondents.
[c] Includes $75,000 and over category.
Source: *Sourcebook of Criminal Justice Statistics 1994* (Bureau of Justice Statistics, 1994), p. 180.

We must incarcerate repeat and violent juvenile offenders and at the same time intervene at an early age in an attempt to educate and habilitate juveniles at risk of becoming criminals."

Shorstein took the proactive and unprecedented step of hiring a career educator to act as a programming coordinator and liaison with Jacksonville schools. Members of his office including himself and other attorneys and staff members regularly make presentations at schools. These presentations warn young people that juvenile delinquency will no longer be tolerated in Jacksonville. As he reports, "I have sent several letters to all schools in Jacksonville to let students know the consequences of criminal behavior. If juveniles continue to break the law in Jacksonville or if they commit a violent act, they will be treated as adults and will be sentenced to up to one year in the Duval County Jail or to lengthy terms in the Florida State Prison. The response to these letters has been overwhelmingly supportive. Parents, teachers, and law enforcement officers have all been in support of our efforts to curb juvenile crime."

Shorstein also stresses that parents must do their part: "My investigators have arrested deadbeat parents for not sending their children to school. In Clay County my office successfully prosecuted a woman who refused to force her children to attend school. She was sentenced to sixty days in jail. My staff is lobbying for more effective laws to hold parents responsible for their children's school attendance."

In 1994 Shorstein began the Juvenile Justice Awareness Summer Program: "We started a hotline for parents to call if they were concerned their children were at risk of becoming involved in juvenile

TABLE 3-15. ATTITUDES TOWARD TREATMENT OF JUVENILES AFTER THEIR SECOND
OR THIRD CRIMES COMPARED TO ADULTS AFTER THEIR SECOND OR THIRD CRIMES
By demographic characteristics, United States, 1994

Question: "Do you think that juveniles convicted of their second or third crimes should be given the
same punishment as adults convicted of their second or third crimes—or should juveniles be
treated less harshly?"

	Treated the same	Treated less harshly	Depends on the circumstances[a]
National	83%	12%	4%
Sex			
Male	85	10	4
Female	81	14	5
Race			
White	83	12	5
Nonwhite[b]	86	12	2
Black	86	13	1
Age			
18 to 29 years	81	17	1
30 to 49 years	85	10	4
50 to 64 years	79	13	7
65 years and older	83	13	4
Education			
College post-graduate	69	25	5
College graduate	75	20	4
Some college	87	8	4
No college	85	11	4
Income			
$75,000 and over	78	17	2
$50,000 and over[c]	81	15	3
$30,000 to $49,999	78	13	8
$20,000 to $29,999	87	8	5
Under $20,000	85	13	2
Community			
Urban area	84	13	2
Suburban area	81	13	6
Rural area	83	10	7
Region			
East	77	15	7
Midwest	88	10	2
South	79	15	5
West	90	8	2

TABLE 3-15, *cont'd*

	Treated the same	Treated less harshly	Depends on the circumstances[a]
Politics			
Republican	85	11	4
Democrat	77	18	5
Independent	86	8	4

Note: The "don't know/refused" category has been omitted; therefore percents may not sum to 100.
[a] Response volunteered.
[b] Includes black respondents.
[c] Includes $75,000 and over category.
Source: *Sourcebook of Criminal Justice Statistics 1994* (Bureau of Justice Statistics, 1994), p. 180.

crime. Dozens of parents called and subsequently participated in the program. We repeated our summer program in 1995 and will again offer the program to the community [in 1996]. To date over 100 juveniles and their parents have benefited from our summer program. One particular parent wrote me to praise the program. She said she could not describe 'the effect the program had on her son.' "

Last but not least, Shorstein has looked for creative and effective ways to get the message across to young people that they should not choose a life of crime. In the beginning of 1994 the State Attorney's Office began to use the Victim Impact Panel (VIP) to let juveniles know how crime affects people's lives: "Actual victims tell juveniles how crime changed their lives. [Students] attend a VIP several weeks after visiting the courthouse. I believe the victim message is an important one and one juveniles relate to. Therefore, we have expanded the use of the panels to interested schools and other institutions."

Of course, neither the no-nonsense incarceration policy nor the tough-love programs have ended crime and delinquency in Jacksonville. But all the data indicate that they have made a real and positive difference. Shorstein and his colleagues have said no to no-fault justice, begun to close the revolving door, and helped address the real root cause of the nation's drug and crime body count—moral poverty. We desperately need more justice officials to do the same.

POLICING MORAL POVERTY: NEW YORK CITY

It is truly amazing how much good can be done by law enforcement officials who take doing justice seriously and muster the human, financial, and administrative resources necessary to address the social disorders that lead to crime. What prosecutor Harry L. Shorstein did in Jacksonville, police chief William J. Bratton did in none other than New York City, with results that were even more amazing.

As Bratton took the helm of the New York Police Department in 1994, serious crime began to drop . . . and drop . . . and drop. For two full years, crime fell in each and every precinct. Murders fell by *39 percent*. Robberies were cut by a third. Burglaries plummeted by about a quarter.

Soon, news of the "Bratton miracle" spread both nationally and internationally. The police chief made the cover of *Time* magazine. Reporters from abroad who only a few years earlier had filed stories on how crime was out of control in New York crowded the chief's office for the latest numbers on how much crime in the city was dropping.

Naturally, a number of criminologists were highly skeptical. Some doubted the numbers; but the numbers were probably the most reliable ever, since Bratton had introduced a new system for checking, double-checking, and triple-checking crime activity and police reports throughout the 76 precincts. Others conceded that the declines were real but attributed them to declines in the number of at-risk juveniles. But, as all the data showed, the number of at-risk juveniles had been stable or growing as the crime rates fell. Still others argued that the real story was the city's increase in police manpower. Manpower matters, but the ranks had already thickened before Bratton arrived.

Instead, what happened in New York under Bratton is foretold in a 1995 essay the chief wrote on "quality of life crimes."[62] As Bratton argued, with "rare exceptions, residents, even in the highest crime areas, usually do not talk about murder, robbery, rape and the other violent crimes that make the headlines. They are frequently more concerned about police problems of a different kind, namely street prostitution, low-level drug dealing, underage drinking, blaring car radios and a host of other quality-of-life crimes that contribute to a sense of disorder and danger on the street. These are the crimes which people see every day, and which they want the police to combat. Naturally, residents want the police to apprehend murderers, robbers and rapists so that they are convicted and imprisoned. But people will not feel safe in their neighborhoods again until the police are also addressing the so-called low-level crimes that undermine people's quality of life."[63]

Under Bratton's leadership, the New York Police Department adopted six crime control strategies:

- Getting guns off the streets.
- Curbing youth violence in schools.
- Driving drug dealers out.
- Breaking the cycle of domestic violence.
- Reclaiming the public spaces.
- Reducing auto-related crime.

Each strategy involved a wide range of policy changes, new procedures, and a renewed commitment to fighting crime. For example, the strategy on youth violence required NYPD precinct commanders to "solicit the help of parents to assist police efforts to remove guns from the possession of young people, to protect children while they are in or are traveling to and from school, and to encourage children to remain in school and take seriously their academic responsibilities."[64] Likewise, the strategy on public spaces required the NYPD to refocus resources "by applying Nuisance Abatement powers on a citywide basis, using lawyers of the expanded Civil Enforcement Division and working with the Office of the Corporation Counsel, to close down illegal indoor businesses such as smoke shops, crack houses, and illegal massage parlors."[65]

Bratton's bet, in effect, was that if the police took enforcing the laws against "minor" crimes and disorders more seriously, not only would they net lots of bad guys, but they would improve police-community relations in ways that would help reduce youth violence and other neighborhood problems:

The NYPD's public spaces strategy and its civil enforcement component are strengthening community policing by providing the organizational means and the tactical knowledge to accomplish community ends—to shut down drug-dealing locations, take noisy cars off streets and deter low-level offenders from coming into New York City neighborhoods. As communities see the police taking effective actions against the problems that they care about, residents will be far more likely to view us as their allies and work cooperatively with us. Working together, we can achieve what every community wants—streets that not only are safer, but feel safer, too.[66]

As the dean of America's policing scholars, Professor George L. Kelling, concluded by the autumn of 1995, Bratton won his bet:

Anecdotes about how well the policy works abound in the department, passed on from cop to cop with the same enthusiasm that transit police felt five years ago when they started arresting fare-beaters at the orders of their then-boss, Bratton, and discovered that these seemingly inconsequential lawbreakers often turned out to be carrying illegal weapons. In the 9th Precinct, a man arrested for public urination provided information about a neighbor who was handling stolen property, especially guns. Police arrested the man and recovered a stash of weapons. What makes these experiences in the NYPD so convincing, even in advance of formal research, is that the department itself has called the shots. It publicly declared it would improve the quality of life in New York, and it is doing so—the virtual elimination of the squeegee nuisance is just one example. It said it would take guns off the streets, and preliminary evidence suggests that it is doing so: in August 1995, for instance, the proportion of arrested suspects who were carrying guns was 39 percent lower than two years earlier. The department has said that taking guns off the streets would reduce violent crime, and statistics show that it has. Because its successes are not random, it's hard to attribute them to luck or to anonymous "larger forces," such as demographics.[67]

POLICING MORAL POVERTY: CHARLESTON

With a mix of tough, innovative police tactics and personal magnetism, [Reuben] Greenberg has cut Charleston's murder, robbery and burglary rates in half, back to levels as low as they were in the early 1960s before violent crime rates soared nationwide. . . . His policies and his politics, he delights in telling people, are as unorthodox as his background as a Southern black Jew. Although he earned two master's degrees from the University of California at Berkeley, his programs are based on old-fashioned notions of strengthening parental authority, imposing a curfew on teenagers and rounding up truant students and transporting them back to school.

—FOX BUTTERFIELD[68]

Chief Reuben Greenberg also targeted "broken windows" in his drive to reduce crime in Charleston, South Carolina. Through an innovative mix of police presence and tough love, his department has lowered the city's crime rate by 40 percent in the seven years 1982–1989.[69] Murder, robbery, and burglary rates have been cut in half.

In the process, Greenberg has achieved what few chiefs have—creating safe public housing, bringing down juvenile crime rates, and lowering street-level drug dealing without overloading city jails. In the past five years, only one person under 17 has been murdered in the city, and the 8 percent of citizens who live in public housing have lower rates of crime and victimization than the rest of the city.

When Greenberg came to Charleston in 1982, there were 17 major open-air drug markets in the city. It was immediately apparent that traditional law enforcement techniques were not impeding their practice—within four hours of arrest, most dealers would be back out on the street. Greenberg decided to redirect his officers to "go after his [the dealers'] market, and make it unprofitable."[70]

He stationed uniformed officers on five of the worst drug corners—standing at least 40 feet from the dealer, to ensure that neither the dealers nor the ACLU could claim invasion of privacy—to simply be there. It had an immediate impact. No one went near the dealer; customers drove by, saw the officer, and left. The dealers tried to move their operations to a new corner but ran into several problems: first, they had no way of telling their customers they had moved; and second, they might infringe on someone else's market. As in real estate, success in this sort of drug dealing is location, location, location, so the police took the location.

Each officer was supplied with several tools, including a Polaroid camera, to take pictures of potential customers, paint to beautify the area by covering graffiti, and a work crew of prisoners to help clean up the area. Greenberg realized that "if you are going to convince people —merchants, citizens, shoppers—that an area is safe, it has to look safe. . . . Within days, when people came around to buy drugs, the area looked a lot different; it looked like someone cared about it."[71] Greenberg estimates that the effort, which drew no additional police resources, drove about 30 percent of the street-level drug dealers out of the drug-selling business.

Greenberg then focused his officers and his creativity on public housing. The police worked with the ACLU and the neighborhood legal system to develop a strategy for ending the victimization of the city's 8,000 public-housing residents. The city gave public housing the same right that other Charleston landlords had, namely, the right to refuse to rent space to convicted felons. Prior to this, public housing could screen for financial status, but those *convicted* of armed robbery, burglary, sexual assault, arson, or child molestation could not be refused space.

The police also set up, on Saturday nights, a barricade to Bayside, one of the complexes where there was a serious drug problem. Each visitor had to have permission from a tenant to enter. Again, the principle was borne out—by not allowing the criminals in, the crime dropped. The department now has three liaison officers assigned to public housing, and a police substation has been set up within the complex to provide a continuous, visible presence.

Chief Greenberg's approach to juvenile crime was equally elegant. He imposed a voluntary curfew on minors, beefed up truancy patrols, and enlisted the kids as partners in monitoring guns. The truancy patrol, which picks up kids from 6 to 17 and returns them to school, decreased crime by 27 percent in its first four years.[72] When questioned about the dedication of four officers to this project, Greenberg responded, ". . . if I pull that resource out, then my crime rate is going to go up 27 percent." As an added benefit, the victimization of juveniles has also plummeted. From 1990 to 1994, he said, "we haven't had a single kid shot, stabbed or beaten up or anything else on public streets."[73] He also made boasting about owning a gun a liability by offering to pay $100 to any student with information on the possession of an illegal handgun.

Greenberg has made the citizens and the police partners in preventing crime. His foot patrol officers cover rich and poor areas of the city, and they are encouraged to become active members of the communities in which they serve. Greenberg and his department have not ended crime in Charleston, but they have made impressive strides in "taking back the streets" from criminal predators.

> *Now public housing is one of the safest places in the city. Taxis now go into public housing and pizzas are delivered there. You can call the Maytag man and he will come. . . . Any city where public-housing residents are victimized and children have to sleep on floors to avoid being shot should be ashamed of itself.*[74]
> —CHIEF REUBEN GREENBERG, CHARLESTON, S.C.

POLICING MORAL POVERTY: HOUSTON

Crime in Houston has plummeted in recent years, and according to police chief Sam Nuchia, "back to basics" policing is at the root of the drop. From 1991 to 1995, the overall crime rate in the city has decreased 27 percent, with murders down by 48 percent to 316, the lowest number in the city since 1973.[75]

Chief Nuchia has developed a strategy that combines neighborhood presence with a zero-tolerance approach to crime. He has increased the police force by approximately 1,000 officers and made patrol areas smaller.[76] This enables his force to do more proactive policing—knowing where problem spots are, and correcting them before trouble breaks out.

When Chief Nuchia came to the force in 1992, Houston had an established neighborhood-oriented policing program. There were storefronts and substations across the city and regular opportunities for citizens and business owners to work with the police to discuss local crime problems. While this was improving community relations, it wasn't significantly affecting gang-related crime or victimization in the most crime-ridden areas of the city.

Nuchia decided to augment neighborhood-oriented policing with a "get tough" strategy targeted specifically at gangs and high-crime areas. He established special gang task forces and a "gang intelligence unit" in each patrol division. These groups track and work to control criminal street gang activity in the city. He has also dramatically increased police presence in high-crime areas through "saturation patrols." Normal police activities in high-crime areas are augmented with zero-tolerance operations where police sweep into an area for several days, arresting perpetrators of nuisance crimes—trespassing, littering, speeding—that enable police to stop, frisk, and run checks on petty criminals who might have not-so-petty backgrounds.

The key to Nuchia's strategy in Houston is the support of the mayor and the city. Nuchia was given the authority to increase the force by almost 25 percent and to use overtime funds to maximize the manpower of the department.[77] He has also changed the composition of the force, insisting that new officers have at least two years of college, and is working to increase minority representation in the department.[78]

"I firmly believe that increasing the number of police on the streets can make a city safer, and I've seen ample evidence that in Houston it does," Nuchia told the Federal Bar Association in 1995. "I believe that policing can effect social change and make a city safer." Houston demonstrates that increasing resources—in conjunction with strategic targeting and a strong community focus—can have a profound effect on crime rates in a relatively short period of time.[79]

Veteran Philadelphia police officer Patrick Boyle suffered the murder of the fellow officer he loved the most—his only son, 21-year-old rookie cop Daniel Boyle.

Out on patrol, Daniel had stopped the driver of a stolen car in North Philadelphia. In a flash, the stolen car's drug-using driver, a street-wise repeat felon named Edward Bracey, fired numerous shots through the windshield of the rookie officer's patrol car. The bullets struck the young officer in the head. A police radio chillingly captured the fatal shots and Daniel Boyle's final words. A few days later, Pat Boyle buried his son. Bracey had been arrested many times for car theft (a "mere auto thief"). Twice he had been released without bail or supervision for failing to show up for trial. In 1994 alone, Philadelphia judges were forced to release defendants in 15,000 cases because a federal judge had imposed a population cap on the city's jails.

Like Bracey, the defendants released because of the judge's order did not go straight with gratitude. Instead, they just kept right on committing crimes. In one 18-month period, Philadelphia police rearrested 9,732 defendants released because of the federal judge's edict. These defendants were charged with 79 murders, 959 robberies, 2,215 drug-dealing crimes, 701 burglaries, 2,748 thefts, 90 rapes, 14 kidnapping charges, 1,113 assaults, 264 gun-law violations, and 127 drunk-driving incidents. "Can anyone explain to me why Danny had to die?" Pat Boyle asked. No one could.[80]

REPRESENTATIVE DEMOCRACY VS. REVOLVING-DOOR JUSTICE

Most average Americans understand perfectly well that government cannot "solve" the nation's crime problem. They understand that government's capacity to prevent crime and protect them from criminals is limited, not limitless. They stand ready to spend more on prisons and other means of restraint, and are aware of the costs of doing so. They even accept, albeit begrudgingly, that some arrested criminals are bound to escape justice on legal technicalities and that every so often a felon out on pretrial release, probation, or parole will elude supervision and commit new crimes.

But what the American people do not accept, and should not be required to accept, is government's prolonged and persistent failure to restrain convicted violent and repeat criminals. Nothing could be more fundamental to the government's holding up its end of the social contract. A government incapable of restraining known criminals in its custody cannot be trusted to do any number of inherently more complicated and costly public chores, domestic or international. A government that passes wave after wave of "get-tough" anti-crime laws but often proves toothless in the execution of those laws is a government well on its way to destroying public confidence in the integrity of lawmakers, in the prudence of judges, and in the competence of public administrators.

In 1993 and again in 1994, there was but one public institution in which the people had less confidence than they did in the U.S. Congress—namely the criminal justice system.[81] Such poll results merely serve to reinforce our keen collective sense, bred by our combined years of public service, personal and professional experience, and intensive study, that government's failure to restrain convicted violent or repeat criminals has done as much as any other policy failure of the last thirty years to bring about the loss of public trust and confidence in our political institutions.

We believe that the war on America's streets will be lost unless the precepts of our representative democracy are honored. That means changing public policies so that government and the justice system give the American people what they have been demanding for years—incarceration for violent and repeat criminals, more community-based cops, an end to revolving-door policies, and deference to public safety and victims' rights over prisoners' rights. It means citizens rising up to do more for themselves—more town watch, more volunteering to work with troubled kids, more charitable giving.

It also means putting our society's human and financial resources, both public and private, where our concerns about drugs, crime, and moral poverty truly are. We cannot will the end without willing the means. The means include more policing, prosecution, prisons, probation, and parole supervision; these are the prosaic and costly realities. As we noted in the preceding chapter, we spend about $100 billion a year on all justice system functions at all levels of government. That's a quarter of what violent crime alone costs us each year, and far, far less than we spend on a wide array of other government programs. When we spend less than a penny per tax dollar to restrain violent and repeat criminals, we are kidding ourselves about promoting public safety, doing justice, and sending an authoritative moral message about crime and disorder.

4

DRUGS, CRIME, AND CHARACTER

If one wants to know immediate causes of much of America's moral poverty, the destruction of large parts of our inner cities, and its record-high crime rate, it is impossible to overlook drug use.

> The seven children, ages 4 to 16, lived in a cramped, fly-infested hovel on the second floor at 5 North Third Street. Their pregnant mother and her boyfriend, the police said, smoked crack around the children. And they clearly indulged squalor.
>
> Today, the kitchen table, the stove, and the sink were piled with dirty dishes and pans containing chunks of old fried food. In the two tiny bedrooms, heaps of clothes a foot or two deep surrounded the ripped mattresses. Near one bed, apparently the one used by the mother, was a big plastic pail containing what appeared to be urine, an inch-deep. A few feet away was a pail brimming with garbage.
>
> Three Paterson police officers discovered the family's sordid

world Sunday night after one child, a 14-year-old girl, called and said her mother had beaten her.

"The stench in the apartment made the officers almost vomit," Detective Robert Vogt said.

Detective Vogt said that an argument over dirty dishes had set off the event that led to the phone call. The mother, Josephine Davis, 34, struck her daughter several times on her shoulders and upper arms with a 3-foot board with a nail protruding from it, he said. Then the girl was locked in an attic room, the detective said. About 7:30 P.M., she got out, ran to a friend's house around the corner on Temple Street and called the police.[1]

If Americans once thought "drug-related violence" was limited to gun battles among drug dealers, it is now all too plain that the families and communities of drug users, dealers, and addicts are the most numerous victims of drug violence.

The Carter family is being stalked here by what the clan's 54-year-old matriarch, Regina, calls a monster—crack cocaine. She has watched it swallow her daughter and now she is fighting it for her grandson's soul.

The 15-year-old boy disappeared from her house six months ago and was found by police officers on Monday, after a half-year odyssey of beating, hunger and sexual abuse, with a tale that is a searing reminder of how desperately those on the front lines are fighting the war on drugs.

Initially the police thought the boy's mother, who has been in jail on an unrelated burglary charge for about two weeks, sold him to dealers to pay off a $1,000 debt, which she has denied.

But after several days of questioning the boy, the authorities say it appears that he went willingly with the dealers but found out, painfully, that he was not as tough as they were.

His grandmother says her grandson told her that he descended into the drug underworld to work off his mother's debt to dealers who had threatened to kill her. The police say he told them that he went with the dealers because he wanted to earn enough money to help his mother move out of the crumbling apartments, abandoned buildings and crack houses where she had spent so many of the last eight years doing almost anything to make the dope man and his monster happy.

But when the boy wanted to leave, after several weeks of selling dope to other people's mothers, fathers, and children, he was tied up and beaten by one dealer, the police said, and later by another.

The boy was given crack to numb his hunger, his grandmother said; his knuckles were burned by cigarettes.

Prosecutors, who have charged a man with criminal sexual conduct, say the dealers offered the boy to female drug customers as a sex toy.

"He was forced to sell drugs," said Inspector Michael Hall of the Detroit Police Department. "He was physically assaulted on a number of occasions. He's a victim. He's just a kid."

Mrs. Carter said she wants her grandson to have an AIDS test. "He needs a lot of help," she said. "Now, he's messed up with the crack just like his mama."

Whatever happened, the story of the Carters illustrates the power of crack to hurt and haunt entire families, from one generation to the next.

"This case has rung a bell that we still have plenty of work to do," said Ronald L. Griffin, the president of the Detroit Urban League, which runs a mentoring program for thousands of young people in Detroit. "There are a lot of boys like Mrs. Carter's grandson," he said. "We have to tighten our belts and start working harder to reach them." [2]

And today, only a willful blindness can obscure the fact that drug use fosters moral poverty and remorseless criminality; that drug use destroys character and brutalizes the lives of users and those around them. It often severs the ties among family members—between parent and child, and child and parent. And often it destroys the bonds between the user and his friends, his community, his understanding of right and wrong, his God, and his common sense.

The homemade video shows a man sitting at a table packaging what looks like crack cocaine, a shotgun and a 9mm handgun at the ready. As the man fills small zip-lock bags and puts them into a larger one, a 4-year-old beside him does the same.

When the man fills a glass from a Seagram's gin bottle and then drinks from the glass, the little boy drinks from the same glass. When the man picks up the 9mm, appears to aim it at someone and then hands it to the little boy, the child also takes aim.

Throughout the video, everything the man does, the boy mimics. And when the man throws another man to the floor and stands over him with the 9mm, the little boy does the same to a younger sibling, standing over the toddler with a toy gun.

Family members who testified late Friday in a neglect hearing concerning the boy and his three siblings said that the weapons were just toys, that the rocklike chunks were really soap flakes, that the gin was water and that no harm was done.

The boy's mother testified that her son and husband merely were acting out "gangsta rap lyrics" for a music video they could sell and "make some extra money for the family."

D.C. Superior Court Hearing Commissioner Evelyn Coburn said she simply didn't believe the family members' versions, but whether crack cocaine or soap flakes, real guns or toy ones, "that children are being taught this behavior at such an early age" is unthinkable. . . .

She ordered all four children in the family placed in shelter care and said she would allow the mother supervised visits with the children only if she submits to drug testing. Neither the mother, her mother nor other relatives showed any emotion as Coburn ordered the children taken from their care.

"To say the least, this is beyond the pale . . . an absolute tragedy," Coburn said.[3]

Drug use is wrong because it degrades human beings. It is an affliction mostly of the young, making young people less than they can and should be. It often robs them of the sense of responsibility to themselves and others, makes them stupid and indifferent, undermines their ability to be productive and prudent, and leads them to mock the demands of virtue. But in our time, it is not fashionable to speak and think seriously in terms of the moral dimension of public policy. As America's preeminent social scientist James Q. Wilson has written:

Even now, when the dangers of drug abuse are well understood, many educated people still discuss the drug problem in almost every way except the right way. They talk about the "costs" of drug use and the "socioeconomic factors" that shape that use. They rarely speak plainly —drug use is wrong because it is immoral and it is immoral because it enslaves the mind and destroys the soul. It is as if it were a mark of sophistication for us to shun the language of morality in discussing the problems of mankind.[4]

Because drugs are pleasurable, they are profitable—and of course they would be profitable *because* they are pleasurable, even if the drug trade were decriminalized. And because drugs are pleasurable and profitable, yet harmful and degrading, they can only be coherently addressed in terms grounded in morality.

DRUGS AND CRIME

In the most direct and truest sense, then, drug use is a catalyst to crime because it makes young men, young women, and even children morally irresponsible. For young people already involved in crime, drugs make criminal activity easier and more severe. They weaken prudential restraints, and in the case of crack, as well as some other drugs, they stimulate aggression and a false sense of invincibility. The Drug Use Forecasting (DUF) program collects the most extensive data on crime committed by individuals while under the influence of drugs. The DUF compiles the results of drug tests (via urinalysis) of a sample of arrestees in over twenty cities throughout the United States. Its latest composite data are reflected in Figure 4-1: a majority of all arrestees tested were using drugs within the 24 to 72 hours prior to their arrest.[5]

But several smaller studies indicate that there may be an even more extensive link between drugs and crime. In one of those studies, 88 male juvenile arrestees in Cleveland were surveyed and tested for drug use via three different methods: self-reports, urinalysis, and hair analysis. Participants in the study were volunteers and the results were anonymous and confidential. While urinalysis is considered reliable for signs of drug use within roughly 24 to 72 hours, hair analysis can detect use as much as 90 days prior to testing. This requires a hair sample cut one and one-half inches from the scalp.

In the Cleveland study (covering marijuana, cocaine, opiates, PCP,

FIGURE 4-1. ARRESTEES TESTING POSITIVE FOR ILLEGAL DRUGS, 1991

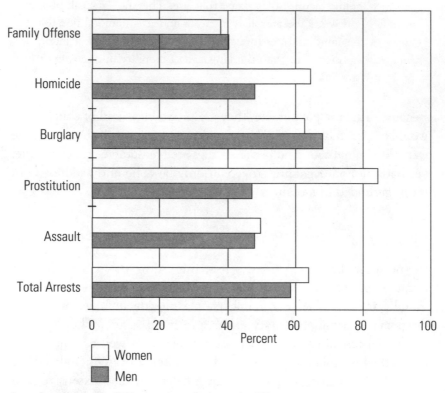

Source: Drug Use Forecasting (DUF) program, last national composite, 1991.

and amphetamines), 6 percent of the male juveniles reported using drugs, 8 percent tested positive for drug use via urinalysis, and 57 percent tested positive via hair analysis.[6] A similar study for cocaine use among 132 female juvenile arrestees in Maryland found self-reported use within the past three days at 6 percent, urinalysis tests for cocaine at 8 percent, self-reported use in the past 90 days at 9 percent, and hair analysis for cocaine at 36 percent.[7]

Not only does drug use in general—and cocaine use in particular—correlate with a wide range of criminality and violent crime but cocaine use has also been linked to victimization. In an examination of the relationship between cocaine use and firearms, a team of researchers analyzed homicides of New York City residents in 1990 and 1991. Of the 4,298 cases of murdered New Yorkers, they focused on the 3,890 instances (90.5 percent of the total) where the victims survived

48 hours or less, and thus medical examiner toxicology reports provided reliable indications of cocaine use prior to death. Thirty-one percent of these murder victims tested positive for cocaine. This was 10 to 50 times *greater* than the estimated rate of cocaine use in the general population for the demographic characteristics studied (age, race, and gender). The researchers also reported: "To our surprise, the use of cocaine prior to being killed was not statistically related to being killed by a firearm rather than by other methods. . . . It is likely that many cocaine dealers are armed and may shoot other dealers and buyers who are using cocaine. Yet cocaine users are killed by means other than firearms in disputes and other situations not related to drug dealing."[8] They noted, "Homicide victims may have provoked violence through irritability, paranoid thinking, or verbal or physical aggression, which are known to be pharmacologic effects of cocaine."[9]

As illustrated in the news stories at the beginning of this chapter, drug use is also a major factor in child abuse—particularly in cases of the most horrifying kind of violence against children. An example: in July 1995 Eric Smith suffered psychotic and paranoid delusions as a result of using methamphetamine. Smith believed his 14-year-old son, Eric Jr., had become a demon about to attack him. The father decapitated his son and tossed his boy's head from his van window along a New Mexico highway. According to Ron Siegel, a UCLA psychopharmacologist who has studied methamphetamine violence, including as many as five such murders a week: "We're seeing everything from serial killing to necrophilia."[10]

In April 1994, *Newsweek* published a feature report on child abuse. It merely repeated what those working in the field have known for years: "Drugs now suffuse 80 percent of the caseload; sexual and physical assaults that once taxed the imagination are now common."[11] Crack burst on the American drug scene in the mid-1980s. Within five years, foster care cases increased over 50 percent nationwide, and over 70 percent of the cases were linked to families in which at least one of the parents was a drug user.[12]

In a 1990 article on welfare reform, Senator Daniel Patrick Moynihan wrote:

> Poverty in the United States is now concentrated in single-parent families. . . . Moreover, starting in 1974, for the first time in our country's

history and possibly for the first time in any advanced society, children became the poorest group in our population.

Such families, moreover, appear to be relatively unreachable by standard economic policy prescriptions. The annual poverty status report recently issued by the Bureau of the Census, for example, provoked concern that the poverty rate seems stuck, that the economic growth and high employment levels of the last decade made no impact on the poverty rate. The number of single-parent families grew. With the advent of AIDS and "crack" the no-parent family appeared.[13]

And on April 24, 1994, the *New York Times Magazine* ran a cover story subtitled "Inside the World of Beggars Who Cajole, Amuse, Shame—And Threaten—Their Way to $100 a Day and More." The story profiled a group of homeless street people in New York City. All the individuals featured were drug addicts.[14] While there is no national estimate of the number of homeless—particularly the most aggressive and crime-prone among them—who are drug addicts, the reality in most areas is very similar to the story reported by the *Times*.

THE GOOD NEWS

In America today, there is no question that the drug problem—the use of illegal drugs—makes every other major social problem much worse: the destruction of families and child abuse; infant mortality; violent crime (particularly domestic violence and juvenile violence), property crime, and prostitution; poverty and homelessness; joblessness; family disintegration; educational failure and the school dropout rate; the social disintegration and economic decay of central cities; and the spread of HIV. And drug use carries its destruction to all social and economic levels of society. It not only draws the children of the poor, but also middle-class and upper-class young people into crime and moral poverty. That is the bad news.

But there is also no question that drug use can be substantially reduced. In fact, the dramatic reductions in drug use from 1979 to 1992 are a demonstration of the crucial power of moral convictions when supported and strengthened by key institutions of society. And that is the good news.

Despite occasional calls for normalizing drug use, the vast majority of Americans have always opposed the legalization of drugs. A 1995 Gallup poll on the subject reported that 85 percent of respondents oppose legalization and 84 percent support increased criminal penalties.[15] The same poll found a resurgence of concern about the drug problem at a level second only to Americans' concern about violent crime. (See Figure 4-2.) Public concern over violent crime and drugs in 1995 exceeded the previous peak of attention to the drug problem in the late 1980s. Since 1981 violent crime and drugs have created far

FIGURE 4-2. WHAT DO YOU THINK IS THE MOST IMPORTANT PROBLEM FACING THIS COUNTRY? 1981–1995

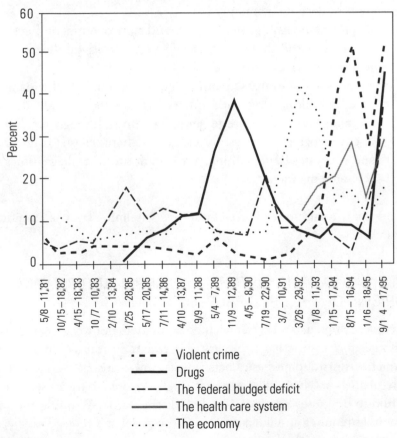

Source: Gallup.

greater alarm than either the federal budget deficit or the economy; for 15 years, when asked to name the most important problem facing the country, twice as many Americans chose violent crime and drugs as those who chose the health care system.

The public's reasons for opposing drug use can be summarized as follows:

- Illegal drugs pose a serious danger—they frequently lead users to harm themselves and to harm others—and they are particularly dangerous to young people.
- Drug use—particularly drug addiction—can destroy the capacity of individuals to be self-governing and responsible. Illegal drugs thus threaten the foundation of American democracy and the roots of decent community life.
- Appropriate legal, governmental, and nongovernmental actions can reduce the threat and the damage caused by illegal drugs without unjust or excessive costs.
- Although there are similarities between some of the dangers posed by illegal drugs and other threats—most of all alcohol consumption and cigarette smoking—and although alcohol is also a recognized catalyst for crime, the harm caused by alcohol and cigarettes is, if anything, a reason not to treat illegal drugs in the same manner.

These judgments are supported by an overwhelming body of empirical data.[16]

CREATING A DRUG CULTURE: THE MORAL AND POLITICAL ORIGINS OF THE DRUG PROBLEM

In order to understand better what does and does not work in anti-drug efforts, it is instructive to review the recent history of drug use in America. First, some basic facts: most Americans have never used illegal drugs and have always been strongly opposed to their use. Opposition to drug use, however, is only half the battle. Winning the war on drugs requires an understanding of the problem's roots. The illegal drug problem in the United States today began as part of the radical political and moral criticism of American culture and the related youthful rebelliousness of the late 1960s and the 1970s—a period distinctly different from that of early-twentieth-century America, the era of the only other national drug use problem. That earlier problem —America's first drug crisis, as it is sometimes called—was spread by medical and pseudomedical views that cocaine and narcotics were harmless health and performance enhancers. They were then widely dispensed in elixirs, tonics, prescriptions, and soft drinks.[17] That crisis was eventually reversed by enforcement changes and a cultural change of attitudes about drugs.

America's second drug crisis was largely driven by political and moral forces. Themes of revolution, liberation, and drugs were inter-twined in popular music, in other parts of the entertainment industry, in the press, on university campuses, and in some quarters of the media. Drug use was "anti-establishment"; it was described as liberat-ing, and at times even presented as a path to "higher consciousness" —a badge of political and spiritual superiority. The moral dimension of these attitudes was also visible in the vilification of drug enforcement personnel—"narcs"—who, among the young and fashionable, were hated as much as the war in Vietnam, with which drug use was so closely, if implicitly, linked.

As it turned out, alarm over the percentage of U.S. troops returning from the Vietnam War as regular heroin (and marijuana) users trig-gered the first phase of the war on drugs. The Nixon administration quickly established screening and treatment programs for returning military personnel. But to the surprise and relief of many, when most heroin- and opium-using GIs returned home, where heroin, in particu-lar, was neither widely available nor acceptable, their use ended.[18] What was true about the availability and acceptability of heroin and opium in the United States was not true, however, of other illegal drugs.

Even though a large majority of Americans have always disapproved of drug use, a substantial—and culturally influential—minority stimu-lated a drift toward the de facto legalization of drug consumption during the 1970s. Penalties and enforcement were reduced. In 1960, 90 drug offenders were incarcerated for every 1,000 drug arrests. By 1980, that figure had dropped to 19 of every 1,000 arrests.[19]

Drug use became fashionable, and among the young it grew well beyond the rare phenomenon it had been previously. When national measurement began in 1975, a *majority* of high school seniors reported trying an illegal drug at least once prior to graduation. For the next 15 years, the typical life experience of a high school senior included experimentation with illegal drugs. Voices calling for the legalization of drugs grew louder and became more influential.

The legalization movement reached an apex in March 1977 when the special assistant to the president for health issues, Dr. Peter Bourne, testified before the House Select Committee on Narcotics Abuse and Control in favor of the decriminalization of marijuana, joined by officials from the Justice Department, the State Department, the Department of Health, Education, and Welfare, and the U.S. Customs Service. At the time, Dr. Bourne and others also considered cocaine a prime candidate for decriminalization.[20]

Shortly thereafter, Dr. Bourne resigned following charges he had used cocaine and improperly written a prescription for a controlled substance. The Carter administration suddenly faced growing popular concern that it was leading the country in a dangerous direction on the drug issue. Drug use was at or very near historically high rates, however, with cocaine use still rising during the first term of the next administration. In 1974, one of the first national surveys found an estimated 5 million Americans had used cocaine at least one time in their life. By 1982, that number had more than quadrupled to 22 million.[21]

Two groups of events triggered a reverse in the growing acceptance of cocaine. The first was the shocking violence that Colombian cocaine traffickers—the "cocaine cowboys"—brought to Florida. The cocaine trade created a new type of wealthy and violent criminal gang. And as the use of cocaine spread, it brought with it a viciousness never before seen in American cities.

Then cocaine use took an even more ominous turn with the creation of crack in the early 1980s. The pure, intense high of crack made it the most powerful addictive pleasure ever encountered. It was too good. Reports of "almost instant addiction" and crack and cocaine use by adolescents began appearing in the national media. Then, in 1986, two events occurred that left a deep impression on the national psyche: Len Bias, on his way to what many predicted would be professional basketball stardom via the University of Maryland, and professional football player Don Rogers died within days of each other. Both died as a result of cocaine use. The death of these two young men, in outstanding physical condition, put emphatic warnings about cocaine use—and illegal drug use in general—on the front page.

The media now described a crisis: an unprecedented, wealthy, powerful, ruthless, foreign criminal cartel was marketing a deadly addictive substance on a massive scale, with even grade-school children becoming victims. Illegal drug use generally was portrayed as an enemy within—a cancer of sorts, threatening all segments of society, particularly young people.

The drug problem quickly became a trial of national character. More and more criminal sanctions, government spending, and a national mobilization were called for, culminating in 1988 in the creation of the Office of National Drug Control Policy (ONDCP), whose director—popularly known as the "drug czar"—would report directly to the president, with the sole job of waging the nation's "drug war." The "drug czar" was to take charge and provide a vigorous, coordinated, and effective federal anti-drug campaign.

Parents' groups had already mobilized to fight illegal drug use by young people at the end of the Carter years, long before there was a national "drug czar." They received an important boost when First Lady Nancy Reagan made their cause her own. Many in the media and elsewhere were critical of her "Just Say No" campaign. In his speech at the 1988 Democratic convention the Reverend Jesse Jackson said: "It's a cop-out to just say to children, 'Just Say No to Drugs. . . .' Children do not buy $150 billion worth of drugs. . . . Children do not grow the drugs, do not run the cartels."[22] But that, of course, was not the point of Mrs. Reagan's simple moral message to children. Despite such ridicule, her campaign grew and it and other prevention efforts began to have an effect. As the evidence of harm caused by drugs mounted, she made the moral imperative not to use drugs fashionable. And not only the young got the message. As can be seen in Figure 4-3,[23] use declined during the 1980s, and by 1992 overall illegal drug use was less than half what it was at the measured peak in 1979. Declines in cocaine use lagged behind this general trend a bit. With the creation of crack, cocaine use grew in the early 1980s, reaching a peak in 1985. Then it, too, fell, with current or monthly cocaine use (usually referred to as casual or nonaddicted use) dropping almost 80 percent between 1985 and 1992. This was important because casual drug use is the vector by which drug use spreads—from

FIGURE 4-3. CURRENT (MONTHLY) DRUG USERS, AGE 12 AND OLDER,
1979–1994

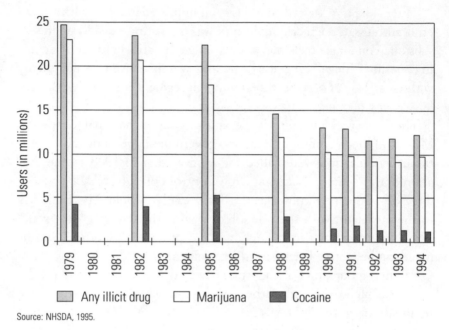

Source: NHSDA, 1995.

friend to friend—and while not every casual user goes on to become
an addict, virtually every addict starts as a casual user.

Even more important were the dramatic reductions in drug use by
young people during the 1980s and early 1990s. Annual use of any
illicit drug by high school seniors dropped from 54.2 percent in 1979
to 27.1 percent in 1992, and cocaine use fell from an annual rate of
13.1 percent at its peak in 1985 to 3.1 percent in 1992.[24] This meant
not only that fewer young people were exposed to the dangers of drugs,
but also that in the future fewer adults would be drug users—and
addicts. As a detailed study of responses to the National Household
Survey on Drug Abuse found, "Regardless of the time (be it the 1970's,
80's, or 90's), respondents who have not tried a drug by the time they
reach their mid-twenties are unlikely to ever do so."[25]

A more detailed look at some of the data regarding use (Figure 4-4)
is instructive for three reasons.[26] First, they show the extent of illegal
drug use and its decline between 1985 and 1992—and the subsequent

rise between 1992 and 1994 (that will be discussed later)—for the age group 12 to 17. Second, they make clear that both the decline in drug use between 1985 and 1992, and its rise between 1992 and 1994, did not merely involve a shifting from one drug to another or from illegal drugs to cigarettes and alcohol (as critics sometimes suggest). Finally, as Figure 4-4 shows, illegal drug use fell at a greater rate proportionately than did cigarette and alcohol use between 1985 and 1992, despite extensive education campaigns against tobacco and alcohol use by the young. Although it is difficult to dissect such human phenomena with scientific precision, it is clear that the categorical legal prohibitions against drugs—actively enforced—played an important part in keeping drug use smaller and making it decline more rapidly.

Thus, between 1977 and 1992 illegal drug use went from being fashionable and liberating to unfashionable and dangerous. Overall, casual drug use by Americans dropped by more than half. For the population age 12 and over, monthly cocaine use between 1985 and 1992 dropped by *78 percent*, from 2.7 percent of the population

FIGURE 4-4. CURRENT USE OF ILLICIT DRUGS, CIGARETTES, AND ALCOHOL, AGES 12–17, 1985–1994

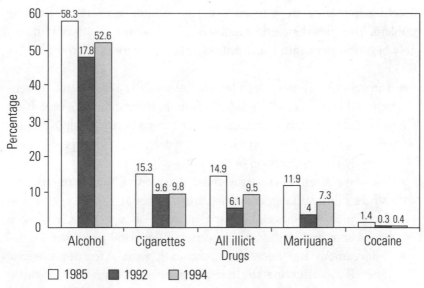

Source: NHSDA, 1996.

(5,294,000) to 0.6 percent (1,305,000).[27] And for high school seniors, the decline between 1985 and 1992 was *81 percent,* from 6.7 percent to 1.3 percent.[28]

To put these developments into a larger context, consider: this decline in illegal drug use marks the most successful attack on a serious social problem in the last quarter century. Think for a moment what the reaction would be today if we diminished by 50 to 80 percent the high school dropout rate, out-of-wedlock births, the spread of HIV, or the rate of violent crime. Imagine the cheers if, say, air pollution or the rate of rain forest loss were sliced by two-thirds. That is precisely what happened with illegal drug use in the United States between 1979 and 1992. But not only is the fact not cheered, it is not even known. And not only is it not known but there is a widespread impression that the nation's anti-drug efforts have been a complete failure. For whatever reasons, many people have refused to accept genuinely encouraging, unambiguous, empirical good news.

THE CLINTON ADMINISTRATION'S RECORD

When President Clinton took office the problem of illegal drugs had undergone a sea change in just a little more than a decade. Instead of directing measured steps to address the residual aspects of the drug problem, the president and members of his administration immediately began undermining anti-drug efforts on a variety of fronts:

- During the Clinton presidency, the morally serious and tough-minded leadership of Presidents Ronald Reagan and George Bush was replaced with such Clinton-era messages as "I didn't inhale" and the former Surgeon General Joycelyn Elders's repeated calls to study the legalization of drugs.[29]
- Just days after the inauguration, President Clinton moved the White House office created to direct national anti-drug efforts— the Office of National Drug Control Policy (ONDCP)—to a backwater, and slashed its personnel by over 80 percent.[30]
- Enforcement has been de-emphasized, with Attorney General Janet Reno decrying the harshness of federal mandatory minimum prison terms for drug crimes and complaining that too many dealers are in prison.[31] And the number of individuals prosecuted

for federal drug violations dropped from 25,033 in 1992 to 23,114 in 1993, and still lower to 21,905 in 1994—a 12 percent drop in just two years.[32]

- The administration also slashed drug interdiction.[33] The number of ships and aircraft devoted to the interdiction of drugs from South America was cut 50 percent between 1993 and 1994.

- On January 10, 1995, the *New York Times* carried a front-page story, "Tons of Cocaine Reaching Mexico in Old Jets." It detailed the traffickers' use of Boeing 727s and French-made Caravelle jets to fly six tons or more of cocaine in each flight from Colombia to Mexico.[34]

- On February 13, 1995, the *Los Angeles Times* reported: "The amount of cocaine seized from Mexican trucks and cargo at the border plummeted last year, as U.S. Customs officials pressed on with a program to promote trade by letting most commercial cargo pass into this country without inspection. Not a single pound of cocaine was confiscated from more than two million trucks that passed through three of the busiest entry points along the Southwest border where federal officials say most of the drug enters the country."[35]

We believe, then, that the record is clear: the illegal drug problem simply ceased to be a national priority; there has been little sustained effort by the federal government. This is not a partisan or idiosyncratic view. Democratic congressman Charles Rangel expressed the opinion of many when two and a half years ago he said, "I've been in Congress over two decades, and I have never, never, never found any administration that's been so silent on this great challenge [illegal drug use] to the American people."[36] That said, we do not want to suggest that the single or even the most important determining factor in drug use is the action of the federal government. It can obviously make a difference. But this country is too large and the causes of drug use too complex and varied to lay all of the blame for the increase in drug use on the Clinton administration. Still, lack of presidential leadership on this issue makes most other anti-drug efforts more difficult. In particular, it becomes virtually impossible to sustain a visible, national moral imperative against drugs when the president himself appears to be indifferent, detached, unengaged.

THE ALARMING RESURGENCE OF TEENAGE DRUG USE

The administration's mismanagement of anti-drug efforts has coincided with a rapid worsening of the drug problem. In December 1995, the University of Michigan announced that drug use—particularly marijuana use—by eighth-, tenth-, and twelfth-graders rose sharply in 1995, as it did in 1994 and 1993, following more than a decade of virtually steady decline (see Figure 4-5).[37] Among the 1995 class of high school seniors, a third used marijuana at least once during their senior year; more than a fifth were current or monthly users; and nearly one in 20 (4.6 percent) were daily users. Researchers also warned that LSD, amphetamine, stimulant, and inhalant use was rising among high school students. Moreover, the survey team found troubling signs of increases in heroin use, which, though small in comparison to the use of other illegal drugs, increased two to three times in the past few years. A majority of the eighth-, tenth-, and twelfth-graders reporting heroin use indicated they had smoked or snorted the drug. The Uni-

FIGURE 4-5. USE OF ANY ILLICIT DRUG BY EIGHTH-, TENTH-, AND
TWELFTH-GRADERS, 1975–1995

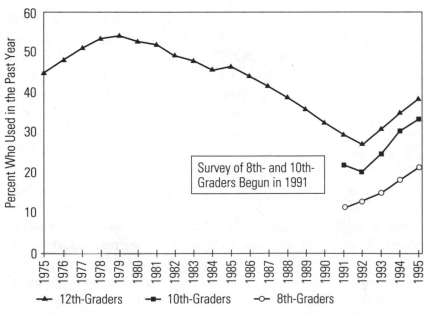

Source: Monitoring the Future Study, 1995.

FIGURE 4-6. TRENDS IN THE PERCENTAGE OF TWELFTH-GRADERS DISAPPROVING
OF MARIJUANA USE AND THE PERCENTAGE USING MARIJUANA, 1975–1995

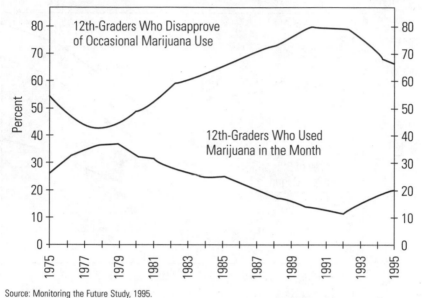

Source: Monitoring the Future Study, 1995.

versity of Michigan study revealed (see Figure 4-6) that student attitudes were becoming significantly less hostile toward illegal drug use,
indicating that further increases in use can be expected in the future.

Following the 1994 increase in use by high school students, the
Center on Addiction and Substance Abuse (CASA) at Columbia
University warned, "If historical trends continue, the jump in marijuana use among America's children (age 12–18) from 1992 to 1994
signals that 820,000 more of these children will try cocaine in their
lifetime. Of that number, about 58,000 will become regular cocaine
users and addicts."

CASA has summarized the available data on teenage marijuana use
and the later use of cocaine as follows:

While a biomedical or causal relationship between the two has not been
established, 12 to 17 year-olds who smoke marijuana are 85 times more
likely to use cocaine than those who do not. Adults who as adolescents
smoked marijuana are 17 times likelier to use cocaine regularly. Sixty
percent of adolescents who use marijuana before age 15 will later use
cocaine. These correlations are many times higher than the initial rela-

FIGURE 4-7. CURRENT (PAST MONTH) DRUG USE BY EIGHTH-, TENTH-, AND
TWELFTH-GRADERS, 1988–1995

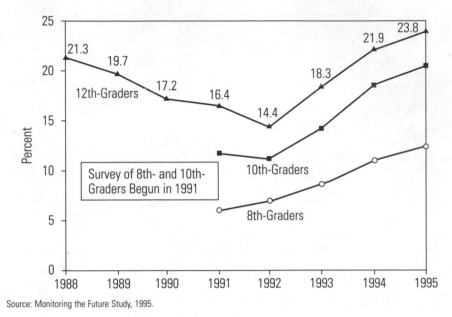

Source: Monitoring the Future Study, 1995.

tionships found between smoking and lung cancer in the 1964 Surgeon
General's report (nine to ten times), high cholesterol and heart disease
in the Framingham study (two to four times), and asbestos and lung
cancer in the Selikoff study (five times).[38]

ADDICTS ARE GETTING SICK AND DYING AT RECORD RATES

In May 1995, the Clinton administration released the results of a 1993
survey of 145 medical examiners in 43 metropolitan areas on the
number of deaths that were either solely the result of illegal drug use
(a "drug-induced" death resulting from a drug overdose) or where drug
use "contributed to the death, but was not its sole cause."

The survey found a total of 8,541 such deaths, of which 75 percent
were male, 24 percent female; 56 percent were white, 30 percent
black, 12 percent Hispanic. In addition, 70 percent of black cases
involved cocaine, compared with 51 percent of Hispanic cases and 33
percent of white cases. And total drug abuse deaths measured by this

survey found increases between 1992 and 1993 of 16 percent for blacks, 8 percent for whites, and 7 percent for Hispanics—with an overall 1992–93 increase of 11 percent. And it is important to emphasize that this report is only a narrow measure of deaths tied directly to drug use. Nonuser deaths from violence by individuals under the influence of drugs, deaths associated with the drug trade, and nonuser deaths caused by drug-related accidents are not included. The report also offers no more than a total of the medical examiners surveyed, and contains no estimate of total drug-use deaths—which would certainly be higher because the 145 medical examiners surveyed account for only about 60 percent of all autopsies performed in the United States.[39]

In November 1995 the Clinton administration reported that in 1994, drug-related emergency room cases—dominated by aging, inner-city drug addicts—reached the highest levels ever (in reporting going back to 1978). Cocaine, heroin, and marijuana cases all increased sharply to record levels.[40]

The demographics of the addicted population are difficult to specify with precision (there is no national census of drug addicts), but one useful indicator is the network of hospital emergency rooms that report cases involving drugs. The Drug Abuse Warning Network (DAWN) is managed by the U.S. Department of Health and Human Services. Data from hospitals throughout the nation are compiled on a quarterly basis and annual summaries are also made, presenting a statistically representative picture of emergency room cases for the nation as a whole.

The DAWN reports reveal that more and more cocaine emergency room cases are related to addictive use (see Figure 4-8); that these cases are concentrated in the nation's central cities (see Figure 4-9); and that the population entering emergency rooms for cocaine-related problems is also aging and substantially overrepresents black Americans (see Figure 4-10). Similar demographic trends are reflected in the data on heroin emergency room cases as well.[41]

ON THE PATH TO THE LOTUS-EATERS?

The Clinton administration's 1995 *National Drug Control Strategy* reported that heroin, cocaine, and marijuana were available at lower prices and higher purities than at any time in recent years.[42] By the

FIGURE 4-8. COCAINE EMERGENCY ROOM CASES BY NATURE OF USE, 1988–1994

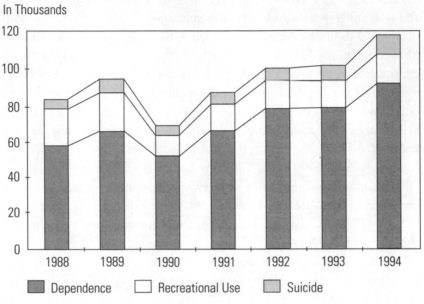

Source: DAWN.

FIGURE 4-9. COCAINE EMERGENCY ROOM CASES BY LOCATION, 1988–1994

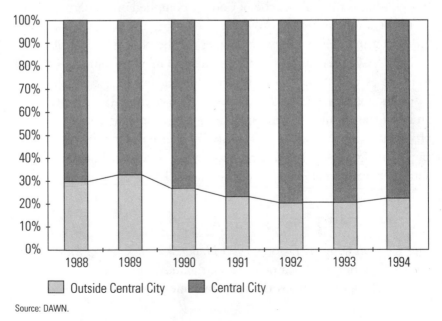

Source: DAWN.

FIGURE 4-10. COCAINE EMERGENCY ROOM CASES BY RACE, 1988–1994

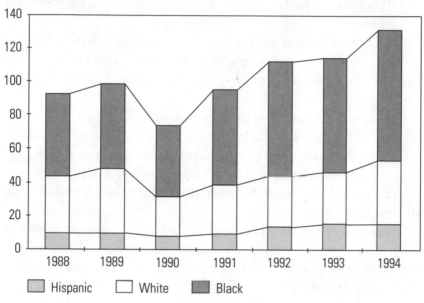

In Thousands

Hispanic ☐ White ■ Black

Source: DAWN.

fall of 1995, the White House drug policy office published even more bad news. The "Pulse Check: National Trends in Drug Abuse" reported:

- The distribution of heroin and cocaine by the same dealers and in the same markets appears in more areas than ever before, adding to evidence that new heroin source areas and new distribution networks have emerged.
- Heroin use is reported to be increasing in most areas. While the majority of users are still reported to be older, established ones, the ethnographers in many areas report increased use among younger, suburban users. These new users are more likely to inhale than to inject the drug.
- Cocaine and crack use continue to level off and are reported to have stabilized in most areas. Despite relatively unchanged availability, cocaine and crack appear to be perceived as less desirable than was true several months ago, particularly among the young.

- Marijuana use continues to increase in all areas, particularly among teens and young adults.
- "Club drugs" like Ketamine, MDMA, and LSD remain popular among middle- and upper-income youth.
- Methamphetamine use appears to be spreading beyond the Western and Southwestern regions of the country into urban areas of the Northwest, and into the South and the Midatlantic region.[43]

To summarize, then: since 1992, the nation has suffered the greatest increase in drug use and the largest expansion in the supply of illegal drugs ever measured. And this has occurred after a reduction of overall drug use of more than 50 percent between 1979 (the peak) and 1992, and a reduction of almost 80 percent in cocaine use between 1985 (the peak for cocaine) and 1992.

The failure by national leaders to support and sustain anti-drug efforts has also encouraged new attacks claiming racial bias in the enforcement of drug laws and a renewed campaign by longtime drug legalization proponents.

RACISM AND CRACK

On October 30, 1995, President Clinton signed legislation preventing a reduction in federal mandatory minimum penalties for the possession of crack cocaine from taking effect, as recommended by the U.S. Sentencing Commission. The legislation overturning the recommendation of the U.S. Sentencing Commission passed the House 332 to 83 and was approved by the Senate unanimously. But the debate over the federal crack penalties—five years in prison for five grams, or roughly 130 "rocks" of crack—focused on two charges: (1) that the law was unjust because the crack penalties were two to six times higher than for a comparable quantity of powder cocaine; and most divisive of all, (2) that the law was racist because over 90 percent of those sentenced under it were black. When the Reverend Jesse Jackson addressed the Million Man March in Washington on October 16, he said of the federal crack law and its enforcement: "That's wrong. It's immoral. It's unfair. It's racist. It's ungodly. It must change."[44]

In fact, it is unlikely the controversy would have arisen if crack were a race-neutral plague. Unfortunately, in the crack trade, both predator and prey come disproportionately from black, inner-city communities. As noted above, cocaine-driven emergency room admissions for African-Americans are at historic high levels—*900 percent* above the rate for the population as a whole.

Yet Reverend Jackson and others maintained, against the evidence, that crack is no different than powder cocaine. And having played the race card, few national leaders ventured to challenge him with the facts:

- Crack is a much more powerful psychoactive agent than powder cocaine. Crack reaches the brain in just 19 seconds, making it far more addictive than snorted powder.
- Crack use is associated with the explosion in the most horrifying cases of child abuse in recent years. And while drug addiction has long been a path to prostitution, crack has created what is called on the street the "freak house" phenomenon, where female crack addicts (variously known as "rock stars" or "toss-ups") gather to trade sex for their next five-dollar piece of crack.
- Crack dealers are notorious for raising violent drug trafficking to new extremes: the trial of Washington, D.C.'s First Street Crew, for example, was marked by the shooting of eleven witnesses— five of them fatally. When federal law enforcement agencies have assisted local officials in apprehending crack organizations like the First Street Crew, their actions disproportionately *benefited* minority inner-city residents who have to put up with the drive-by shootings and the unlivable neighborhoods.

As Tal Fair, president of the Urban League of Greater Miami, told a Senate staffer bluntly: "[Crack dealers] sell death to my community. They destroy the fabric of peace and harmony in my community by virtue of what they choose to do." John Jacob, former president of the Urban League, put it this way: "Drugs kill more blacks than the Klan ever did. They're destroying more children and more families than poverty ever did."[45]

Opponents of tough crack laws argue that their enforcement snares mostly young, nonviolent minority defendants. But according to the

U.S. Sentencing Commission itself, the typical dealer is caught selling 109 grams of crack—the equivalent of 3,000 "rocks." He (90 percent of crack defendants are male) is more likely to have carried a weapon than other traffickers, and he is more likely to have had an extensive criminal record at the time of arrest. There is no creditable evidence that there was any racist intent behind the federal crack laws when they were enacted in the late 1980s. No one claims that those who are convicted are innocent. And no one has credibly claimed that federal enforcement patterns reflect bias.

In fact, very few federal crack defendants are low-level, youthful, and nonviolent. According to the U.S. Sentencing Commission, of the 3,430 crack defendants convicted in 1994, there were just 51 youthful, small-time crack offenders with no prior criminal history and no weapons involvement (48 of the 51 were black).[46] And under the so-called safety valve provision of the 1994 Crime Act, which repealed mandatory minimum penalties for first-time, nonviolent offenders, cases similar to these 51 are now eligible for specially lenient sentences.

What the Reverend Jackson actually did in charging racism was to identify the interests of the black community with a small number of predatory criminals, instead of with the millions of inner-city residents who have equal rights to safe neighborhoods. He used race to argue for denying the protection of law to black Americans.

TURNING UP THE VOLUME FOR LEGALIZATION

Early in 1996, William F. Buckley, Jr., devoted an entire issue of his *National Review* magazine to a call for drug legalization. This was not a new stance by Buckley, and neither he nor the other longtime legalizers who contributed articles to the issue offered a single piece of new empirical evidence. Nonetheless, the issue inspired *New York Times* columnist Anthony Lewis to join in the Buckley call for legalization.

Actually, most of the arguments advanced in this new round of "let's end the drug war" campaign were simply false. The most basic premise—that the drug war failed—simply ignored some crucial and inconvenient facts, namely, the 50 to almost 80 percent reductions in drug use during the 1980s and early 1990s. The argument also failed to note that despite the recent increases in use of some drugs among teenagers in particular, the number of users is still greatly below the peaks of the 1970s and early 1980s.

Mr. Buckley and his colleagues also falsely claimed that "nearly 50 percent of the million Americans who are in jail today" are there for violations of the drug laws.[47] As discussed previously, this is not even close to the reality of who's in prison and why.

But Buckley and Princeton's Ethan Nadelmann have gone further to argue that drug use really isn't that dangerous. Buckley claimed, "Americans who abuse a drug, here defined as Americans who become addicted to it or even habituated to it, are a very small percentage of those who have experimented with a drug or who continue to use a drug without any observable distraction in their lives or careers."[48] And Nadelmann seconded this assertion, writing, "Most people can use most drugs without doing much harm to themselves or anyone else, as Mr. Buckley reminds us, citing Yale Law School Professor [Steven B.] Duke. Only a tiny percentage of the 70 million Americans who have tried marijuana have gone on to have problems with that or any other drug."[49]

Here, again, the most reliable data indicate something quite different. The ratio of experimental and casual drug users to heavy users of certain drugs is as low as two to one. The best and latest (1993) estimates by the Office of National Drug Control Policy indicate that there are more than 4 million casual users of cocaine (defined as those who use it less than once a week) and over 2.2 million heavy (at least weekly) users. And ONDCP reports an estimated 229,000 casual users of heroin and 500,000 heavy, addicted users.[50]

The legalizers also consistently pretend that the extensive research literature on the health problems associated with marijuana does not exist. Columbia University's Center on Addiction and Substance Abuse summarized the available research as follows: "While not as dangerous as snorting cocaine or shooting heroin, smoking marijuana is clearly detrimental both physically and mentally." The center noted that marijuana weakens the immune system, impairs judgment and short-term memory, reduces the ability to concentrate, and diminishes motor control functions. In addition, "prenatal use of marijuana by the mother appears to reduce significantly the IQ of babies."[51] Nationally, emergency room admissions for cases involving marijuana and hashish totaled over 40,000 in 1994.[52] And in 1994, the Office of National Drug Control Policy reported that in some areas of the country the number of individuals seeking treatment for marijuana dependence exceeded those seeking treatment for heroin addiction, and that many of those dependent on marijuana also had become dependent on other drugs.[53] Moreover, Buckley, Nadelmann, and others who seek to downplay the risk of marijuana use fail to mention that such use by teenagers appears to increase the danger that they will go on to use cocaine more than eightyfold.[54]

The legalizers also generally fail to mention the comparative rates (see Figure 4-11) of teenage use of illegal drugs versus teenage use of cigarettes and alcohol (all of which are illegal for teenagers, but only drugs are also illegal for adults). Even the comparative rates of use for the population as a whole suggest that the illegality of drug use is associated with dramatically less drug use (see Figure 4-12).[55] It is certainly true that the legalization of marijuana, cocaine, and heroin would not make the vast majority of Americans begin to use them. But legalization would surely increase the use of those drugs significantly, particularly among teenagers. As the Center on Addiction and Substance Abuse at Columbia University has noted:

FIGURE 4-11. PAST MONTH USE OF ALCOHOL, CIGARETTES, MARIJUANA, AND COCAINE, AGES 12–17, 1994

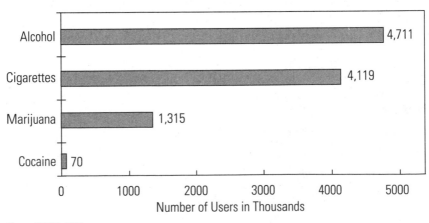

Source: NHSDA, 1994.

FIGURE 4-12. PAST MONTH USE OF ALCOHOL, CIGARETTES, MARIJUANA, AND COCAINE, AGES 12 AND OLDER, 1994

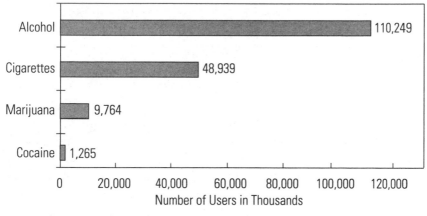

Source: NHSDA, 1994.

Despite assertions to the contrary, the evidence indicates that presently drugs are not accessible to all. Fewer than 50 percent of high school seniors and young adults under 22 believe they could obtain cocaine "fairly easily" or "very easily." Only 39 percent of the adult population reported they could get cocaine; and only 25 percent reported that they could obtain heroin, PCP, and LSD. Thus, only one-quarter to one-half of people can easily get illegal drugs (other than marijuana). After legalization, drugs would be more widely and easily available. Currently, only 11 percent of individuals reported seeing drugs available in the area where they lived; after legalization, there could be a place to purchase drugs in every neighborhood. Under such circumstances, it is logical to conclude that more individuals would use drugs.[56]

Of course, it is impossible to predict the results of legalizing drugs with precision, but there is more evidence of potential harm than the advocates admit. For example, one of the most prominent voices for drug legalization is Baltimore mayor Kurt Schmoke. He is not only an elected official, but another black American opposed to the current drug laws. In the legalization issue of *National Review*, he wrote, "Although I strongly believe that changes in national drug policy must be national in scope, I have nevertheless tried to demonstrate that some reforms can be made on the local level."[57] Mayor Schmoke claims actually to have put his pro-legalization views into action. So, what has been the result?

Mayor Schmoke was first elected mayor of Baltimore in 1987. Although there have been no broad surveys of drug use limited to Baltimore, since 1988 drug-related emergency room admissions in the city have skyrocketed, increasing over 359 percent to become the highest rate in the nation per capita. In 1988, the national average for such admissions was 307.3 per 100,000 population annually; Baltimore's was 379.7. By 1994, the national rate was 384.1 per 100,000 and Baltimore's rate was 1,365.5 per 100,000—the worst in the nation, and three times the rate in Los Angeles and almost twice the rate of New York City. Cocaine emergency room admissions for Baltimore in 1988 were 95.7 per 100,000 (the national average was 46.7), and by 1994, when Baltimore led the nation at 461.5 per 100,000, the national average was 61.8. And heroin emergency room admissions for Baltimore in 1988 were 51 per 100,000 (the national average was 17.5), and in 1994 Baltimore again led the nation with 397.5 per 100,000—almost an eightfold increase—when the national average increased to only 27.9 per 100,000.[58]

Now it is impossible to prove that Mr. Schmoke's policies caused this unparalleled increase. However, it is at least fair to say that his policies did not prevent Baltimore from becoming far and away the national leader in drug-related emergency room admissions. And this record, and the attendant human carnage, seems to trouble the legalizers—William F. Buckley, Jr., Anthony Lewis, and others—not one whit. It is worth noting, we think, that while the drug legalization advocates make a lot of noise now and again, their views carry little real-world political impact. They remain on the outer fringes of the national political debate. To ensure that they stay there, their arguments need to be addressed and exposed. We are encouraged that no national political leader has even flirted with taking a stance in favor of drug legalization—at least not while in office.

There are those who argue that the nation has spent enormous sums of money to no effect, and they assert that the drug trade is too rich, too powerful, and too deeply rooted in human nature to be defeated. But again, this is the "big lie" about the drug problem, and it is demonstrably false. The success of the 1980s and early 1990s gives witness to the lie. The energy and resources devoted to the anti-drug effort during that time, combined with hardening public attitudes, produced dramatic declines in the drug problem.

And while annual federal spending on the drug war was substantial, it only approached $12 billion at the end of the Bush years.[59] At no time did such spending exceed federal spending for, say, NASA. The point here is that neither the space program nor the federal anti-drug effort ever represented a serious burden on the federal budget. And busting the budget today is not required either. Leadership and a properly directed anti-drug effort are the most crucial needs.

MYTHS ABOUT DRUG USE

Two myths present serious obstacles to reducing drug use. First is the mantra that the root causes of drug use are poverty, racism, and "low self-esteem." And second is the more general view that therapy by a team of counselors, physicians, and specialists is the only effective way to reduce drug use. At their core these myths deny individual responsibility and assume that drug use is not the product of an individual's decision—that decisions are somehow made in a vacuum where things like fear of getting caught, public disgrace, and punishment are never considerations. At their core, those prescriptions for addressing the drug problem manifest a moral ignorance in public policy itself. Reversing recent increases in drug use, and finishing the job of reducing drug use begun in the 1980s and early 1990s, requires restoring common sense and, more important, common moral sense about the drug problem. And this means recognizing the primary importance of those things contemporary liberalism has sought to undervalue: law enforcement, individual responsibility, and reducing the supply of drugs on our streets.

Drug enforcement and individual responsibility are important because drug use can be intensely pleasurable. The desire for drugs must be countered by certain moral precepts: drug use is wrong, and those who use and traffic in illegal drugs deserve to be punished. A responsible community teaches these things by what those in positions of authority—parents, religious leaders, teachers, friends, employers, and political officials—say about drugs and how they act toward drug use and sale. If those in authority do not address the issue seriously, they teach that drug use is not a serious matter. And if they say drug use is intolerable but fail to act effectively to stop and punish those who sell and use drugs, their actions convey a much different and more powerful lesson than their words.

Drug use—whether by nonaddicts or addicts—is fueled not merely by the desire to use but by the ease with which those who want drugs can obtain them. A nation that permits wide availability of dangerous drugs is sending an unwitting message: we are basically indifferent to drug use. The wide availability of drugs entails the normalization of drug use. The harsh reality is that drug use often begins with experimentation, with a substantial portion escalating to addiction, which often ends in death. It seems clear to us that a humane and civilized society ought to display a special intolerance for those things that eviscerate people's character and, eventually, destroy their lives as well.

HOW DRUG USE BEGINS AND HOW TO PREVENT IT

Drug use most often begins in childhood and adolescence with experimental or so-called casual use. When twelfth-graders[60] who reported using marijuana in the past year were asked why they had done so, the most common reasons given were: "to feel good or get high" (73.7 percent); "to experiment—to see what it's like" (71.1 percent); and "to have a good time with my friends" (64.1 percent). The same three reasons were also the most common ones given by seniors who had used cocaine in the past year—experiment (75.9 percent), get high (64.6 percent), and good time with friends (43 percent). It turns out that drug use spreads among peers and almost never by an adult "pushing" drugs on a young person. As such, the level of drug use by teenagers is linked to the acceptability of experimentation and getting high and on the availability of drugs.

In a parallel section of the national survey of high school students, students who reported that they "probably will not" or "definitely will not" use marijuana in the coming year were asked why. They were given a series of 18 reasons and asked to rank their importance. Of the reasons cited as "very important," four answers were most prominent: "don't feel like getting high" (62.4 percent); "concern about possible psychological damage" (60.9 percent); "concern about possible physical damage" (59.7 percent); and "my parents would disapprove" (58 percent). When students who said they would not use cocaine or crack were asked why, 80 percent or more expressed concern about five areas of harm: becoming addicted, physical damage, psychological damage, that it could lead to stronger drugs, and losing self-control. The next most prominent reason given (by 70 percent of the students in the case of crack and 71.9 percent in the case of powder cocaine) was "concern about getting arrested." Fear of the personal harm drug use can cause, a sense of self that is opposed to getting high and abandoning self-control, and fear of the disapproval of parents and society (in the form of arrest) are precisely what common sense might suggest as the central forces for preventing drug use.

The Partnership for a Drug-Free America, formed in the late 1980s, became famous for its frying-egg "this is your brain on drugs" public service ads. The partnership sponsored a detailed study of adult, teenage, and preteen attitudes about drugs during 1995, paralleling a survey it conducted in 1993.[61] It found that 13- to 18-year-olds in 1995 saw "significantly less physical and social risks in marijuana and drugs, and perceive more 'benefits' in drug use—i.e., more teens believe drugs help you relax and that getting high feels good." Marijuana, in particular, was increasingly viewed as "no big deal" by the teenagers surveyed in 1995.

The partnership study offers several possible reasons for the change in teen attitudes toward drugs. First, teens are receiving less anti-drug information. Drug-related stories airing on the three major television networks dropped from 518 in 1989 to 82 in 1994, a decline of 84 percent. Media donations of broadcast time and print space for the partnership's ads declined by 22 percent between 1991 and 1995. Second, popular music and the media have increasingly presented more favorable views of drugs and drug use—particularly marijuana use. The partnership study reported: "Select music groups encourage legalization of marijuana, and some artists dedicate entire CDs to the drug; more examples of drug use, especially marijuana use, being portrayed lightly and/or as a non-consequential behavior are appearing on television and in movies; a marijuana fashion craze began in the early 90s attracting widespread media attention." It also noted that "the continuing public debate on the legalization of drugs may be having a detrimental impact on teens' perceptions of drugs and drug use."

Comparing responses from teens and the parents of teenagers, the partnership found that while 95 percent of the parents claim to have talked to their children about drugs, only 77 percent of the teens say they have had such a conversation. And while 14 percent of the parents believed it was possible that their teenagers may have experimented with marijuana, 38 percent of the teens reported doing so. Ginna Marston, the partnership's director of research and strategic development, warned parents and others concerned about the welfare of today's teenagers that "music, media and fashion have a profound influence on the way young people see the world around them. And what they're seeing is a world that increasingly tells them that smoking pot is fun, cool, inconsequential and a normal part of growing up." [62]

The lesson is obvious: normalize drug use and more young people will take drugs, stigmatize drug use and there will be less of it. Parents are justified in their increasing concern about the danger, even if some of them may underestimate its magnitude. The same partnership study cited above found that "77 percent of parents of teenagers say parents should forbid their kids to use any drugs at any time" even though 60 percent of those baby-boomer parents admit they have tried marijuana. Only 9 percent said they "worry about feeling hypocritical when talking to their kids about marijuana."

Parents should increase their efforts to convey why drug use is wrong and why it is dangerous. But it has become such a commonplace to tell Americans that they need an expert to advise them on every aspect of life, that even the task of talking to one's own children about drugs is frequently viewed as requiring specialized materials and "training." It doesn't. The best place to start is by example and by explaining honestly why you as an adult do not use drugs and oppose their use by others. It will ring true and have a more lasting effect as a result. For those who still want further assistance, there are many sources of free drug prevention information. The federal government operates a clearinghouse for such material; most state and local governments also offer it through education, public health, and public safety offices; and most youth organizations have such materials for both young people and parents.

Another pressing task is to get other key institutions to support, rather than undermine, parents in this task. The biggest change in the past several years is the withdrawal of such support by national leaders and the institutions of popular culture. Children will learn what they are taught. And in too many ways they are being taught directly and indirectly, by the behavior of prominent individuals and of institutions, that drug use is accepted and even expected. To reverse the recent rise in drug use by teenagers they must hear and see a different lesson.

THE VIRTUAL LEGALIZATION OF DRUGS—
OPEN-AIR DRUG MARKETS

Open-air drug markets are the most visible sign of the acceptance of the drug trade in our nation. It is a national disgrace that such markets are tolerated in virtually every major American city. Where they exist, crime, victimization, and addiction flourish. Yet many communities have demonstrated that forcing drug dealers from open spaces makes their lives more difficult and dangerous and hence their activities less frequent.

One such community success story is that of the Miami Coalition. It has helped organize a wide range of local anti-drug activities, not the least of which was pressing Dade County officials to demolish more than 2,000 crack houses. The coalition claims that crime in the area has been reduced by 24 percent and annual drug use has decreased by 40 percent as a result of its efforts. [63]

Another success story is the Safe Streets Campaign in Tacoma, Washington. It has involved 8,000 community members, including 2,000 young people, in its activities (i.e., closing down local drug markets and neighborhood prevention efforts). The campaign, formed in 1989, claims to have closed over 600 drug markets, reduced 911 calls by 23,000, and removed all graffiti from the more than 3,000 blocks it has organized. [64]

And in San Antonio, Texas, San Antonio Fighting Back has created a partnership between the community and the police to fight crime and drugs. Burglaries decreased by 19 percent and auto theft by 23 percent in one year. Resident reports to police of criminal activity increased substantially. Eighty-five crack houses have been closed, and an abandoned nursing home that became a haven for transients, drug users, and criminals on the run was demolished. A special effort for young people called Mentors Fighting Back claims to have substantially reduced criminal behavior, improved student attendance by 25 percent, and improved student grades by 30 percent.[65]

Throughout the nation thousands of neighborhoods and communities have organized themselves to confront street crime, drug dealing, and drug use. They range in sophistication from little more than neighborhood watch efforts to large programs including prevention activities in homes, schools, and workplaces and treatment and rehabilitation services. There is even a national organization, Community Anti-Drug Coalitions of America, located in Alexandria, Virginia, that serves as a clearinghouse for information and technical assistance. One of their recent publications, "Procedures for Establishing a Community-Based Curfew Intervention Program Through Religious Organizations," is a how-to manual prepared in collaboration with the American Bar Association. Community coalitions are important because they provide a means of enlisting local energies under local leadership and they produce results.

Many communities have demonstrated that creating a law enforcement presence and maintaining it in response to relocation efforts by drug dealers is doable—but only if closing drug markets is made a priority. In the next year, mayors, city councils, and police chiefs should pledge to close all open-air drug markets in their communities. Citizens should demand such a pledge and make clear that they will insist that these officials keep it. We need to stop claiming that the crime and drug problem in our communities is someone else's responsibility. Decisive action can be taken by local officials and community members now.

THE ADDICTED AND THE RECORD OF THE DRUG TREATMENT SYSTEM

The most obvious casualties of the fad of drug use in the 1960s, 1970s, and 1980s are today's drug addicts. Figure 4-13 reveals that while the drop in casual cocaine use in particular has been rapid—and thus the

FIGURE 4-13. ESTIMATED NUMBER OF HEAVY AND CASUAL USERS OF COCAINE
AND HEROIN, 1988–1993

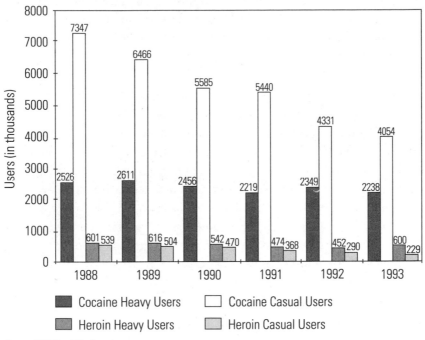

Cocaine Heavy Users   ☐ Cocaine Casual Users

Heroin Heavy Users   Heroin Casual Users

Source: ONDCP and Abt Associates.

source of potential new addicts has been curtailed—the heavy, addicted cocaine and heroin user populations remained roughly the same size.[66]

Heavy cocaine and heroin users also tend to use a variety of other drugs (marijuana, heroin, sedatives, and others) and alcohol.[67] Both heavy cocaine and heroin users are predominantly male, unmarried (most never married), and most commit crimes and are frequently involved in the criminal justice system. They commit crimes—including selling drugs—as a means of income to purchase drugs. But heavy cocaine users in particular also commit crimes as a result of "the effects of the drug itself (they become disinhibited and commit crimes), or because of a life-style choice (they participate in both drug use and criminal activity)."[68]

In one of the more intensive studies of heroin addicts, the Clinton administration's Office of National Drug Control Policy reported: "More users initiated heroin use in 1968, 1969, and 1970 than in any other years. . . . Twenty-five years after the last heroin epidemic, we are still suffering its effects." This study also reported that "public assistance is a major—and perhaps the single largest—source of income for heroin users."[69]

Feeding Waste and Mismanagement in the Drug Treatment Bureaucracy

The Clinton administration began by calling for a reorientation of national drug control efforts focusing on treating hard-core addicts. Some very fine drug treatment programs have proven their usefulness,[70] but the government treatment bureaucracy is manifestly ineffective. The Clinton administration's claim that it will improve the drug problem by increasing treatment slots for hard-core addicts is contradicted by the facts found in the recent record of treatment funding and the number of persons served.[71] As shown in Figure 4-14,

FIGURE 4-14. FEDERAL DRUG TREATMENT SPENDING AND NUMBER OF PERSONS TREATED, 1988–1994

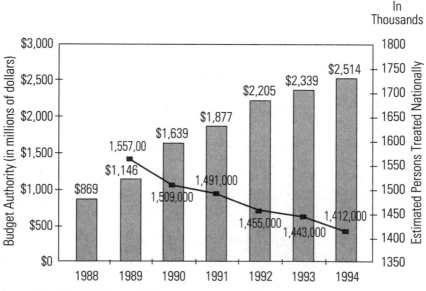

Source: National Drug Control Strategy, 1994.

although federal drug treatment spending almost tripled between 1988 and 1994, the number of treatment slots remained virtually unchanged and the estimated number of persons treated declined—from 1,557,000 in 1989 to 1,412,000 in 1994.[72]

Nonetheless, existing treatment capacity, measured in terms of persons served per year, is equivalent to more than half the total estimated number of cocaine and heroin addicts (see Figure 4-15).[73] So it is important to ask: bureaucratic waste and inefficiencies within the treatment system aside, why hasn't the system reduced the number of addicts?

Most addicts have been through treatment more than once. The fact is that drug addicts like using drugs (even though most of them also dislike some aspects and consequences of their drug use). They sometimes admit themselves to treatment programs, not to stop using drugs, but to regain greater control over their drug use. But the overwhelming majority of the addicts entering treatment with the goal of ending their use are coerced to do so by the courts, family members, or an employer.[74]

A substantial number of addicts have been through many treatment

FIGURE 4-15. ESTIMATED HEAVY COCAINE AND HEROIN USERS AND ESTIMATED NUMBER OF PERSONS RECEIVING DRUG TREATMENT NATIONALLY, 1989–1993

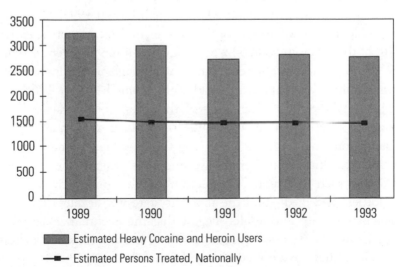

Estimated Heavy Cocaine and Heroin Users

Estimated Persons Treated, Nationally

Source: ONDCP.

programs. Some of those programs are simply not effective, but there are insufficient structures monitoring performance to force them out of business. Sometimes addicts and programs are not matched properly.[75] When the cocaine epidemic started, many heroin treatment slots were unfilled, but not enough slots for those needing treatment were tailored for cocaine addiction. Government can, and should, act to increase accountability (insist that programs receiving federal funds demonstrate they are effective) and increase service capacity in target areas, but the federal government is a very blunt and rather slow instrument for getting this done. The federally funded portion of the treatment system is estimated to be less than half the total national spending on drug treatment, and federal measures for accountability and targeting must attempt to reach through multiple layers of bureaucracy—in the federal government, and in state and local governments.

In addition, more and more of the addict population seems to be a fixed, aging cohort, with a long history of addiction from early adulthood—so-called hard-core addicts. Many of them are addicted to a variety of drugs and suffer from a range of pathologies, including severe mental disorders. The best treatment programs can still offer some hope of recovery, but it is also likely that for a substantial percentage of the most severely addicted there may be no effective treatment today, particularly if drugs remain widely available.

A long-term study of heroin addicts, published in 1993, highlights this problem in stark terms. Five hundred eighty-one narcotics addicts (most of them heroin addicts) were studied at intervals over 24 years. The group originally entered treatment through a criminal justice program, the California Civil Addict Program, between 1962 and 1964. A 1985–86 follow-up study of this group found that only 25 percent of them tested free of opiates, 6.9 percent were in a program of methadone maintenance (receiving the drug methadone to block the high resulting from heroin use and thus remove the strongest reason for such use), and 27.7 percent (of the group now in their late forties) had died—and the mortality rate was accelerating. The researchers warn: "The results suggest that the eventual cessation of narcotics use is a very slow process, unlikely to occur for some addicts, especially if they have not ceased use by their late 30's."[76]

Another study of heroin addicts released in November 1994 found:

Only 15 percent of the heroin users in the study (23 of 150) had never participated in substance abuse treatment. Of the 85 percent who had received treatment, one-third (42 of 127) were currently enrolled in a treatment program. . . .

Among users with treatment experience, the median number of times enrolled in treatment was five. However, more than a fourth reported having been in treatment on more than ten occasions. One user reported 67 treatment experiences.[77]

On August 9, 1993, Clinton administration Drug Policy Director Lee Brown released a research paper, "Characteristics of Heavy Cocaine Users." That study contained a similar, sobering conclusion regarding the success rates of treatment programs for cocaine addicts:

> While many users benefit from treatment, compulsive use is most frequently a chronic condition. The Treatment Outcome Prospectives Study (TOPS) showed that for every 10 clients who used cocaine regularly during the year prior to treatment, six clients had returned to heavy use one year after treatment, and eight clients had relapsed into heavy use within three to five years after treatment. These statistics do not accurately reflect the success of treatment outcomes. (The TOPS study is the most recent large-scale study of treatment outcomes. Many smaller scale treatment studies show results with better long-term outcomes.) Nevertheless, the TOPS data suggest that treated cocaine users are more likely than not to return to drug use.[78]

Those who assert that treatment is the answer, and those who advocate legalizing drugs and retrieving those who become addicted by expanding drug treatment, never confront the fact that today a significant portion of those who are addicted to cocaine and heroin will die of that addiction if treatment alone is the principal vehicle society employs to save them.

The 1994 crime bill contained large sums for drug courts. These provisions were highlighted by spokesmen who announced that they were being "smart and tough." The model, and essentially the justification, for this funding was the Miami Drug Court and Attorney General Janet Reno's personal involvement with it as a prosecutor.

But in August, as the crime bill fight was near its peak, the *Miami Herald* published a lengthy report raising serious questions about the effectiveness of the program.[79] In particular, the program established to divert first- and second-time drug offenders into treatment instead of prison was being used by robbers and burglars to serve as little as 45 days. And in December the *Herald* reported that the chief judge overseeing the Miami Drug Court ordered an audit of the entire program, expressing alarm that it "had no mechanism to measure whether it was succeeding."[80] A central flaw in the rush to embrace drug courts as a major answer to addiction and crime is that a very large number of addicted offenders today are long-term, hard-core addicts who are poorly suited for diversion programs. Drug courts, properly run, hold promise for treating young addicts in the early stages of addiction. But young addicts in the early stages of addiction are not the primary addiction problem. Moreover, drug courts generally depend on the same probation, parole, and pretrial supervision system that is now unable to prevent a third of all violent crime from being committed by individuals under its "custody." These institutions are not a promising source of the close supervision and imposition of sanctions for resorting to drug use or withdrawing from treatment required for drug courts to be effective.

In 1994, two groups of studies were released that purport to demonstrate the effectiveness of drug treatment and its superior cost-effectiveness to all other categories of drug enforcement and supply control. One, funded by the California Department of Alcohol and Drug Programs, received attention for its conclusion that treatment "averages [a] $7 return for every dollar invested." But it included both alcohol and drug addiction and was thus too broad to be enlightening in regard to the cost-effectiveness of treating cocaine, and particularly crack, addiction—the most destructive addiction threat today. Moreover, the study relied on two sample groups with only a 50 percent and 46 percent response rate. Despite efforts to impute outcomes for nonrespondents from respondents, it is probable that the nonrespondents constitute very high—with the precise level unmeasured—treatment failures.[81] In addition, none of the sympathetic news reports noted that such benefits-to-society-for-every-dollar-invested studies for expenditures on prisons and jails have produced estimates as high as 17 to 1.[82]

A second widely reported study was funded in part by the White House drug office, and conducted by the RAND Corporation. It was entitled "Controlling Cocaine," and concluded that "treatment is seven times more cost effective in reducing cocaine consumption than the best supply control program."[83] Most of the press reports on the release of this study failed to mention that even Clinton administration drug office officials participating in the release distanced themselves from the reliability of the methods RAND used to measure the effectiveness of supply control programs.[84] And to our knowledge none of the press reports explained what the study actually found in regard to the effectiveness of programs treating cocaine addicts.

In reviewing all forms of cocaine treatment, RAND reported that 20 percent of addicts continue using drugs while in treatment and only 13.2 percent of the cocaine addicts treated reduce their drug use below weekly or more frequent use (what RAND defined as "heavy use") during the year following their treatment. Overall, RAND reported, only "6 percent of heavy users leave heavy use each year [i.e., to something less than heavy use, not to be equated with no use]. About two-thirds of that outflow is apparently due to existing treatment programs . . . [and] one-third of the total annual outflow from heavy use is estimated to be due to unassisted desistance from heavy use."[85]

In other words, overall, the cocaine treatment system was only 4 percent effective in reducing heavy use and only 2 percent more effective in reducing heavy use than no treatment at all. And if effectiveness were measured in terms of the percentage of addicts who stopped using cocaine altogether and for good, the results would have been much worse.

While support for treatment programs should continue, the harsh reality of cocaine and crack addiction is that most addicts—and most of them are hard-core, long-term addicts today—are likely to die from the effects of their addiction sometime in their forties, if not earlier. This is yet one more compelling reason why preventing casual drug use by young people—the first step on the path to addiction—is so important.

As long as the drug problem is discussed in terms of treatment versus enforcement or supply versus demand, it will remain fundamentally misguided. These positions are at odds with both reality and common sense. An effective drug policy should begin with this assumption: as long as young people and those who receive treatment reside in communities where the supply of dangerous, addictive drugs remains plentiful—i.e., where there is de facto legalization—prevention and particularly treatment efforts will be severely undercut and, for purposes of national policy, not very effective.

THE ILLEGAL DRUG TRADE, SUPPLY REDUCTION, AND ADDICTION

What is increasingly an addict-driven trade today is still dominated by cocaine, as can be seen in Figure 4-16.[86] Roughly three-fifths of the total spent on illegal drugs is spent on cocaine—and for the most part, that means crack.

As can be seen in Figure 4-17, working with cocaine source countries (Colombia, Peru, and Bolivia) on reducing coca[87] crops stopped the increase in cultivation that occurred during the 1980s, but did not substantially reduce the crop size.[88] Eradication of the plants from

FIGURE 4-16. ESTIMATED U.S. EXPENDITURES ON ILLICIT DRUGS, 1988–1993

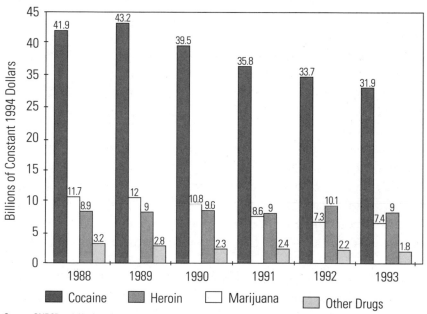

Source: ONDCP and Abt Associates.

FIGURE 4-17. TOTAL COCA CULTIVATION, 1986–1994

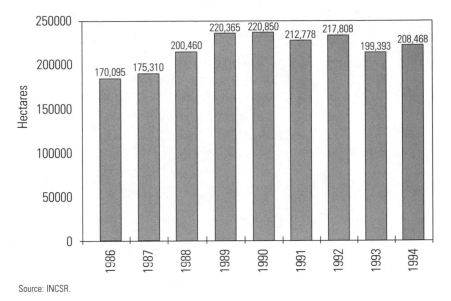

Source: INCSR.

which illegal drugs are extracted was a principal emphasis of U.S. anti-drug policy in the 1980s. It produced disappointing results, however. Since 1987, eradication efforts in cocaine source countries have produced less than a 10 percent reduction in estimated potential cocaine production, and it only came close to 10 percent in one year— 1992 (see Figure 4-18).

Much more encouragingly, interdiction of cocaine within the source countries and in transit from them to the United States has substantially reduced the amount of cocaine available to American markets. What could arrive, based on what could be produced, minus what was seized, declined between 1989 and 1992 (see Figure 4-19).[89] Seizures within South America increased dramatically, and U.S. assistance, particularly military detection and tracking assistance, supported interdiction throughout the hemisphere.

In 1992, half or more of potential cocaine production was seized (see Figure 4-20). Not only did interdiction stop almost twice as much cocaine as that actually consumed, supply reduction efforts actually seem to have contributed to a reduction in cocaine emergency room cases and a reduction in the population of cocaine addicts.

The Colombian government's broad and intense attack on the co-

FIGURE 4-18. POTENTIAL COCAINE PRODUCTION, 1987–1994

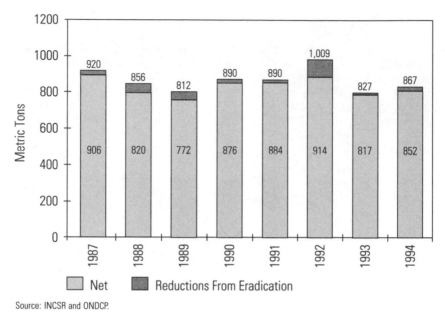

Source: INCSR and ONDCP.

FIGURE 4-19. ESTIMATED COCAINE AVAILABLE TO THE U.S. MARKET,
1987–1994

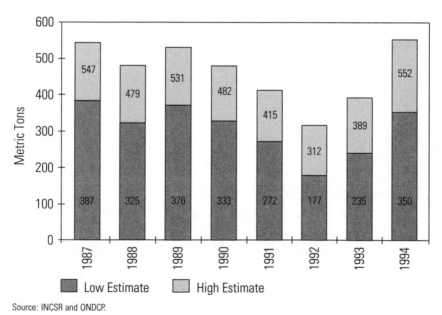

Source: INCSR and ONDCP.

FIGURE 4-20. ESTIMATED COCAINE DISTRIBUTION, 1992

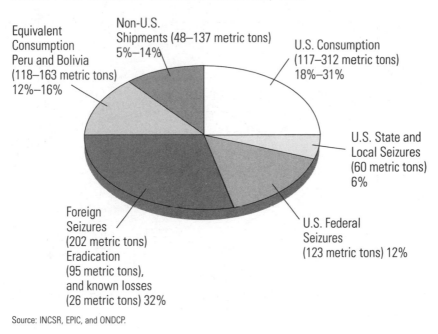

Source: INCSR, EPIC, and ONDCP.

caine cartel produced a substantial disruption in the cocaine supply to the United States from the very end of 1989 into 1991, although there are no exact measures of the magnitude of that disruption (and the previous estimates of potential production cannot fully capture it). Nonetheless, there are important indicators of significant disruption with beneficial consequences, particularly for heavy cocaine users.

The U.S. Drug Enforcement Administration's data on cocaine prices throughout the nation reveal (see Figure 4-21) that in gram amounts—the accepted retail quantity—the downward trend in prices and upward trend in purity through early 1989 abruptly reversed.[90] The magnitude of this change in availability is perhaps best represented by using a standardized price, that is, by calculating the cost of a 100 percent pure gram of cocaine at each point of measurement.[91] And this reduction in the availability of cocaine—driving the price up and the purity down—coincided with a 27 percent reduction in cocaine emergency room cases between 1989 and 1990, as can be seen in Figure 4-22.[92]

FIGURE 4-21. RETAIL COCAINE PRICE AND PURITY IN THE U.S., 1988–1992

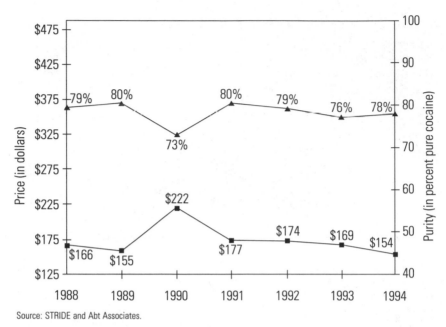

Source: STRIDE and Abt Associates.

Medical examiner reports of deaths related to cocaine use during this period also declined. Analysis has found cocaine price increases, purity reductions, and declines in cocaine emergency room cases, deaths, and cocaine use among arrestees for all the more than 20 largest U.S. cities for which the data are available.[93] Further, this cocaine supply reduction also coincides with the estimated decline in number of heavy cocaine users previously cited.[94]

What conclusions can we draw based on the limited available data? The reduction in cocaine availability seems beyond question, and that it was a causal factor in the decline in cocaine use, particularly heavy use, is the most obvious and reasonable conclusion in light of the data. But this cannot be proven with the precision that might be demanded in circumstances where the available data were more extensive.

Second, while nonaddictive users consume a much smaller quantity of cocaine than heavy or addicted users, an almost 80 percent drop in nonaddictive users between 1985 and 1992 certainly reduced demand

FIGURE 4-22. COCAINE EMERGENCY ROOM CASES AND STANDARDIZED COCAINE
PRICE, 1981–1993

In Thousands

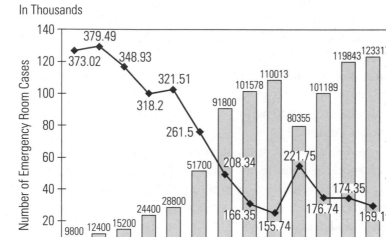

Source: DAWN and Abt Associates.

in a significant, if limited, extent (which is not measurable by existing
surveys and analyses). In order to increase cocaine retail prices and
reduce purity, supply-reduction efforts would have to cut supply beyond the amount that would have satisfied the reduced demand. So
the actual supply disruption may be even greater than the change in
the price and purity data.[95]

Finally, such analysis must consider whether cocaine traffickers may
have manipulated supply to increase profits or for some other purpose.
In fact, in smaller transactions and at the wholesale level in particular
areas, law enforcement investigators have reported efforts by particular groups to influence prices by withholding supply, but these have
been limited in both scope and duration. There is no evidence of
either large-scale efforts to manipulate availability or the ability to
do so.

If measured strictly by results, our national prevention efforts produced impressive achievements—dramatic declines in casual cocaine

use in particular—and, contrary to conventional opinion, interdiction and cocaine source-country programs seem to have been a crucial factor in the reductions in heavy or addictive cocaine use.

Why didn't the reduction in cocaine supply continue throughout 1991 and beyond? The movement of U.S. military resources to the Persian Gulf for Desert Shield and then Desert Storm, beginning in the summer of 1991, reduced interdiction coverage, particularly in regard to some of the most powerful airborne and surface naval systems. Those resources were never returned and interdiction resources were slashed even further.

We believe the supply of drugs—measured in their retail price and purity (which can be stated as their standardized price as cited above) —bears a direct relationship to the number of people who will enter emergency rooms with drug-related emergencies, not only for cocaine, but for heroin and marijuana as well, as can be seen in Figures 4-23 and 4-24.[96] In short, greater supply at lower cost means greater demand. It is the economics of mass, discount marketing.

FIGURE 4-23. HEROIN EMERGENCY ROOM CASES AND STANDARDIZED HEROIN PRICE, 1981–1993

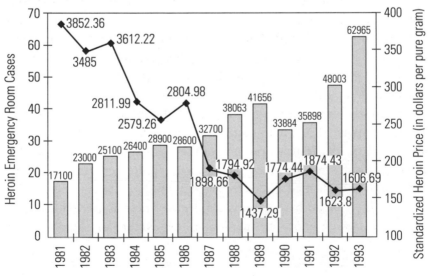

Source: DAWN and Abt Associates.

FIGURE 4-24. MARIJUANA/HASHISH EMERGENCY ROOM CASES AND AVERAGE MARIJUANA PRICE, 1988–1993

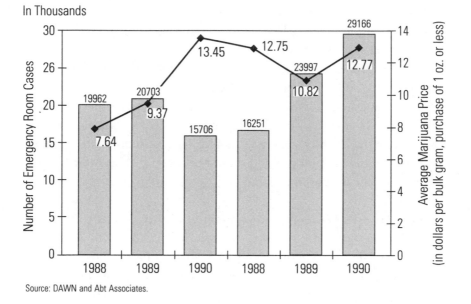

Source: DAWN and Abt Associates.

PRIORITIES FOR EFFECTIVE ACTION

TEACH THE YOUNG THAT DRUG USE IS WRONG

Preventing young people from using drugs is central to all effective anti-drug efforts. After all, young people who do not use drugs in their teens are unlikely to ever do so as adults. But each generation must be taught that illegal drug use is wrong. And this lesson must be taught by the community of adults. Specifically, children learn about drugs by what the adults around them say and do. Parents teach by precept and example. The same is true of schools and the communities. If drug use and sale is not aggressively opposed and prevented, children learn it is acceptable, despite what some adults may occasionally tell them. It will always fall to parents to provide that education in the home and to ensure that schools and their communities are teaching this lesson effectively. This task is easier, of course, if national leaders set the right example and speak in support of parents. But parents, churches, schools, youth organizations, and communities have always been, and will always remain, the first—and most important—line of defense.

Put Open-Air Drug Markets Out of Business

Open-air drug markets feed addiction and are a visible sign of the toleration of the drug trade in our nation. Aggressive street-level policing can force drug dealers from open spaces and make their lives more difficult and dangerous—and hence their activities less frequent. Many communities have demonstrated that creating a law enforcement presence and maintaining it in response to relocation efforts by drug dealers is doable—but only if closing drug markets is made a priority. Decisive action can and should be taken by local officials and community members immediately.

Sanction Foreign Nations That Are the Source of Drugs

The federal government can also do what no parent or local community can: diminish the flow of drugs reaching local communities.

The United States regularly threatens and initiates trade sanctions to protect business interests—to protect copyrights and force foreign nations to open their markets to American goods, for example. We believe there are more compelling reasons to use trade sanctions to protect American young people from drugs. Those who properly support the goal of free trade ought to recognize that their goal cannot be defended if free trade means accepting the drug trade.

America needs once again to forge an anti-drug partnership with Colombia and other Latin American nations.[97] Otherwise the cartels' grip on Colombia will not only tighten, but the leaders of the drug trade will grow stronger in many nations of South America and in Mexico. The cartels are moving rapidly toward the goal of ending all threat of serious enforcement action against their operations in this hemisphere, outside the United States. And Americans will face a virtually unrestricted flow of cocaine, heroin, and marijuana—at lower and lower prices and higher and higher purities.

Only the threat and, if necessary, the imposition of trade sanctions will mobilize the legitimate interests in the Latin American nations to force their governments to attack drug trafficking seriously.

MAKE INTERDICTING DRUGS A TOP NATIONAL SECURITY PRIORITY

It is time to put the U.S. military in charge of stopping the flow of illegal drugs from abroad. Law enforcement agencies currently responsible for drug interdiction should be placed under the overall command and control of the military. We realize that some in the military will object to this nontraditional mission and its cost. And some inside and outside the military will object to what they will call the "militarization" of the drug war. Those are legitimate concerns. But the fact is, no law enforcement organization will ever have the intelligence-gathering resources, radar, tracking, and apprehension capabilities for the interdiction task that the military already possesses. Those military capabilities should be dedicated in a much larger, more sustained, and integrated manner to the interdiction mission—with the military in charge of that mission outside our borders. The national security capabilities of a superpower give the United States overwhelming superiority over even the richest and most ruthless drug lords. Yet this superiority remains substantially unused. The drug trade —in the magnitude that it exists today—can only operate if the federal government fails to apply the national security resources to cripple it.

DESTROY THE MAJOR DRUG-TRAFFICKING ORGANIZATIONS OPERATING WITHIN THE UNITED STATES

The drug trade inside the United States relies on sophisticated senior management. Despite periodic law enforcement successes, federal domestic enforcement agencies have produced no disruption of major trafficking operations and no sustained reductions in availability. This needs to change.

Right now federal drug enforcement lacks sufficient accountability. This could change by requiring the attorney general to prepare a report every six months identifying all major drug-trafficking organizations known to be operating in the United States[98] and a plan to deploy federal enforcement personnel to dismantle them. Congress can even impose such a policy by making funds for federal drug enforcement agencies contingent on effectively implementing it.

Most Americans' opinions about the drug problem conform remarkably to the best available research. Americans have remained steadfast in their opposition to drugs despite the arguments advanced by legalization advocates. But that steadfast conviction must be conveyed more forcefully—particularly to today's young people. To put it another way: the issue is less about public opinion (which is strongly against drug use) than the intensity of that opinion and how well (or poorly) it translates throughout society. The majority of the American public rightly believes that drugs are a cause of moral poverty, often destroying the strongest human bonds of love and affection—among parents and children, husbands and wives—in their wake. The majority of the public is right, too, in its conviction that drugs feed and intensify violent crime. The key here as elsewhere, of course, is to act on that conviction. We know what needs to be done—at the level of the federal and state governments, within communities, in our schools, and in individual lives. A successful and serious anti-drug effort will require once again taking up the proven, purposeful, and successful steps we have taken in the past.

5

ABOUT MORAL POVERTY: SOME THINGS WE NEED TO DO

In 1967, the President's Commission on Law Enforcement and Administration of Justice issued *The Challenge of Crime in a Free Society*. The first page of the report began with these disturbing words: "There is much crime in America, more than ever is reported, far more than ever is solved, far too much for the health of the Nation."[1]

The commission used crime statistics on robbery to illustrate the point: "Consider the crime of robbery, which, since it involves both stealing and violence or the threat of it, is an especially hurtful and frightening one. In 1965 in America there were 118,916 robberies known to the police"—in other words, 6 reported robberies for every 10,000 Americans.[2]

Now consider that in 1994 in America there were 1,299,000 robberies, some 719,000 of them known to the police—in other words, 27.5 reported robberies for every 10,000 Americans (and 4.6 times the 1965 rate).[3]

Even before the 1967 report, a 1962 White House Conference on Narcotics and Drug Abuse was convened because "drug traffic and abuse were growing and critical national concerns," and "the informed public was becoming increasingly aware of the social and economic damage of illicit drug taking."[4] A three-sentence entry on "cocaine" stated in part: "This drug is included as a narcotic under Federal and other laws but, unlike the opiates, it is a powerful stimulant and does not create tolerance or physical dependence. . . . At present it is not the major drug of abuse that it once was."[5]

By the late 1980s, one did not need to be "informed" to know that drug abuse was doing tremendous damage to Americans, and that cocaine in the form of crack was stimulating a major violent crime wave.

In one of the most widely cited passages of the report, the commission declared that "warring on poverty, inadequate housing, and unemployment is warring on crime."[6] To this day, the report is remembered by many for its emphasis on government anti-poverty programs, racial injustice, and more across-the-board spending on the justice system and other activities. "Money is needed for everything," according to the commission.[7]

But on the same page as the commission declared that the war on crime should be fought as a war on economic poverty, it also declared that the "activities of almost every kind of social institution with which children come in contact—schools, churches, social-service agencies, youth organizations—are predicated on the assumption that children acquire their fundamental attitudes toward life, their moral standards, in their homes." And then this: *Offering opportunities is not the same thing as providing moral standards.*"[8]

We couldn't agree more emphatically.

In 1969, another presidential commission issued *Violent Crime: The Challenge to Our Cities*. The report warned that "increasingly powerful social forces are generating rising levels of violent crime which, unless checked, threaten to turn our cities into defensive, fearful societies."[9] One edition of the report reprinted a ten-point plan for urban renewal developed by Professor Daniel Patrick Moynihan—then a Harvard professor and counselor to President Richard Nixon.[10]

These reports are instructive if for no other reason than that they place our current crime situation in historical context and clearly reveal two things: one is that the nation has gotten much more dangerous in the past thirty years. The other is that we have become in many ways inured to the trauma.

What is so striking today is not simply the increased *number* of violent crimes, but the *nature* of those crimes. It is no longer "just" murders that we see but murders with a prologue, murders accompanied by acts of unspeakable cruelty and inhumanity.

In the 1980s the inner-city problem with drugs and crime became the urban nightmare about which the 1969 commission had warned. In 1989, Senator Daniel Patrick Moynihan wrote about the horrifying ills of the inner-city underclass.[11] And in 1993, Senator Moynihan wrote about "defining deviancy down," by which he meant that we now passively tolerate levels of social disorder—out-of-wedlock births, drug abuse, child abuse, crime, and public disorder—that but a generation ago would have been unthinkable.[12] And in the process we are losing a once-reliable sense of civic and moral outrage.

Listen to this story from former New York City Police Commissioner Raymond Kelly:

> A number of years ago there began to appear, in the windows of automobiles parked on the streets of American cities, signs which read: "No radio." Rather than express outrage or even annoyance at the possibility of a car break-in, people tried to communicate with the potential thief in conciliatory terms. The translation of "no radio" is: "Please break into someone else's car, there's nothing in mine." These "no radio" signs are flags of urban surrender. They are hand-written capitulations. Instead of "no radio," we need new signs that say "no surrender."[13]

As we have argued throughout this book, moral and not economic poverty is the real "root cause" of the nation's drug and crime problem.

As a polity, we are astonishingly close to the point where it takes juvenile super-predators to shock and outrage us—and just barely, at that. We are therefore in danger of succumbing to the drug and crime culture, and of defining down even homicidal behavior.

We should bring to the task of alleviating moral poverty the same passion that an earlier generation trained on alleviating economic poverty. But we need to learn from the failures of that earlier effort, too. And so we need to conjoin passion with prudence, wisdom, and realism. We should commit ourselves to a redistribution of sorts—not of wealth but of basic standards and a vivid sense of civic and personal responsibility. To be successful, our approach to making progress against drugs and crime must focus on the nature of the problem itself —namely, on matters cultural. Revolving-door justice and anemic anti-drug activities are the symptoms that must be treated. But moral poverty is the root cause that must finally be addressed.

At this point, our views are clear enough: combatting moral poverty must include a full-scale, concentrated, intense effort at combatting drugs and crime. But the effort *cannot* be limited merely to the efforts of the criminal justice system; it must be prosecuted through any number of institutions—families, churches, schools, and the mass media, among others.

So where have we been since we introduced this book with a trumpet call to arms—or, rather, the sound of chimes at midnight? We have demonstrated that violent crime in America is by far the worst in the industrialized world; violent crime is a problem of massive proportion; recent drops in violent crime rates, while encouraging and important, constitute only a small decrease from record high figures; the crime problem (for demographic reasons) is likely to get worse before it gets significantly better; there is a new young breed of super-predators who have been raised in practically perfect criminogenic environments, who are already destroying lives and, as their ranks thicken and unless radical changes are made, may soon terrorize our nation; while there are a variety of sources that are (more or less) contributing causes to crime, all roads lead back to moral poverty; revolving door justice is real but can be corrected; drugs are a particularly insidious threat given what crack does to sunder the bonds of human and familial ties; alcohol plays a much more prominent role in contributing to violent crime and moral poverty than most people realize; and what can be done to reduce violent crimes and the use of drugs.

Here we want to reissue a warning made at the beginning of this book: unchecked freedom can often unintentionally turn into its opposite. Unless we combine self-regulation with freedom, and unless we soon restore order to our communities and make advancements against spreading social anarchy, we will see an increase in state coercion. And then we will be only a short step away from achieving a quasi-police state. As the old saying goes, we can pay now or we can pay later.

We would like to conclude *Body Count* by attempting to put crime, drugs, and moral poverty in their larger cultural context. We want to leave you with a sense of where we think we are, socially and morally, as a nation, as well as with a sense of some of the things we think need to be done.

Body Count has discussed how moral poverty contributes to violent crime. But what are the factors that have contributed to moral poverty? In what ways are they manifested? And what are some of the things we can do in government and beyond government to reverse the trend?

Social pathologies have become a seemingly permanent feature of late-twentieth-century America. We have experienced an astonishing degree of social regression. Consider: at the midpoint of this century, America was the preeminent military power in the world. And at the close of this American century, the United States is still the undisputed military leader. But morally it has been on a very steep slide.

How steep? Between 1960 and 1990 we made a tremendous financial investment in an attempt to alleviate various social ills. Social spending by all levels of government increased (in constant dollars) by more than fivefold. But during the same 30-year period there was not only an enormous increase in violent crime but also a huge increase in the rates of out-of-wedlock births, the percentage of children living in single-parent homes, the teenage suicide rate, and the divorce rate. During this period we witnessed the worst decline in the history of American education. In short, we have experienced an unparalleled degree of economic prosperity *and* an unprecedented degree of social regression.

Widespread moral poverty is the inevitable result of the enfeebled condition—in some places in our society, the near-complete collapse —of our character-forming institutions. In a free society, families, schools, and churches have primary responsibility for shaping the moral sensibilities of the young. The influence of these institutions is determinative; when they no longer provide moral instruction or lose their moral authority, there is very little that other auxiliaries—particularly the federal government—can do.

Among those three institutions, the family is preeminent; it is, as Michael Novak once said, the original and best department of health, education, and welfare. But the family today is an agency in disrepair. Writes David Popenoe:

> This period [the 1960s through the 1990s] has witnessed an unprecedented decline of the family as a social institution. Families have lost functions, social power, and authority over their members. They have grown smaller in size, less stable, and shorter in life span. . . . Moreover, there has been a weakening of child-centeredness in American society and culture. Familism as a cultural value has diminished.[14]

Now, in the mid-1990s, more than 30 percent of all births and more than 70 percent of all black births are out of wedlock.[15] By the turn of the century, according to reliable projections, 40 percent of all American births and 80 percent of all minority births will be out of wedlock.[16] Each night in America, four out of 10 children go to sleep without fathers who live in their homes, and upward of 60 percent will spend some major part of their childhood without fathers.[17] This is "the most socially consequential family trend of our generation" (in the words of David Blankenhorn of the Institute for American Values),[18] and it has seismic social implications. Senator Moynihan warned 30 years ago that a society which allows a large number of young men to grow up without fathers in their lives asks for and almost always gets chaos. We have come to the point in America where we are asking prisons to do for many young boys what fathers used to do.

WHAT WENT WRONG

What accounts for America's social and moral regression? What is the intellectual soil from which moral poverty has grown? One explanation has to do with a marked shift in the public's attitudes. According to Professor Wilson, "The powers exercised by the institutions of social control have been constrained, and people, especially young people, have embraced an ethos that values self-expression over self-control." [19]

The pollster Daniel Yankelovich finds that we Americans now clearly place less value on what we owe others as a matter of moral obligation; less value on sacrifice as a moral good, on social conformity, respectability, and observing the rules; less value on correctness and restraint in matters of physical pleasure and sexuality; and correspondingly greater value on things like self-expression, individualism, self-realization, and personal choice. [20]

If the self, in the late Allan Bloom's withering assessment, has become "the modern substitute for the soul," [21] we are also living in an era in which it has become unfashionable to make judgments on a whole range of behaviors and attitudes. This unwillingness to judge has resulted in unilateral moral disarmament, as dangerous in the cultural realm as its counterpart is on the battlefield. With the removal of social sanctions in the name of "tolerance" and "open-mindedness," and the devaluing of the idea of personal responsibility, is it any wonder, for instance, that in a recent survey, 70 percent of young people between the ages of 18 and 34 said that people who generate a baby out of wedlock should not be subject to moral reproach *of any sort?* [22]

A number of pernicious, destructive ideas made their way into the mainstream of American life. It became unfashionable to make value judgments. Moral relativism became the de facto and defining doctrine of modern American life. We witnessed an expansive notion of "rights" and an attenuated sense of personal responsibility. "If it feels good, do it," "Do your own thing," and "You only go around once in life, so you have to grab *all* you can" became the words to live by. These seemingly innocuous phrases masked a destructive underlying philosophy. This is not merely an abstract academic debate we are talking about. In many parts of urban America, we are seeing a cruel social experiment being played out, namely, what happens when the trend-setting ideas of the influential rich and upper class—in this case, the celebration of unfettered freedom mixed with moral relativism— eventually spread to the rest of society. It turns out that the social damage—the body count—is *not* evenly dispensed. It is not even close. The underclass suffer disproportionately. An analogy helps make the point: when the rich and famous in Beverly Hills get hooked on drugs, they check into the Betty Ford Clinic. Fine. But when the poor and not-so-famous in Watts get hooked on drugs, there is no Betty Ford Clinic for them. Instead, many of them walk and sleep in the streets. They prey on the innocent. And eventually they, too, die on the streets.

In addition, a whole series of misguided social policies were championed. As we have already demonstrated, in the area of criminal justice, an anti-incarceration outlook took hold that said, in effect, society's response to criminal behavior should be rehabilitation, not punishment. In education, schools replaced moral education with "values clarification"—perhaps the single most harmful idea to take hold in America in the last three decades. Standards were abandoned, and homework forgotten. As the number of out-of-wedlock births hit critical mass, the opprobrium disappeared. It has now reached the point where, as reported by scholar Maggie Gallagher, almost one-third of the 70 girls in Indiana's Tipton High School's senior class are either pregnant or already unwed mothers. Tipton County, Indiana, is "not the kind of place most of us imagine when we think about the problem of illegitimacy," according to Ms. Gallagher. "It is white and rural, churchgoing Norman Rockwell country."[23]

These facts, and others detailed in this book, are ample evidence of substantial social regression. But there are other signs of decay, particularly of the cultural variety—ones that do not so easily lend themselves to quantitative analyses. Much of "gangsta" rap music celebrates the abuse and torture of women. Advertisements on television and on street corner billboards are increasingly erotic, even perverse. Many of our most successful and critically acclaimed movies celebrate brutality, casual cruelty, and twisted sex. And television shows make a virtue of promiscuity, adultery, homosexuality, and gratuitous acts of violence.

In a society where traditional institutions are in a state of decline, mass culture often fills the gaps. Where traditional institutions fear to or do not enter, other cultural forces rush in. As the hand of family, church, and school loosens, the grip of popular culture grows stronger. It is our opinion that, overall, television has become an increasingly dominant and destructive force on our social landscape. This is not to say that television has done no good, or that there are no quality shows on the air, or that television is responsible for most of our social ills. But taken in its totality—both in terms of broadcast content as well as things endemic to the medium—television is doing a good deal of damage. There is now a solid body of evidence which indicates that television increases rates of aggression and violence among children. Television viewing crowds out time that can be better spent on, say, homework (teenagers watch television an average of 23 hours per week,[24] which is a good deal more time per week than they spend on homework).[25] And there is increasing evidence that television is responsible for undermining America's civic culture by fostering increased levels of pessimism, passivity, and atomization.

Our social crisis is most often discussed with reference to, and focus on, the problems of the underclass. It is true enough that our modern-day "tangle of pathologies" is densely concentrated in urban centers and inner cities. That is where the fire burns hottest, where moral poverty is most pronounced, where the pathologies are most obvious, most intense, most intractable. Indeed, these subjects have been much of the focus of *Body Count*.

But there is trouble in River City, on Main Street, and in the Hamptons, too. And while the problems there are somewhat different in nature (e.g., prolific divorce remains more widespread than illegitimacy), they pose no less a threat to the nation's long-term prospects. A free society depends ultimately on the beliefs, behavior, and standards of the average citizen. What makes our situation today different from previous periods in American history—and fundamentally more serious—is the "de-moralization" of much of middle- and upper-middle-class life. The ballast that was once there isn't there any longer.

We moderns are reluctant to admit that much of what has gone wrong has not been done to us, that we have done it to ourselves. It is self-delusion to think that the American people have been unwittingly and reluctantly drawn into a culture of permissiveness.

Boston University president John Silber has spoken about a phenomenon he called the "invitation to mutual corruption." In a familiar usage: "I won't judge you if you won't judge me." Many of us moderns are hesitant to impose upon ourselves a common moral code because we want our own exemptions. "If it feels good, do it" has a wider appeal on all of us than we like to admit. The consequences are not good. Large segments of America are characterized by moral confusion, indolence, indifference, and distraction.

There is some legitimate good and encouraging news on the cultural scene. There are exciting and consequential cultural reclamation movements like Promise Keepers, the National Fatherhood Initiative, and Best Friends. There is fresh interest in moral education, and a new intensity of child nurture in some quarters (as indicated by things like the boom in home schooling). Some would say there is a spiritual ferment in the air. We are seeing community leaders—Reverend Eugene Rivers in Boston and Charles Ballard in Cleveland, for example —take an active and constructive role in helping restore neighborhoods to civic health. And a seismic shift has recently taken place in our public discourse. A set of issues once thought beyond the purview of politics is now driving much of the public debate as more and more Americans worry that the social wheels are coming off. The rising body count, the daily atrocity stories, the mounting social science evidence, the horrifying signs of urban decay all around us have seared a deep impression upon the public imagination. The common citizenry knows that great chunks of America are in the midst of serious moral decline.

Indifference and denial are being replaced by an awakened recognition. What we are seeing, we think, are social antibodies reacting against a 30-year cultural virus. But awakened recognition is merely the first step toward healing. An analogy helps to make the broader point. The recognition of a drug problem is the first step toward an addict's recovery. But much more is required. The addict still needs to *act*. This requires a willingness to change and to persevere.

Specifically, then, what needs to be done? One thing we need to do is to set higher expectations, to instill in our children worthy aspirations, and to eschew cynicism. We need to point to individuals who possess qualities of human excellence that are worth imitating and striving for. But for a variety of reasons, many people today seem contemptuous of the very notion of heroes or moral excellence. This kind of corrosive cynicism is dangerous. It puts children's ideals, aspirations, and notions of self-worth in jeopardy. Children need to know what deserves to be emulated, loved, and nurtured. We must publicly admire that which warrants admiration—and much does.

Through political leadership, cultural icons, and other influential voices, in every area society needs to affirm once again the message that having a child is the most important thing a person will do in life. This act entails certain obligations. There is no substitute for parental and moral guidance. Parenthood must once again be understood as including the following: logging lots of time, doing chores and errands together, playing together, reading together, and patiently explaining the way the world works and the way people ought to live. Children need to be taught by example and precept; they need specific reference points. But above all, they need the discipline and love of a caring adult. And please note the word "adult." A recent study compared two groups of Americans: those who finished high school, got married, and reached age 20 before having their first child, and those who didn't. Of the children in the latter group, 79 percent live in poverty; in the former, the rate was 8 percent.[26] Eight percent. Surely we can rededicate our efforts to get more people to satisfy those three conditions.

Cornell psychologist Urie Bronfenbrenner once said, "In order to develop, a child needs the enduring, irrational involvement of one or more adults in care and joint activity with the child." When someone asked him to explain what he meant by "irrational involvement," he said, "Somebody has got to be crazy about that kid!"[27]

We also need to fight back. As Flannery O'Connor put it, "You have to push as hard as the age that pushes against you."[28] The main problem that afflicts America today is not that we are in a state of complete moral decadence. We are not. What is most striking to us is the paucity of resistance against so much violent crime and destitution. Have we so defined deviancy down that we are getting used to decadence? Whatever the case, in America today there is too much reticence, too much indifference, too *little* civic and moral outrage. This is what the novelist Walker Percy most worried about. When asked what concerned him most about the future of America, he answered:

> Probably the fear of seeing America, with all its great strength and beauty and freedom . . . gradually subside into decay through default and be defeated, not by the Communist movement . . . but from within by weariness, boredom, cynicism, greed and in the end helplessness before its great problems.[29]

One arena in which we can fight back—though by no means the only or even the most effective one—is in the area of government policy. There are a number of actions government can take that would amount to constructive and far-reaching reforms. However, we would stipulate a general point that should guide any discussion of public policy solutions. We borrow from an old principle of medicine: *primum non nocere*—first, do no harm. In many cases, the best thing government can do is stop doing what makes the problem worse. With that in mind, government does have a role to play in improving our social condition. The likelihood that any governmental action—regulation, legislation, or executive act—will have a salutary impact on the causes of our explosion in violent crime is proportional to the care given to its effect on moral poverty. We believe legislators need to ask these related questions before writing and passing legislation: "Will this law replenish or drain our stock of moral capital? Will it increase or decrease the chance that a responsible adult will communicate right and wrong to a child?"

These questions should be applied on a wide range of issues. In welfare, for example, we should not advocate policies that virtually guarantee high rates of illegitimacy (i.e., subsidizing women to have children out of wedlock) while at the same time cut benefits to those welfare recipients who do an honest day's work. Neither should we penalize couples who marry (through the "marriage penalty" in the tax code) or make marriage one of society's easiest contracts to nullify (through "no-fault" divorce). In education we should advocate policies which allow parents to send their children to schools that affirm and reinforce their deeply held beliefs.

Since we have no desire to close on a tedious list of public policy reforms, let us consider in some detail but a single example of the sort of federal initiative that fits the model we are talking about: adoption. We choose this issue because it is one that, if legislated intelligently and carefully, can help to strengthen the ties between children and adults. Needless barriers to adoption should be eliminated. Only 50,000 children are adopted each year in the United States;[30] at any given time, 1 million to 2 million homes are waiting to adopt. Unfortunately, in addition to the prohibitively high cost of private adoption (the National Council of Adoption estimates that the average cost of domestic adoption is $20,000),[31] many couples are automatically excluded from consideration due to race, financial background, age, disability, or home size. Studies show that there is no adverse effect on black children when they are adopted by white families, demolishing the racially polarizing arguments made by groups like the National Association of Black Social Workers.[32] Other couples are scared away by lax confidentiality laws, nonbinding adoptions, and the expanded rights of the biological father to reclaim legal custody.

Availability of adoption is also severely limited. Unwed mothers are often denied information about adoption in prenatal counseling; others decide to abort their pregnancy for economic reasons. Indeed, it may be partly for this reason that abortion has increasingly become a problem of juveniles: of the 1 million teenage pregnancies each year, about 400,000 now end in abortion. Finally, with the stigma of illegitimacy all but gone in this country, for many young, unwed pregnant women, single motherhood has become a more attractive option than giving up a child for adoption.

The greatest hope lies in reforms that prohibit the use of race and/or ethnicity as a qualification for would-be foster or adoptive parents (in practice this has affected whites seeking to adopt nonwhite babies); expedite adoption procedures for infants and children who have been abandoned by their parents and are living in limbo in hospitals, group homes, and/or foster care; terminate parental rights and thus make a child available for adoption if by the age of six months—in the case of infants born with positive toxicology—maternal drug use has not ceased, or if a child has been severely abused by its parents; enact model legislation that will require courts to consider the best interests of the child first in all cases concerning custody; establish uniform rules making voluntary surrender/adoption irrevocable at any point past 72 hours after birth; restrict payments to biological parents by adoptive parents to necessary expenses related directly to the pregnancy and adoption; and ensure that adoptive families are treated with the same respect as other families, free of the fear of intrusion by the state or other parties after an adoption has been finalized.

We are quite encouraged by the recent passage of the Adoption Promotion and Stability Act of 1996, which aims to penalize state adoption agencies that restrict interracial adoption and provides a $5,000 tax credit for expenses incurred for an adoption. This is relevant because we have argued throughout this book that the problem is that inner-city children are trapped in criminogenic homes, schools, and neighborhoods where high numbers of teenagers and adults are no more likely to nurture, teach, and care for children than they are to expose them to neglect, abuse, and violence. Children cannot be socialized by adults who are themselves unsocialized, or worse, families that exist in name only, schools that do not educate, and neighborhoods in which violent and repeat criminals circulate in and out of jail.

In our view, situations will arise that may warrant the removal of a child from the care of his or her parent(s). To be sure, this should only happen in desperate circumstances and as a last resort. But we cannot ignore the plain fact that there are more and more horrifying cases of abuse, neglect, and parental malfeasance.

While adoption is the best alternative in such circumstances, the concept of orphanages, or group-care homes, should not be dismissed. Such institutions pretty much disappeared from the national scene when government began distributing money in the expectation that poor parents, with federal assistance, would do a better job of raising their children. But in far too many cases that expectation has been resoundingly refuted by experience.

When parents cannot care for their children's basic material, psychological, medical, and moral needs, it is time to look to other institutions. The orphanage—call it a boarding school without tuition—may then be in their best interest. And please, spare us the *Oliver Twist* demagoguery. Can anyone seriously argue that some boys would be worse off living in Boys Town than in, say, the Cabrini Green housing project in Chicago, considered by its residents a virtual war zone?

REMEMBERING GOD

We have spent a good portion of our professional lives thinking about public policies. One of the impressions we have come away with is how little has been done, on the most commonsensical level, to address the problems that confront us and that have escalated in both number and intensity over the past thirty years. And so we believe that thinking concretely about specific, practical reforms offers the hope that, if they are part of a concerted national effort, we might yet begin to alleviate some of the worst manifestations of these ills and even, in time, to reverse course.

And yet, even if we were to enact desired reform in almost every area of social policy, we would still be a long way from having healed the broken families in America. Smart, intelligent public policies can and do make a difference. But political solutions are not, ultimately, the answer to problems that are at root moral and spiritual.

"Manners," wrote Edmund Burke two centuries ago,

> are of more importance than laws. Upon them, in a great measure, the laws depend. The law touches us but here and there, and now and then. Manners are what vex or soothe, corrupt or purify, exalt or debase, barbarize or refine us, by a constant, steady, uniform, insensible operation, like that of the air we breathe in. They give their whole form and color to our lives. According to their quality, they aid morals, they supply them, or they totally destroy them.[33]

Can government supply manners and morals if they are wanting? Of course it cannot. What it can supply, through policy and law, is a vivid sense of what we as a society expect of ourselves, what we hold ourselves responsible for, and what we consider ourselves answerable to. There can be little doubt that in this last period of time the message our laws have been sending our young people and their parents has been the profoundly demoralizing one that we expect little, and hold ourselves answerable for still less.

By changing and improving our laws, we might not thereby bring about, but we would certainly *help* to bring about, a climate that would make it easier rather than harder for all of us to grow more civilized; easier rather than harder for us to keep our commitments to one another; easier rather than harder for us to recapture the idea of personal and civic responsibility. This, in turn, would make it easier rather than harder for us to raise our children in safety to adulthood —something that at the moment we are not doing very well at all.

In 1991 the number of juveniles in custody increased from earlier years to nearly 58,000. By our estimate, we will probably need to incarcerate at least 150,000 juvenile criminals in the years just ahead. In deference to public safety, we will have little choice but to pursue genuine get-tough law enforcement strategies against the super-predators. But some of these children are now in diapers, and they can be saved. It is really up to us.

Jeremy Bentham once observed that the way to be comfortable is to make others comfortable; the way to make others comfortable is to appear to like them; and the way to appear to like them is to like them in reality. Today there are an awful lot of children who need to be loved in reality. To "love in reality" is above all the responsibility of parents. But one of the grim facts of modern life is that children who are most in need of love, order, and moral instruction are the children whose parents are most often missing in action. So the job now falls to the rest of us—not necessarily to be surrogate parents, but to begin to play a much more active role in the lives of these children, to create surroundings that make it easier and not harder for children to grow up to be morally responsible adults, and to support the institutions (including religious institutions) that can make the most positive difference in the lives of these kids.

We face a simple, stark choice. We can continue on our present course, which means another generation of children who will grow up having received virtually no love or sound moral instruction. They will be meaner, and angrier, and more violent than the current generation of super-predators. They will be more radically self-regarding, more radically present-oriented, more unsocialized and more uncivilized, and completely devoid of "empathic impulses" (as scholars of prison rehabilitation phrase it). In that case we will see, in the years ahead, more prisons, drug treatment centers, juvenile delinquent homes—and many more grave sites.

The other choice is to heed the wisdom of Aristotle, who believed that the care of the community is the common business of good citizens. The "common business" we now face is the nurture, protection, and moral education of the rapidly increasing number of unattended and neglected young in our midst. It will require of us hard work and sacrifice—in terms of our time, our comfort, our leisure, our money. But that may well be the cost of citizenship in late-twentieth-century America, as well as the "cost of discipleship" for those of us who share a common religious faith.

A lot is at stake. If we do nothing, we may well be on the way to the ruin of our civilization. If we act responsibly, purposefully, and quickly, we will redeem the true promise of this nation, which Lincoln called an "inestimable jewel"—indeed, the "last, best hope of man on earth."

But we want to be very clear on this point: the arena in which our cultural struggle will ultimately be won or lost is within the human heart. Oliver Wendell Holmes, Jr., said that the main remedy to some of the evils of our time is for us to grow more civilized. And so it is. As we approach the end of the last decade of this century, it is worth restating an obvious but often overlooked truth: social regeneration depends on individual citizens living better, more committed, more devoted lives. Not perfect lives, mind you. Just lives that reflect the basic and modest character traits—self-discipline, civic-mindedness, fidelity to commitments, honesty, responsibility, and perseverance—that the Founding Fathers understood to be the sheet anchor of a free republic. And to accomplish these things, it would be no small help, as Aleksandr Solzhenitsyn and others have urged us, to remember God.

It is on that subject—God—that we close. We have argued throughout this book for the need to address the moral poverty of our children and of the institutions that serve them. This naturally brings us to the religious dimension of moral poverty—which we believe to be the most important dimension of all.

There are many arguments one can marshal on behalf of the crucial role religion can play in assuaging and reversing moral poverty. There is, for example, the growing body of scientific evidence from a variety of academic disciplines which indicates that churches can help curtail or cure many severe social pathologies. There is also the argument that is well known to every serious student of American history who is familiar with the writings of the founders—namely, the compelling civic case for religion (i.e., religion as an aid and friend of the constitutional order, providing society with a moral anchor and taming the baser appetites, passions, and impulses of citizens).

But the reader will recall how we define moral poverty: the poverty of being without loving, capable, responsible adults who teach children right from wrong. In essence, what we are talking about is child abuse, neglect, and abandonment on a mass scale—an unprecedented severing of the bonds of affection, devotion, and love between adults and children, between parents and child.

How do we restore these bonds? We believe the most obvious answer—and perhaps the only reliable answer—is a widespread renewal of religious faith and the strengthening of religious institutions. Many people have ignored or forgotten something that almost everybody once knew: *the good requires constant reinforcement and the bad needs only permission*. Religion is the best and most reliable means we have to reinforce the good. True religious faith enlarges the human heart; inspires us to revere and honor those things that are worthy objects of our attention; reminds people of their basic responsibilities and commitments; provides society with reliable moral and social guardrails; helps the impulse of compassion take on the name of action; and allows the "eyes of our heart" to see our fellow citizens not merely as distant body count statistics or as enemies or aliens or "other" but as moral and spiritual beings, as children of God.

For that is, in fact, what they are.

APPENDIX: OFFICIAL CRIMINAL HISTORIES OF 40 "LOW-LEVEL" WISCONSIN PRISONERS AND PROBATIONERS

PROFILES OF "LOW-RISK" OFFENDERS SENTENCED TO "INTENSIVE SANCTIONS"

1.

MOST RECENT CRIME AND SENTENCE

Armed robbery
5 years—Intensive Sanctions
During the crime "the subject . . . entered a dry cleaning store. On duty were two employees. . . . The subject stated 'don't move, I swear don't move' [and] grabbed one of the employees and acting as if he had a gun in a paper sack, pressed it into her side. . . ."

ADULT AND JUVENILE CRIMINAL RECORD

Adult Arrests: 12
Adult Incarcerations: 3

Juvenile: None
Adult: Burglary, robbery, unlawful restraint, attempted criminal sexual assault, attempted aggravated criminal sexual assault.
Parole or Probation Violation(s): Yes
Violent Crime(s): Yes

OTHER BACKGROUND
From state's presentence investigation:

"The defendant stated he has been on SSI for about one year . . . that he would use up his entire check smoking crack and drinking."
"Prior convictions are for armed robbery, burglary, robbery, attempted criminal sexual assault. . . ."
"One must question why the judge sentenced such an individual to the DIS [Division of Intensive Sanctions] program."

2.

MOST RECENT CRIME AND SENTENCE

Burglary and auto theft
5 years—Intensive Sanctions
While on probation for a 1993 battery to a child, the subject burglarized a woman's home and stole the car of another woman.

[Less than two months after being sentenced to Intensive Sanctions, he escaped from a minimum security prison in Milwaukee.]

ADULT AND JUVENILE CRIMINAL RECORD

Adult Arrests: 2
Adult Incarcerations: 1

Juvenile: Burglary, auto theft, auto theft, auto theft, attempted auto theft, and 1st-degree sexual assault of a child.
Adult: Battery to a child.
Parole or Probation Violation(s): Yes
Violent Crime(s): Yes

OTHER BACKGROUND

From state's presentence investigation:

Burglary victim said it "has affected her life a great deal because her privacy was invaded and she had to move because she was so afraid. She said it felt like being raped without being touched." Auto theft victim said "she has quit going into the area where her van was stolen so she does not visit her friends that live in that area."

The subject "was constantly running in the streets and involved with the Black Gangster Disciples gang. . . . Even though [he] admitted . . . both offenses . . . he expressed little or no remorse for his actions or empathy for his victims."

From state's prison intake report:
The subject "has been involved in various probationary terms [and] juvenile placements. . . . He has been seen as assaultive, not cooperative, and manipulative by various staff in those placements. He has also tended to run away from juvenile placements."

3.

MOST RECENT CRIME AND SENTENCE
Burglary
4 years—Intensive Sanctions
Subject "and several accomplices [burglarized] a Milwaukee residence [and] confiscated several personal items including jewelry. . . ."

[State files show three different escapes from the program in the course of four months during 1993.]

ADULT AND JUVENILE CRIMINAL RECORD
Adult Arrests: 8
Adult Incarcerations: 3

Juvenile: Theft, theft, disorderly conduct (amended from original charge of burglary).
Adult: Receiving stolen property, drug possession, attempted burglary, robbery, burglary.
Parole or Probation Violation(s): Yes
Violent Crime(s): Yes

OTHER BACKGROUND
From state's presentence investigation:

"The defendant has been in the criminal justice system on an almost non-stop basis since 1985. During this time [he] had difficulties reporting to his supervising agents as ordered, became involved in further criminal behavior, and refused to cooperate with drug treatment referrals. . . . He was involved in some incidents of domestic violence and a robbery in which the elderly victims were threatened. . . ."

From state's prison intake report:
Subject "fails to learn from his past as he continues to involve himself in criminal-like behavior and drug usage . . . needs to face the consequences of his unacceptable behavior and be held accountable."

4.

MOST RECENT CRIME AND SENTENCE
Burglary
5 years—Intensive Sanctions
"Subject and two accomplices burglarized [a Milwaukee retail store]."

ADULT AND JUVENILE CRIMINAL RECORD
Adult Arrests: 6
Adult Incarcerations: 2

Juvenile: Auto theft and operating an auto without a license.

OTHER BACKGROUND
From state's presentence investigation:

"[H]e is basically unmotivated . . . and has no constructive plan to

[Two months after being sentenced to Intensive Sanctions, escaped from a minimum security prison in Milwaukee.]

Adult: Robbery, burglary, possession of cocaine, fleeing, burglary.
Parole or Probation Violation(s): Yes
Violent Crime(s): Yes

change his life . . . has demonstrated no motivation in his life and little desire to change."

Record on community supervision includes violation of robbery probation in 1982, burglary on probation in 1986, and multiple positive drug tests while on parole in 1988. Three months after being discharged from probation in 1990 he was arrested for cocaine possession and fleeing an officer on city streets at speeds of 75–80 mph.

5.

MOST RECENT CRIME AND SENTENCE
Armed Burglary
5 years—Intensive Sanctions
With two accomplices, "kicked in the front door" of a home to burglarize it and was found by police with "a loaded .380 semi-automatic pistol."

ADULT AND JUVENILE CRIMINAL RECORD
Adult Arrests: 1
Adult Incarcerations: 1

Juvenile: Criminal damage to property, drug delivery, auto theft, robbery, theft from person, battery.
Adult: No prior adult record.
Parole or Probation Violation(s): Yes
Violent Crime(s): Yes

OTHER BACKGROUND
From state's presentence investigation:

"It is . . . respectfully recommended that [the subject] be sentenced to [prison]. . . . Because of the nature of the crime [armed burglary] the defendant is not appropriate for referral to [Intensive Sanctions]."

"The defendant drinks excessively [and] doesn't see a problem with drinking eight 16-ounce bottles of beer a day. . . . This attitude alone is a problem that will lead him back into criminal behavior."

6.

MOST RECENT CRIME AND SENTENCE

Burglary
5 years—Intensive Sanctions
Stole a shovel and bicycle from an open garage and "stated that he wanted money to buy alcohol and drugs."

[Two separate escapes in 1993 from separate minimum security prisons in Milwaukee.]

ADULT AND JUVENILE CRIMINAL RECORD

Adult Arrests: 8
Adult Incarcerations: 4

Juvenile: 9 counts of burglary, burglary and receiving stolen property, drug possession, burglary, burglary, possession of burglary tools.
Adult: Burglary (juvenile, waived to adult court), criminal damage and theft, burglary, battery to a police officer, burglary, entry into locked vehicle, habitual criminality.
Parole or Probation Violation(s): Yes
Violent Crime(s): Yes

OTHER BACKGROUND

From state's presentence investigation:

"The defendant has a long-standing pattern of being irresponsible and mismanaging his life. . . . He has been offered help many times . . . and has not cooperated or responded in a satisfactory manner. . . . He is quick to blame external factors . . . for his lack of any success. . . . While he says he can change . . . this is hard to believe. . . . All this talk [of change] is motivated by the fact that it will help to avoid serious consequences. . . ."

"He has a prior record for assaultive behavior."

"The Department of Corrections does not recommend a sentence to Intensive Sanctions."

7.

MOST RECENT CRIME AND SENTENCE

Burglary
4 years—Intensive Sanctions
"The subject entered a residence and stole $9,500 worth of stereo equipment. The subject had been at the residence earlier working as part of a cleaning crew."

ADULT AND JUVENILE CRIMINAL RECORD

Adult Arrests: 4
Adult Incarcerations: 2

Juvenile: Theft from auto, entry into a locked vehicle, attempted theft and obstructing an officer, entry into a locked vehicle, auto theft, burglary, 2 counts of auto

OTHER BACKGROUND

From state's presentence investigation:

His "lengthy record of criminal behavior and the fact that treatment needs can best be met while serving a lengthy period of incarceration would make a sentence to [Intensive

theft, escape from custody, armed robbery, burglary, auto theft, and receiving stolen property.
Adult: Auto theft, drug delivery, auto theft.
Parole or Probation Violation(s): Yes
Violent Crime(s): Yes

Sanctions] inappropriate." Supervisor concurred.

The subject "first became involved in the correctional system at the age of 11 [and] has established a very lengthy criminal record. . . . He has substantially ignored the orders of the Court and continued to violate his parole on many occasions."

Subject says he got in trouble because "he hung around with the wrong people" and "recent offenses took place due to his trying to support his drug habit."

From state's prison intake report:
"He does not yet appear to accept responsibility for his actions."

8.

MOST RECENT CRIME AND SENTENCE
Auto theft (3 counts)
5 years—Intensive Sanctions
Convicted in connection with 3 separate auto thefts over a 2-week period. Subject "explained [that] his acquaintances encouraged him to become involved and he earned easy money by stealing cars."

ADULT AND JUVENILE CRIMINAL RECORD
Adult Arrests: 3
Adult Incarcerations: 1

Juvenile: No information (raised in Puerto Rico).
Adult: Auto theft and entering a locked vehicle.
Parole or Probation Violation(s): Yes
Violent Crime(s): No

OTHER BACKGROUND
From state's presentence investigation:

"On 5-1-91 [subject] was placed on probation . . . four months later he became involved in another offense . . . he was released from custody and placed on the Electronic Monitoring Program. On 12-23-91 he was again placed on a two-year probation for entering a locked vehicle while on electronic monitoring. Current offense [3 counts auto theft] occurred while on probation."

"His previous terms under probation supervision have not benefited him, due to his rejection of supervision, nevertheless another opportunity may be appropriate. . . ."

9.

MOST RECENT CRIME AND SENTENCE	ADULT AND JUVENILE CRIMINAL RECORD	OTHER BACKGROUND

Auto theft (3 counts), fleeing an officer, resisting arrest, and escape
5 years—Intensive Sanctions
Stole a car from the Northridge Shopping Center parking lot; stole a car and led police on 75 mph chase (wrecked car but escaped apprehension); and used a friend's car without permission, and struck an officer in the face attempting to avoid arrest.

Following initial sentence to Intensive Sanctions, escaped from a minimum security prison in Milwaukee, was apprehended and convicted and recommitted to Intensive Sanctions.

Adult Arrests: 7
Adult Incarcerations: 3

Juvenile: Burglary, loitering, burglary, shoplifting, burglary, theft, theft, burglary, theft, operating a vehicle without a license, burglary, entering a locked building, receiving stolen property, auto theft.
Adult: Auto theft, auto theft, retail theft, burglary, auto theft.
Parole or Probation Violation(s): Yes
Violent Crime(s): No

From state's presentence investigation:

The subject's "criminal history is extensive and dates back to the age of 9. . . . [He] is a criminally oriented individual, who has exhibited no respect for the property of others. . . . He denies or minimizes his involvement in the last two [offenses and] expressed no remorse for the victims. . . ."

"His criminal behavior seems to be ingrained and the substance abuse issue allows him to legitimize his behavior. . . . For the past 16 years [he] has done little to improve himself, his lifestyle, or to become a responsible member within the community. [He] seems to maintain the attitude he had as a child, which was to take whatever he wanted."

10.

MOST RECENT CRIME AND SENTENCE

Forgery, auto theft, theft
7 years—Intensive
Sanctions
The recent offense of theft (a camcorder and sunglasses) from a residence where he was living occurred while subject was "on escape status" from probation for prior conviction of forgery and auto theft.

[Subject has two prior escapes from Intensive Sanctions and has been terminated from Intensive Sanctions and returned to prison.]

ADULT AND JUVENILE CRIMINAL RECORD

Adult Arrests: 7
Adult Incarcerations: 2

Juvenile: None
Adult: Speeding, concealing stolen property, possession of a switchblade, underage drinking, speeding, speeding, speeding, disorderly conduct, speeding, operating a vehicle after revocation, theft by fraud, disorderly conduct, theft by fraud, operating after revocation.
Parole or Probation Violation(s): Yes
Violent Crime(s): No

OTHER BACKGROUND

From state's presentence investigation:

Following most recent escape from Intensive Sanctions, confinement in a structured correctional setting is necessary to address the risk concerns of the community. This is evidenced by [his] convictions of 9 new offenses [auto theft, 2 escapes, theft by fraud, etc.]. . . ."

"To allow [him] to remain within the community would not only enable his continual pattern of non-compliance, it would also encourage other [Intensive Sanctions] inmates to defy the rules . . . and seriously jeopardize the integrity of the [Intensive Sanctions] program."

11.

MOST RECENT CRIME AND SENTENCE

Burglary (1 count and 4 read-ins)*
File unclear as to sentence
While on parole, on 9/23/93, defendant "broke into a home . . . with two co-defendants. . . . The three men stole 3 clocks, a brass apple, a pair of men's

ADULT AND JUVENILE CRIMINAL RECORD

Adult Arrests: 8
Adult Incarcerations: 3

Juvenile: None
Adult: Burglary, larceny, possession of controlled substance, armed robbery, obstructing, auto theft, escape.

OTHER BACKGROUND

From state's presentence investigation:

While serving a sentence for armed robbery and auto theft, subject "was [paroled] from prison. . . . He reported three times for parole supervision and boots, and a leather coat."

Four other residential burglaries were read-in, but not charged. They occurred over a 5-month period and typically involved stereos, TVs, CD players, and CDs.

* Read-in: charge dismissed but "read-in" for purposes of restitution.

Parole or Probation Violation(s): Yes
Violent Crime(s): No

then absconded" and committed current burglaries.

As an "Alternative to Revocation," the "Department of Corrections is seeking a formal [commitment] to the Division of Intensive Sanctions due to current convictions for burglary."

In the same report recommending Intensive Sanctions, the state says subject "does not feel directly responsible [for the victims]." Report also says he "has become very skillful in attempting to manipulate the [criminal justice] system to his advantage. He alluded [sic] prosecution for 4 years on his previous armed robbery . . . and openly admitted to changing jobs so he would not get caught for absconding from parole supervision."

In addition to burglaries, defendant "has been active in purchasing stolen property [from his accomplices] for 6 months . . . [the accomplices] may have been involved in up to 150 burglaries . . . and obviously this would not be financially rewarding if there was not an individual willing to buy this property. The end result is that there are many terrified members of the community who are experiencing the same difficulties as the 5 victims

interviewed for this
report."

**From state's prison intake
report:**

". . . his motivation to
truly change . . . is
somewhat suspect. The
subject is in denial. . . . It
is thought the presiding
judge will sentence him
to" Intensive Sanctions,
based on the department's
recommendation.

12.

MOST RECENT CRIME AND SENTENCE
Burglary (2 counts)
8 years
Following probation and
parole violations for
burglary, subject "was
paroled to the Division of
Intensive Sanctions" and
subsequently escaped from
a Milwaukee halfway
house and was found to
have stolen property from
the halfway house and
used drugs.
    [Has been terminated
from Intensive Sanctions
and returned to prison.]

ADULT AND JUVENILE CRIMINAL RECORD
Adult Arrests: 7
Adult Incarcerations: 2
Juvenile: Burglary,
burglary, burglary.
Adult: Burglary, burglary.
**Parole or Probation
Violation(s):** Yes
Violent Crime(s): No

OTHER BACKGROUND
**From state's Case History
Review Summary:**

He was paroled to
Intensive Sanctions in
1993, despite this narrative
submitted from the state
to a judge: the subject
". . . has a history of
burglary offenses dating to
1982. [He] has a burglary
12/1/82 [and] three months
later 3/1/83 a second
burglary [and] seven
months later a third
burglary. . . . [He] was
placed on adult probation
3/18/89 [followed by]
another burglary
conviction within six
months . . . at that time
[the judge] suggested
electronic monitoring . . .
however [the subject] was
incarcerated for a new
burglary . . . therefore
electronic monitoring was
rejected. . . . After serving

a one-year period in jail
. . . he was placed at the
Bridge Halfway House
[but] was terminated from
the Bridge . . . after one
month and eight days due
to his lack of cooperation
with the program [and his
failure] to comply with the
AODA Program at DePaul
. . . and withdrew from
DePaul without
completing the program."

**From state's 1989
presentence investigation:**
"The defendant indicated
that on the night of the
offense he had run into the
wrong people. . . ."

"[He] displays criminal
thinking and anti-social
values which would appear
to be a major contributing
factor in his adjustment to
society."

". . . first smoked
marijuana at age 16 [and]
would smoke 1 or 2 joints
a day . . . began to use
cocaine about one year ago
. . . his use increased to
$200 worth of cocaine a
week . . . once he was no
longer employed he began
to steal to get money to
buy cocaine."

13.

MOST RECENT CRIME AND SENTENCE	ADULT AND JUVENILE CRIMINAL RECORD	OTHER BACKGROUND
Possession of firearm by a felon **4 years** While "on active probation supervision for Possession of Short-Barreled Shotgun . . . the inmate received [an Intensive Sanctions] sentence for Felon in Possession of Firearm . . . after it was discovered during a routine traffic stop that inmate did not have a valid operator's license. . . . When the vehicle was searched a loaded .22 caliber Derringer [and] ten .22 caliber live rounds of ammunition" were found. Discharge and parole "dates adjusted accordingly" to reflect "escape status" for 22 days from Intensive Sanctions.	**Adult Arrests: 2** **Adult Incarcerations: 2** **Juvenile:** Yes (gang member). **Adult:** Possession of short-barreled shotgun. **Parole or Probation Violation(s):** Yes **Violent Crime(s):** No	**From state's prison intake report:** Subject "associated fairly regularly with gang members and was in fact a gang member. . . ." Earned his high school equivalency degree "in the Wisconsin State Prison System." Subject "has matured and made positive changes in his life . . . was driving a car with ammunition and a gun due to fear relating to" earlier gang beating.

PROFILES OF IMPRISONED "PROPERTY OFFENDERS"

1.

MOST RECENT CRIME AND SENTENCE

Theft
9 months (added to prior sentence)
While on parole for burglary, subject was arrested and convicted of theft. His parole was revoked and he received a 9-month extension to his prior sentence of 5 years and 9 months.

ADULT AND JUVENILE CRIMINAL RECORD

Adult Arrests: 12
Adult Incarcerations: 3

Juvenile: Runaway from correctional facility; original crime not documented.
Adult: Theft, theft, burglary, burglary, escape.
Parole or Probation Violation(s): Yes
Violent Crime(s): No

OTHER BACKGROUND
From state's prison intake report:

Subject "is, at times, inclined to function irresponsibly and without regard for consequences. . . . [He] behaves childishly and impulsively. . . . When confronted he denies, makes excuses, and slavishly promises to do better."

". . . record notes pattern of not reporting [or] absconding while on adult probation." This includes at least three probation revocations and one parole revocation.

Escaped from minimum security Milwaukee prison four months after intake report identified "little reason to believe he will be a security risk."

Subject "admit[s] to a period of using cocaine [and] describes a pattern of 'snorting' 1–2 times a week. . . ."

2.

MOST RECENT CRIME AND SENTENCE

Burglary, criminal damage to property
6.5 years
Used a pry bar to break into a residence, "kicked and smashed two plate glass windows" to enter an apartment.

ADULT AND JUVENILE CRIMINAL RECORD

Adult Arrests: 14
Adult Incarcerations: 3

Juvenile: Robbery, robbery.
Adult: Armed robbery, robbery, escape, battery, battery, violation of domestic abuse restraining order.
Parole or Probation Violation(s): Yes
Violent Crime(s): Yes

OTHER BACKGROUND

From state's presentence investigation:

Several earlier crimes committed on parole or probation.
  Earlier offenses of battery and violating domestic abuse restraining order include following a female "to her bedroom, where he struck her in the mouth, choked her and pushed her to the floor [and] threatened to kill her if she would not continue seeing him." Seven months later he "punched [her] in the face and choked her, causing swelling to her face and neck."
  Subject drinks a fifth of gin or vodka every day, uses $50 of cocaine every day, and is an occasional marijuana user.

3.

MOST RECENT CRIME AND SENTENCE

Theft by fraud (2 counts)
20 years
Defrauded employer of more than $500,000 over a period of several years.

ADULT AND JUVENILE CRIMINAL RECORD

Adult Arrests: 1
Adult Incarcerations: 1
Juvenile: None
Adult: No prior adult record.
Parole or Probation Violation(s): No
Violent Crime(s): No

OTHER BACKGROUND

From state's prison intake report:

"There is no prior history of criminal activity. . . . She has always maintained a responsible lifestyle except for the offenses which brought her to prison. . . . Potential [Intensive Sanctions] eligibility."

4.

MOST RECENT CRIME AND SENTENCE

Arson (3 counts)

6 years

ADULT AND JUVENILE CRIMINAL RECORD

Adult Arrests: 3

Adult Incarcerations: 1

Juvenile: Four separate detentions (crimes not specified).

Adult: Arson and negligent handling of burning material.

Parole or Probation Violation(s): Yes

Violent Crime(s): No (see "Other Background").

OTHER BACKGROUND

From state's prison intake report:

"Subject has an assaultive history and has stated that during a domestic dispute she had stabbed a boyfriend; however, there were no charges."

"Subject was placed on probation 6/18/86 for the offense of arson . . . was again placed on probation for negligent handling of burning materials 11/23/93. She was revoked for failure to complete probation rules and for involving herself in current offense."

5.

MOST RECENT CRIME AND SENTENCE

Theft

2 years

Defrauded an 82-year-old woman of her Wisconsin Homestead Tax Credits, totaling more than $2,000, for home repair and landscaping work never performed.

ADULT AND JUVENILE CRIMINAL RECORD

Adult Arrests: 10

Adult Incarcerations: 3

Juvenile: Burglary, burglary, theft, burglary.

Adult: Criminal damage to property, disorderly conduct, endangering safety by conduct regardless of life, unfair home improvement trade, theft by contractor (2 counts), bail jumping, theft by contractor, theft by contractor, theft by contractor, theft by contractor.

Parole or Probation Violation(s): Yes

Violent Crime(s): Yes

OTHER BACKGROUND

From state's presentence investigation:

After conviction and before sentencing, canceled multiple appointments for presentence interview. "On 11/2/94 defendant's girlfriend called stating she had kicked him out because he was back on cocaine."

State's probation and parole agent "spoke with the victim. She is extremely upset regarding this offense. [She] is 82 years old and lives on a fixed income. The money she paid the defendant to fix up her residence were [sic] her Homestead tax returns."

The victim "called this agent crying because she was afraid of losing all the money . . . she was very upset and had to go to the hospital . . . for 10 days and therapy for 17 days. She was upset because she thought her children would be angry at her, which they were and did not support her."

Based on numerous probation and parole violations, "the defendant has not complied with the goals and objectives of the Department of Corrections. . . . [He] does not accept any responsibility for his behavior [and] has no remorse for the current offense."

"It would appear to this agent the defendant's main concern is one of self-gratification without any regard for those he hurts or misuses. . . ."

6.

MOST RECENT CRIME AND SENTENCE
Forgery
7 years
Attempted to purchase several hundred dollars of merchandise with a stolen credit card.

ADULT AND JUVENILE CRIMINAL RECORD
Adult Arrests: 56
Adult Incarcerations: 7
Juvenile: None
Adult: Theft, prostitution, theft, violation of Illinois credit card act, possession of stolen property, criminal

OTHER BACKGROUND
From state's presentence investigation:

A 40-year-old female with a 22-year record of adult crime.

She "is a professional thief [who] has covered a

trespass, prostitution, theft, prostitution, theft, theft, retail theft, theft, forgery (5 counts), obstructing justice, escape. **Parole or Probation Violation(s):** Yes **Violent Crime(s):** No

lot of the United States doing crimes and has served relatively little time. . . . She is presently wanted by Nevada and Illinois for felony-level offenses. . . . Her life is out of control."

7.

MOST RECENT CRIME AND SENTENCE
Retail theft
Sentence unclear
While on parole for felony and misdemeanor retail theft, stole tools from a parked truck.

ADULT AND JUVENILE CRIMINAL RECORD
Adult Arrests: 15
Adult Incarcerations: 5
Juvenile: Theft, uncontrollable behavior, drug possession, shoplifting, battery, auto theft, "etc."
Adult: Retail theft, retail theft, retail theft, retail theft, retail theft, retail theft, obstructing, burglary, retail theft, retail theft, theft, attempted theft (habitual), retail theft, "and other arrests [retail thefts, drug possession, credit card violations]."
Parole or Probation Violation(s): Yes
Violent Crime(s): Yes

OTHER BACKGROUND
From state's prison intake report:

The juvenile and adult record summarized in the previous column characterizes the subject as "low-risk."

8.

MOST RECENT CRIME AND SENTENCE
Theft (repeater)
3 years
While on probation for theft, subject "robbed an elderly priest of $74 . . . subject shoved [the priest]

ADULT AND JUVENILE CRIMINAL RECORD
Adult Arrests: 17
Adult Incarcerations: 5
Juvenile: None
Adult: Forgery, forgery, burglary, theft, attempted theft, auto theft, burglary.

OTHER BACKGROUND
From state's prison intake report:

Regarding pending robbery charge, the priest victim of the "theft" was attacked at 12:15 A.M. "and laid [sic] against a kitchen chair and onto the floor."

[The robbery charge and related revocation proceedings were pending at the time of this study, with subject still showing on state records as a current property offender.]

Parole or Probation Violation(s): Yes
Violent Crime(s): Yes (based on pending charge).

there in great back and leg pain until approximately 5 A.M. when he managed to get to a telephone. . . . The victim continues to be in pain and is in a wheelchair unable to walk for more than a few steps."

"Subject admitted he had been consuming alcohol and smoking cocaine prior to the offense."

Prior to pending robbery, subject's history of 16 arrests and 4 incarcerations was described as making him "low-risk."

9.

MOST RECENT CRIME AND SENTENCE
Burglary
3.75 years
After having been paroled in early 1994, subject was arrested and parole was later revoked for stealing and then forging a payroll check from a temporary help agency.

Nine months were added to prior 3-year sentence.

ADULT AND JUVENILE CRIMINAL RECORD
Adult Arrests: 10
Adult Incarcerations: 4
Juvenile: None
Adult: Burglary, burglary, battery. "In addition to these convictions, the subject has been arrested on other occasions on charges of burglary, second degree sexual assault, false imprisonment, and battery. The disposition of these charges is unknown."
Parole or Probation Violation(s): Yes
Violent Crime(s): Yes

OTHER BACKGROUND
From state's prison intake report:

Prior to current parole violation, subject was deemed a "low-risk" offender by the state. Previously, subject was paroled in 1989 for burglary, convicted 18 months later for theft, and "violated his probation on or about 7/28/93 when he entered [an establishment] in the city of Milwaukee and while pointing a gun at an employee did take money belonging" to the business.

From the state's 1995 parole revocation report:
Subject "is a career criminal and continues to

pursue illegal behavior regardless of the known consequences. . . . His continuous disregard for the laws of the community needs to be addressed."

Notwithstanding the above, "A packet has been submitted to the Division of Intensive Sanctions for review."

10.

MOST RECENT CRIME AND SENTENCE

Forgery
3 years

Subject "impersonated a security company employee and talked to an 81-year-old burglary victim about putting bars on the windows and other safety equipment. . . . The subject went to [the victim's] restroom and took blank checks and credit cards from the victim's purse in the bedroom next to the bathroom."

Subsequent investigation determined that the suspect recently committed a burglary at the victim's home to scare her and make her more receptive to security equipment fraud. A burglary charge was dismissed but read-in for purposes of restitution.

ADULT AND JUVENILE CRIMINAL RECORD

Adult Arrests: 3
Adult Incarcerations: 1
Juvenile: Aggravated assault, theft.
Adult: Theft, retail theft. Also two other arrests for theft, "but neither have a disposition listed," and "municipal tickets for disorderly conduct and resisting" that were "permanently stayed."
Parole or Probation Violation(s): No
Violent Crime(s): Yes

OTHER BACKGROUND

From state's presentence investigation:

The 81-year-old burglary and forgery victim "has been extremely nervous about anyone coming to the house. She won't answer the door unless she knows who is coming, and when I went to visit her I had to call right before I got there. . . . The victim has been highly traumatized by the events and it has affected her lifestyle and her physical health."

". . . I believe the defendant's involvement in the crime is more extensive than she admits to. It was an especially brazen crime involving a vulnerable victim."

The defendant "has stolen from at least one other elderly victim."

11.

MOST RECENT CRIME AND SENTENCE

Burglary, escape
Current sentence unclear
In 1979 subject and an accomplice burglarized a Milwaukee home while the owner was asleep.

[Subject received a 6-year sentence and escaped after 2 years. He was located in Texas and reincarcerated four years later, in 1984.]

ADULT AND JUVENILE CRIMINAL RECORD

Adult Arrests: 10
Adult Incarcerations: 3
Juvenile: Threat of bodily harm, uncontrollable, criminal damage to property, theft, drinking, endangering health, morale, and welfare, disorderly conduct, runaway, truancy, auto theft, burglary, disorderly conduct, drinking, sexual misconduct, truancy, runaway, obstructing an officer, delinquency.
Adult: Sexual intercourse without consent, disorderly conduct, failure to support wife and child, disorderly conduct, strong-arm robbery, forgery, theft, hindering.
Parole or Probation Violation(s): Yes
Violent Crime(s): Yes

OTHER BACKGROUND
From state's 1979 presentence investigation:

The subject "has been on both parole and probation supervision. He has not once completed any term successfully. . . . He has not reported to his agents as directed, has failed to keep his agents truthfully informed of his whereabouts and activities, has failed to remit court-ordered financial obligations and continued his involvement in criminal activity."

12.

MOST RECENT CRIME AND SENTENCE

Burglary
4 years
Subject "broke into a bar in the City of Milwaukee" and was arrested as he was attempting to leave with stolen merchandise. Received 4-year probation sentence.

[Pending at the time of this study in 1995 were several charges for offenses

ADULT AND JUVENILE CRIMINAL RECORD

Adult Arrests: 4
Adult Incarcerations: 1
Juvenile: Strong-arm robbery.
Adult: Carrying a concealed weapon and shoplifting. Also pending is battery and retail theft. See "Other Background."
Parole or Probation Violation(s): Yes
Violent Crime(s): Yes

OTHER BACKGROUND
From state's prison intake report:

At time of this study, pending "violations prompting probation revocation proceedings began when the subject committed a substantial battery to an individual by hitting him several times to the head causing massive swelling to the

while on probation. See
next two columns.]

eyes and forehead. . . .
Subject failed to report to
Batterers Anonymous
[and] absconded from
supervision [and] was
arrested for retail theft
[and] failed to complete
. . . the Salvation Army
Adult Rehabilitation
Program."

While awaiting
revocation proceedings at
Milwaukee County's House
of Correction, "the subject
was observed by an officer
striking with his hands and
feet another inmate . . .
resulting in injuries severe
enough that the inmate
required [outside] medical
attention. . . . "

Identified as "low-risk"
before current offense.

13.

MOST RECENT CRIME AND SENTENCE
Burglary
8 years
While on probation for
retail theft, committed a
burglary involving the
stealing of women's
undergarments for sexual
stimulation.

ADULT AND JUVENILE CRIMINAL RECORD
Adult Arrests: 25
Adult Incarcerations: 3
Juvenile: None
Adult: Criminal trespass,
burglary, auto theft, theft,
battery, theft, disorderly
conduct, obstructing an
officer, burglary,
shoplifting, failure to
support a child, burglary,
burglary, burglary, battery,
battery, burglary, retail
theft, drug possession,
criminal trespass, retail
theft, possession of drugs
and burglar tools, burglary.
**Parole or Probation
Violation(s):** Yes
Violent Crime(s): Yes

OTHER BACKGROUND
**From state's presentence
investigation:**

Beginning "in 1975
[subject] was in need of
specialized treatment
under the Sex Crimes Law.
. . . In 1979 he was
released from the
Winnebago Mental Health
Institution even though he
continued to demonstrate
many of the adjustment
problems that originally
brought him to the
institution."

Victim of a recent
burglary of women's
undergarments
encountered the subject,

who fled, when she
returned to her residence.
She "still feels intruded
upon, thinks about it on a
daily basis and checks out
each floor of her home
completely on her return.
She has a difficult time
being at home alone and is
now easily frightened. . . ."

14.

MOST RECENT CRIME AND SENTENCE
Auto theft
2 years
While on probation for
robbery, a police officer
followed an auto that had
been reported stolen and it
"accelerated to a high rate
of speed . . . the officer
pursued the auto at a high
rate of speed [until] the
fleeing auto collided with
a pile of debris . . . the
driver fled on foot and was
apprehended."

ADULT AND JUVENILE CRIMINAL RECORD
Adult Arrests: 2
Adult Incarcerations: 2
Juvenile: Recklessly
endangering safety.
Adult: Robbery and theft.
**Parole or Probation
Violation(s):** Yes
Violent Crime(s): Yes

OTHER BACKGROUND
**From state's prison intake
report:**

"In July 1989 [the subject]
and two other individuals
beat a female victim, took
her money and her car. . . .
He was convicted of
robbery and received a
withheld sentence and was
placed on 10 years
probation [consecutive] to
a prison term for theft."

**From state's presentence
investigation:**
The 1989 robbery
"involved pulling an
elderly woman into [her]
van and stealing her
money . . . he and his
accomplices beat her up
and threw her out of the
moving van."
Despite this and other
"assaultive offenses" cited
in the report, the report
said he "is eligible for the
Division of Intensive
Sanctions" but not
recommended for the
program.

15.

MOST RECENT CRIME AND SENTENCE

Burglary
7 years
Details of 1994 burglary not available in file.

ADULT AND JUVENILE CRIMINAL RECORD

Adult Arrests: 3
Adult Incarcerations: 3
Juvenile: Robbery, runaway, runaway, theft, shoplifting, theft, runaway, possession of burglary tools.
Adult: Burglary, escape, burglary.
Parole or Probation Violation(s): Yes
Violent Crime(s): Yes

OTHER BACKGROUND

From state's 1987 presentence investigation:

At the time of first adult burglary conviction and lengthy juvenile crime record, "he does not seem to understand the seriousness either of his offense history, current offense, or his consistent failure to capitalize on treatment opportunities offered . . . he has become quite adept at manipulation. . . . Burglarizing for [him] is a way of making a living."

PROFILES OF IMPRISONED "DRUG OFFENDERS"

1.

MOST RECENT CRIME
AND SENTENCE
Possession WITD*
2.3 years
While on probation for a
1993 drug-dealing
conviction, arrested and
convicted for a new charge
of possession with intent
to deliver cocaine base.
* WITD: with intent to
deliver.

ADULT AND JUVENILE
CRIMINAL RECORD
Adult Arrests: 2
Adult Incarcerations: 1
Juvenile: Battery, auto
theft.
Adult: No prior adult
record.
**Parole or Probation
Violation(s):** Yes
Violent Crime(s): Yes

OTHER BACKGROUND
**From state's presentence
investigation:**

At the time of his first
conviction for drug
dealing, subject "indicated
he thought [selling drugs]
was easy, quick money. . . .
He takes full responsibility
and does show some
remorse. He indicated this
was the first time he had
sold drugs and I wonder if
he is not minimizing the
situation. This is his first
offense as an adult but the
defendant has served two
probationary periods as a
juvenile."

In connection with his
first arrest, "the defendant
stated to police officers
that this was the first time
he had ever sold any drugs
and that he needed some
quick money to buy a car."

2.

MOST RECENT CRIME
AND SENTENCE
**Possession WITD while
armed and within 1,000
feet of a school**
13 years
After being paroled in late
1994 for a drug offense,
subject was arrested and
convicted in January of
1995 for the same type of

ADULT AND JUVENILE
CRIMINAL RECORD
Adult Arrests: 12
Adult Incarcerations: 2

Juvenile: Auto theft.
Adult: Burglary, marijuana
dealing, numerous
domestic violence
offenses, criminal damage,

OTHER BACKGROUND
**From the subject's
probation/parole agent's
report:**

"[Subject's] correctional
experience has consisted of
numerous offenses and
negative behavior. He has
been involved in the

crime. Revocation of two separate parole cases is pending.

bail jumping, probation violations.

Convicted of dealing cocaine within 1,000 feet of a school. Paroled, then committed current offense.
Parole or Probation Violation(s): Yes
Violent Crime(s): Yes

criminal justice system for more than 20 years. . . . [H]e has been charged with a number of domestic charges in Milwaukee Co. for offenses against" his ex-girlfriend.

From the subject's social worker's report:
In the drug offense for which the subject was paroled in 1994, subject denied he was selling drugs, saying that he was "dropping drugs off at houses and picking up the money for someone else."

Prior periods of community supervision "did not curtail his negative behavior within the community as he continued to have numerous contacts with the correctional system."

3.

MOST RECENT CRIME AND SENTENCE
Possession WITD
2 years
Offense occurred while on probation for prior dealing of drugs. "According to the Milwaukee Police, the total amount of cocaine found on the subject weighed a total of 0.13 grams."

ADULT AND JUVENILE CRIMINAL RECORD
Adult Arrests: 5
Adult Incarcerations: 3
Juvenile: Burglary, receiving stolen property, burglary.
Adult: Armed robbery, resisting/obstructing an officer, auto theft, endangering safety by conduct regardless of life, drug dealing. Numerous violations for operating a vehicle after revocation. Retail theft.
Parole or Probation Violation(s): Yes

OTHER BACKGROUND
From state's presentence investigation:

A habitual parole and probation violator: "[Subject] seems to rationalize his behavior and blames his drug usage as being the reason why he has engaged in new criminal behavior. . . . This agent does feel that the defendant seems to like his current lifestyle and has shown little effort to change it. . . . His past behavior has shown a

Violent Crime(s): Yes

blatant disregard to the community and the Department by engaging in new criminal activity."

4.

MOST RECENT CRIME AND SENTENCE
Possession WITD
5 years
While on probation for 4th-degree sexual assault, subject fled police attempting to question him and was apprehended with baggies containing cocaine and marijuana.

ADULT AND JUVENILE CRIMINAL RECORD
Adult Arrests: 3
Adult Incarcerations: 1
Juvenile: None
Adult: 4th-degree sexual assault, possession of marijuana.
Parole or Probation Violation(s): Yes
Violent Crime(s): No (excluding 4th-degree juvenile sexual assault).

OTHER BACKGROUND
From state's presentence investigation:

"[Subject] stated he got involved with the drug deliveries for the money. It was easy money."

"[Subject] . . . has had people in his short life who have tried to reach out to [him] in an effort to facilitate a positive change. Unfortunately, each time [the subject] pushed these people away. It appears that [the subject] lacks the maturity and insight needed. . . ."

From state's prison intake report:
The subject "placed too much credit to his family history as a determinant of his present behavior. . . .
He stated that he laced his marijuana cigarettes with cocaine approximately two times per week."

5.

MOST RECENT CRIME AND SENTENCE

Possession WITD while armed

5 years

Parole violation for similar offense pending. Original offense: while conducting an investigation, the police patted down the subject and "discovered a .38 caliber gun in his coat pocket. . . . [Officers] also recovered 2 plastic bags . . . containing three bundles of cocaine." At the parole revocation hearing the judge said, "This is the sixth violation report on the client in seven months of parole supervisions, which includes one month in absconder status."

ADULT AND JUVENILE CRIMINAL RECORD

Adult Arrests: 3

Adult Incarcerations: 1

Juvenile: Robbery, auto theft (two counts), armed robbery.

Adult: Auto theft, resisting/obstructing an officer, possession with intent to deliver cocaine while armed.

Parole or Probation Violation(s): Yes

Violent Crime(s): Yes

OTHER BACKGROUND

From state's presentence investigation:

"[Subject did not] express any remorse or emotion for being involved in criminal activity. . . . [The subject] had no explanation for failing to follow through with his probation agents' referrals for drug treatment. . . . [H]e totally lacks self-control and he fails to consider how his actions could affect his life in the long term. . . . Probation was of minimum significance to him."

From the state's revocation decision:
"The one year and four months the client has served had done little to protect the community from the client's criminal acts."

6.

MOST RECENT CRIME AND SENTENCE

Delivery of cocaine

1.8 years

From state's revocation summary:
While on probation for armed robbery, the subject's "negative adjustment to supervision includes Operating a Motor Vehicle Without a Valid Driver's License,

ADULT AND JUVENILE CRIMINAL RECORD

Adult Arrests: 5

Adult Incarcerations: 2

Juvenile: Third-degree sexual assault, theft.

Adult: Burglary, robbery, possession of a controlled substance.

Parole or Probation Violation(s): Yes

Violent Crime(s): Yes

OTHER BACKGROUND

From state's revocation summary:

"[The subject's] violations clearly show his unwillingness to be supervised . . . he has continually possessed illegal narcotics, had demonstrated assaultive and aggressive behavior toward his girlfriend. . . ."

missing appointments with
his agent, domestic
violence, not disclosing
his whereabouts and
activities, not fulfilling his
court ordered obligations,
several positive urines for
drug usage . . . and the
current violation of
Delivery of a Controlled
Substance where [subject]
sold the cocaine . . . to a
Police Officer."

7.

MOST RECENT CRIME AND SENTENCE
**Drug delivery and
possession of firearm
by felon
7 years**
Police "executed a search
warrant at [subject's]
Milwaukee apt., 15 'dime'
bags of rock cocaine and a
loaded .44 caliber
handgun were found in a
closet."

ADULT AND JUVENILE CRIMINAL RECORD
**Adult Arrests: 8
Adult Incarcerations: 3**

Juvenile: Theft, auto
theft, burglary.
Adult: Burglary,
hindering, miscellaneous
drug offenses, delivery of a
controlled substance,
resisting an officer,
obstructing an officer,
criminal damage, criminal
trespass.
**Parole or Probation
Violation(s):** Yes
Violent Crime(s): No

OTHER BACKGROUND
**From state's prison intake
report:**

"When evaluated in 1988
reference was made to . . .
numerous violations for
Disrespect, Fighting,
Failure to Follow Orders,
and [urinalyses] positive for
cocaine. . . . Subject relates
he was using cocaine
(snorting, smoking, and
occasionally injecting) and
this was 'out of control'
this past summer (1993).
He denies he was regularly
involved in selling drugs."
    Judged "low-risk" until
current firearm offense.

8.

MOST RECENT CRIME AND SENTENCE

Possession WITD
10 years
Subject was "approached by officers and fled. During the chase . . . subject threw a plastic baggie from his pocket, a baggie found to contain 39 clear green gem packs of crack cocaine. . . . He maintains his innocence. He denies the drugs were his or that he was involved in dealing drugs at this time."

ADULT AND JUVENILE CRIMINAL RECORD

Adult Arrests: 15
Adult Incarcerations: 4
Juvenile: None
Adult: 5 retail thefts, burglary, injury by conduct regardless of life, 2 resistings, multiple drug offenses.
Parole or Probation Violation(s): Yes
Violent Crime(s): Yes

OTHER BACKGROUND

From state's presentence investigation:

"The defendant primarily associates with people who gamble, drink, do drugs, and look for girls. . . . He is a user and seller of drugs and seems to see no problem with this. . . ."

"He minimizes his criminal involvement in past incidences and has an answer for everything. . . . Crime is a way of life for [him] and he seems very reluctant to give it up . . . has been convicted of 13 crimes in as many years."

From state's social worker's report:
"In simplest terms [subject] states: 'I ain't chemical dependent on drugs whatever. . . . In my mind I don't need treatment.' "

9.

MOST RECENT CRIME AND SENTENCE

Possession WITD
2.5 years (probation)*
"Several officers were conducting surveillance of street drug dealing when subject was observed conducting what appeared to be two drug transactions . . . subject was detained and the

ADULT AND JUVENILE CRIMINAL RECORD

Adult Arrests: 2
Adult Incarcerations: 1
Juvenile: 4th-degree sexual assault, theft, retail theft, battery, disorderly conduct, 4th-degree sexual assault.
Adult: Drug trafficking, auto theft, fleeing (pending).

OTHER BACKGROUND

From state's prison intake report:

Excluding the juvenile crime record resulted in a "low-risk" offense rating.

"It is unfortunate that subject was not able to complete his probation. Subject violated his supervision only 15 days

search revealed" multiple packets totaling more than 7 grams of marijuana.
* Although sentenced to probation, subject was incarcerated at the time of this study with pending charges of auto theft and fleeing an officer in a high-speed chase that ended with a crash into a concrete light pole and a bus stop sign.

Parole or Probation Violation(s): Yes
Violent Crime(s): Yes

after being placed on supervision. . . . Subject did not take seriously the conditions of his supervision and rapidly re-offended. . . . It is hoped that during this period of incarceration [his first] that subject will successfully participate in the recommended programming and assume a pro-social value system and lifestyle once he is released back into the community."

From state's presentence report:
"While on intensive probation [as a juvenile] for 4th-degree sexual assault . . . [he] reported he had violent and sexual hallucinations. He said he imagines himself raping young women." His Safe Path Program for Sex Offenders counselor "is afraid of these hallucinations because he may rape someone."

10.

MOST RECENT CRIME AND SENTENCE
Possession WITD
1.5 years
"The subject was observed backing up a vehicle at a high rate of speed by a local police officer. The subject did not have a valid driver's license and a search was conducted [that] discovered 20 corner

ADULT AND JUVENILE CRIMINAL RECORD
Adult Arrests: 2
Adult Incarcerations: 1
Juvenile: Reckless driving.
Adult: Driving after revocation (3 counts), felony battery.
Parole or Probation Violation(s): No
Violent Crime(s): Yes

OTHER BACKGROUND
From state's prison intake report:

"At age 13 he began involvement with marijuana and alcohol . . . upon his arrest he continued to use marijuana until the day of sentencing. He identifies his cocaine use as cut baggies containing cocaine . . . and 10 additional corner cuts of cocaine. . . ."

situational and does not want to identify himself as a drug dealer. . . . Based [on other self-reported information] he is viewed as someone who uses cocaine and marijuana on a regular basis and as someone who is selling cocaine to support his drug use."

11.

MOST RECENT CRIME AND SENTENCE

Delivery of cocaine within 1,000 feet of a school; possession WITD within 1,000 feet of a school; possession of a short-barrel shotgun
13 years

"An undercover officer made a controlled buy at subject's residence . . . asking to purchase cocaine and a transaction occurred . . . for cocaine base. The officer observed the subject leave the premises and a no-knock search was conducted . . . at which time they found a 12-gauge loaded shotgun . . . the subject returned . . . and was apprehended."

ADULT AND JUVENILE CRIMINAL RECORD

Adult Arrests: 8
Adult Incarcerations: 1

Juvenile: None
Adult: Possession of controlled substance, possession WITD cocaine, multiple arrests (dispositions unclear in file) for carrying a concealed weapon, possession of a controlled substance and possession WITD, attempted 1st-degree murder, battery-domestic abuse.
Parole or Probation Violation(s): No
Violent Crime(s): Yes

OTHER BACKGROUND
From state's prison intake report:

"The offenses include the subject having a loaded 12-gauge shotgun in the residence with the safety off. The potential for violence appears very high. By the subject's own admission he made contact with other drug dealers for the purpose of selling and [these] transactions took place on the grounds of North Division High School."

12.

MOST RECENT CRIME AND SENTENCE

Possession WITD within 1,000 feet of a school 5 years

Police "executed a search warrant [at subject's home] . . . a person was attempting to get out and dropped a baggie [containing 7.91 grams] of marijuana in paper folds. On the floor of the closet . . . was a bag with 23 smaller bags . . . containing . . . cocaine base. Also in the closet was a sawed-off 12-gauge shotgun and a short-barreled rifle, both of which were loaded. Another loaded gun was found under the mattress. This was a .357 magnum revolver. . . . A .38 revolver was found under the mattress. . . . In the living room police found a scale, ziplock bags, two pagers and a 6mm Browning pistol."

ADULT AND JUVENILE CRIMINAL RECORD

Adult Arrests: 1
Adult Incarcerations: 1

Juvenile: None (arrests but no disposition for robbery and resisting/ obstructing an officer).
Adult: No prior adult record.
Parole or Probation Violation(s): No
Violent Crime(s): No

OTHER BACKGROUND

From state's presentence report:

Referring to the circumstances of the arrest and crime scene, "the defendant admitted he lived there [and] denied any knowledge [of the weapons] and said he did not sell drugs. He said he had been on his way to play basketball at North Division High School, which was within 1,000 feet."

"He was able to live in that residence because his grandfather owned the house. . . . From the beginning he said different friends of his hung around and that they had drugs and eventually he realized they were selling drugs from his place."

"Because of the amount of drugs involved and the number of weapons, this certainly must be viewed as a serious offense."

NOTES

CHAPTER 2: THE ROOT CAUSE OF CRIME: MORAL POVERTY

1. *Criminal Victimization 1994* (Bureau of Justice Statistics, April 1996), p. 2.

2. *Highlights from 20 Years of Surveying Crime Victims* (Bureau of Justice Statistics, October 1993), p. 6; *Criminal Victimization 1993* (Bureau of Justice Statistics, May 1995), p. 2; and *Crime in the United States* (Federal Bureau of Investigation, 1994), p. 58.

3. Mark A. Cohen et al., *Crime in the United States: Victim Costs and Consequences* (Research Report, National Institute of Justice, December 1995), p. 29.

4. *Sourcebook of Criminal Justice Statistics 1994* (Bureau of Justice Statistics, 1995), p. 2.

5. Douglas J. Besharov, "The Children of Crack: A Status Report," *Public Welfare*, Winter 1996, p. 33.

6. *Murder in America* (International Association of Chiefs of Police, May 1995), p. 13.

7. Alfred Blumstein, "Youth Violence, Guns, and the Illicit-Drug Trade," *The Journal of Law and Criminology*, Fall 1995, pp. 19–20.

8. David G. Walchak, "President's Message," *The Police Chief*, December 1995, p. 6.

9. *Losing Ground Against Drugs: A Report on Increasing Illicit Drug Use and National Drug Policy* (Senate Committee on the Judiciary, December 19, 1995); and *Facing the Future: The Rise of Teen Drug Abuse and Teen Violence* (Senate Committee on the Judiciary, December 1995).

10. James Alan Fox, *Trends in Juvenile Violence* (Bureau of Justice Statistics, March 1996), p. 2.

11. Ibid.

12. Alfred Blumstein, "Prisons," in James Q. Wilson and Joan R. Petersilia, *Crime* (Institute for Contemporary Studies, 1995), p. 412.

13. Fox, *Trends in Juvenile Violence*, p. 2.

14. *Young Black Male Victims* (Bureau of Justice Statistics, December 1994), p. 1.

15. Ibid., p. 2.

16. Glenn Loury, "The Impossible Dilemma," *The New Republic*, January 1, 1996, pp. 21–25.

17. Carrie Dowling, *USA Today*, February 6, 1996, p. 3A.

18. Calculated from *Uniform Crime Report—1990* (Pennsylvania State Police, 1991), pp. A2–A4.

19. Don Russell and Bob Warner, "Fairhill: City's Deadliest Turf in '94," *Philadelphia Daily News*, January 9, 1995, pp. 4–5.

20. *Violence in America: Mobilizing a Response* (National Academy Press, 1994), p. ix.

21. Peter Anin, " 'Superpredators' Arrive," *Newsweek*, January 22, 1996, p. 57.

22. James Q. Wilson, "Crime and Public Policy," in Wilson and Petersilia, *Crime*, p. 492.

23. Ibid., p. 507.

24. Ibid., p. 493.

25. Debra Dickerson, "Who Shot Johnny?" *The New Republic*, January 1, 1996, pp. 17–18.

26. Marvin E. Wolfgang et al., *Delinquency in a Birth Cohort* (University of Chicago Press, 1972); and Marvin E. Wolfgang and Paul E. Tracy, "The 1945 and 1958 Birth Cohorts," unpublished paper, Harvard University, 1982, as cited in James Q. Wilson, *Thinking About Crime*, rev. ed. (Basic Books, 1983), pp. 223, 279.

27. Professor Marvin E. Wolfgang, interview, May 21, 1996.

28. Marvin E. Wolfgang et al., *From Boy to Man, From Delinquency to Crime* (University of Chicago Press, 1987); Delbert S. Elliott et al., "Self-Reported Violent Offending: A Descriptive Analysis of Juvenile Offenders and Their Offending Careers," *Journal of Interpersonal Violence*, December 1986, pp. 502–3.

29. Robert J. Sampson and John H. Laub, *Crime in the Making: Pathways and Turning Points Through Life* (Harvard University Press, 1993), p. 23.

30. Walchak, "President's Message," p. 6.

31. Ibid.

32. Aristotle, *The Ethics*.

33. *Juvenile Offenders and Victims: A National Report* (Office of Juvenile Justice and Delinquency Prevention, August 1995), p. 58.

34. Ibid., p. 108; and *Weapons Offenses and Offenders* (Bureau of Justice Statistics, November 1995), p. 3.

35. *Murder in America*, p. 11.

36. Ibid., p. 6.

37. *Child Victimizers: Violent Offenders and Their Victims* (Bureau of Justice Statistics, March 1996), p. 3.

38. Ibid.

39. Mark S. Fleisher, *Beggars and Thieves: Lives of Urban Street Criminals* (University of Wisconsin Press, 1995), p. 143.

40. Anne Morrison Piehl et al., "Juvenile Gun Violence in Boston: Gun Markets, Serious Juvenile Offenders and a Use Reduction Strategy," forthcoming, *Law and Contemporary Problems*.

41. John J. DiIulio, Jr., and George A. Mitchell, *Who Really Goes to Prison in Wisconsin?* (Wisconsin Policy Research Institute, April 1996), p. 19.

42. *Youth Crime in Florida* (Florida Department of Law Enforcement, April 25, 1996), pp. 4–5.

43. Ibid., p. 6.

44. *Juvenile Crime: Outlook for California* (Legislative Analyst's Office, May 1995), p. 23.

45. Deborah Coombe and Judy Peet, "Slain Teacher Recorded Her Pleas to Abductor," *Star-Ledger*, March 20, 1996, pp. 1, 2, 19.

46. *Crime and Neighborhoods* (Bureau of Justice Statistics, June 1994).

47. Black Community Crusade for Children, *Overwhelming Majority of Black Adults Fear for Children's Safety and Future* (Children's Defense Fund, May 26, 1994).

48. Michael A. Fletcher, "Study Tracks Blacks' Crime Concerns," *Washington Post*, April 21, 1996, p. A11.

49. U.S. Bureau of the Census, CP-2-1, *U.S. Summary: Social and Economic Characteristics*.

50. V. O. Key, *The Responsible Electorate* (Harvard University Press, 1966), p. 8; Benjamin I. Page and Robert Y. Shapiro, *The Rational Public: Fifty Years of Trends in America's Policy Preferences* (University of Chicago Press, 1991); John J. Dilulio, Jr., and Donald E. Stokes, "The Setting: Valence Politics in Modern Elections," in Michael Nelson, ed., *The Elections of 1992* (CQ Press, 1993), chapter 1.

51. Glenn Loury, "The Impossible Dilemma," pp. 23–24.

52. "Tougher Treatment Urged for Juveniles," *New York Times*, August 2, 1994, p. A16, citing data from a survey of 250 judges by Penn and Schoen Associates for *National Law Journal*.

53. Jennifer L. Hochschild, *Facing Up to the American Dream: Race, Class, and the Soul of the Nation* (Princeton University Press, 1995), p. 205.

54. Robert I. Lerman, "Building Hope, Skills, and Careers: Creating a Youth Apprenticeship Program," in Irwin Garfinkel et al., eds., *Social Policies for Children* (Brookings Institution, 1995), p. 159.

55. Mark A. Cohen, "The Monetary Value of Saving a High-Risk Youth," Urban Institute–National Institute of Justice, November 1995.

56. Wilson, *Thinking About Crime*, p. 6.

57. Ibid., p. 13.

58. Ibid., p. 20, emphasis in original.

59. Ryder, as quoted in ibid.

60. Wilson, *Thinking About Crime*, p. 24.

61. James Q. Wilson and Richard J. Herrnstein, *Crime and Human Nature* (Simon & Schuster, 1985).

62. Ibid., pp. 508–9.

63. James Q. Wilson, "In Loco Parentis: Helping Children When Families Fail Them," *Brookings Review*, Fall 1993, p. 14.

64. David Rubinstein, "Don't Blame Crime on Joblessness," *Wall Street Journal*, November 13, 1992.

65. Alan L. Keyes, *Masters of the Dream* (William Morrow, 1995), pp. 12, 13, 15.

66. National Research Council, *Losing Generations: Adolescents in High-Risk Settings* (National Academy Press, 1993), p. 164.

67. Stephen P. Klein et al., *Predicting Criminal Justice Outcomes: What Matters?* (RAND, 1991).

68. *Correctional Populations in the United States, 1990* (Bureau of Justice Statistics, 1992), and *National Corrections Reporting Program, 1988* (Bureau of Justice Statistics, 1992).

69. *Sentencing in the Federal Courts: Does Race Matter? The Transition to Sentencing Guidelines, 1986–90, Summary* (Bureau of Justice Statistics, 1993).

70. Patrick A. Langan, "No Racism in the Justice System," *Public Interest*, Fall 1994, p. 51.

71. Stanley Rothman and Stephan Powers, "Execution by Quota?" *Public Interest*, Summer 1994, pp. 3–17.

72. Alfred Blumstein, "On the Racial Disproportionality of United States Prison Populations," *Journal of Criminal Law and Criminology*, vol. 73 (1982); Patrick A. Langan, "Racism on Trial: New Evidence to Explain the Racial Composition of Prisons in the United States," *Journal of Criminal Law and Criminology*, vol. 76 (Fall 1985); *Prison Admissions and Releases, 1983* (Bureau of Justice Statistics, 1986).

73. John J. DiIulio, Jr., "My Black Crime Problem, and Ours," *City Journal*, Spring 1996, p. 25.

74. Neil Alan Weiner and Marvin E. Wolfgang, "The Extent and Character of Violent Crime in America, 1969 to 1982," in Neil Alan Weiner et al., eds., *Violence* (Harcourt Brace Jovanovich, 1990), p. 32.

75. Ibid.

76. DiIulio, "My Black Crime Problem, and Ours," p. 26.

77. Ibid., p. 16.

78. Katia Hetter, "A Pittsburgh Court Battles the Tide," *U.S. News & World Report*, March 25, 1996, p. 37.

79. *Prisoners in 1994* (Bureau of Justice Statistics, August 1995), p. 8.

80. Gerald G. Gaes, "Prison Crowding Research Examined," *The Prison Journal*, September 1994, pp. 329–63.

81. John J. DiIulio, Jr., "Prisons That Work: Management Is the Key," *Federal Prisons Journal*, Summer 1990, pp. 7–15, and "Principled Agents: The Cultural Bases of Behavior in a Federal Bureaucracy," *Journal of Public Administration Research and Theory*, July 1994, pp. 277–318.

82. *Sourcebook of Criminal Justice Statistics* (Bureau of Justice Statistics, 1995), p. 14.

83. Ibid., pp. 560–70.

84. Robert Bidinotto, "Must Prisons Be Resorts?" *Reader's Digest*, November 1994, pp. 65–71.

85. John J. DiIulio, Jr., *No Escape: The Future of American Corrections* (Basic Books, 1991), pp. 110–23; Charles H. Logan and Gerald G. Gaes, "Meta-Analysis and the Rehabilitation of Prisoners," *Justice Quarterly*, June 1993, pp. 245–63.

86. John J. DiIulio, Jr., and Anne Morrison Piehl, *Results of the New Jersey Prisoner Self-Report Survey* (New Jersey Sentencing Policy Study Commission, 1993).

87. Neal Shover, *Great Pretenders: Pursuits and Careers of Persistent Thieves* (Westview, 1996), pp. 178–79.

88. Ibid., p. 179.

89. This section is drawn largely from John J. DiIulio, Jr., "Retrieve the Death Penalty from Symbolism," *The American Enterprise*, May/June 1995, pp. 40–41.

90. James W. Marquart et al., *The Rope, the Chain, and the Needle* (University of Texas, 1994).

91. This section is drawn largely from John J. DiIulio, Jr., "Crime," in Henry J. Aaron and Charles L. Schultze, eds., *Setting Domestic Priorities* (Brookings Institution, 1992), p. 143.

92. Department of Justice, *Attorney General's Task Force on Violent Crime: Final Report* (Washington, 1981), p. ix.

93. Wilson, *Thinking About Crime*, p. 262.

94. Gary Kleck, *Point Blank: Guns and Violence in America* (Aldine de Gruyter, 1991); Gary Kleck and E. Britt Patterson, "The Impact of Gun Control and Gun Ownership Levels on Violence Rates," *Journal of Quantitative Criminology*, 1993, pp. 249–87.

95. Philip J. Cook and Mark H. Moore, "Gun Control," in Wilson and Petersilia, eds., *Crime*, pp. 290–91.

96. Robert James Bidinotto, "Subverting Justice," in Robert James Bidinotto, ed., *Criminal Justice?* (The Foundation for Economic Education, 1994), p. 67.

97. Paul G. Cassell, "Miranda's Social Costs: An Empirical Assessment," *Northwestern University Law Review*, Winter 1996, pp. 483–84; Paul G. Cassell and Bret S. Hayman, "Police Interrogation in the 1990s: An Empirical Study of the Effects of Miranda," *UCLA Law Review*, February 1996, pp. 839–931.

98. Cassell and Hayman, "Police Interrogation," p. 840.

99. Wilson, *Thinking About Crime*, p. 260.

100. Matthew Reilly, "In Prison for Life, These Inmates Try Scaring Kids Away from Joining Them," *Star-Ledger*, March 26, 1996, p. 17.

101. Joseph Tierney and Jean Baldwin Grossman with Nancy L. Resch, *Making a Difference: An Impact Study of Big Brothers/Big Sisters* (Public/Private Ventures, November 1995).

102. Aristotle, *The Ethics*.

103. Isabel Wilkerson, "2 Boys, a Debt, a Gun, a Victim: The Face of Violence," *New York Times*, May 16, 1994, p. A1.

104. Robert J. Sampson and John H. Laub, *Crime in the Making* (Harvard University Press, 1993), pp. 95–96.

105. Daniel S. Nagin et al., "Adolescent Mothers and the Criminal Justice System," unpublished paper, Carnegie Mellon University, December 15, 1995, pp. 28, 30.

106. Carolyn Smith et al., "Resilient Youth: Identifying Factors That Prevent High-Risk Youth from Engaging in Delinquency and Drug Use," *Current Perspectives on Aging and the Life Cycle*, 1995, p. 221.

107. *Cycle of Violence* (National Institute of Justice, 1992).

108. Mark S. Fleisher, *Beggars and Thieves*, pp. 262–63.

109. Fox Butterfield, *All God's Children: The Bosket Family and the American Tradition of Violence* (Knopf, 1995), esp. pp. 327–28.

110. This section is drawn largely from John J. DiIulio, Jr., "Saving the Children: Crime and Social Policy," in Irwin Garfinkel et al., eds., *Social Policies for Children* (Brookings Institution, 1996).

111. National Research Council, *Losing Generations*, p. 5.

112. Bureau of Justice Statistics, *National Update* (1992), p. 7; and Ellen Schall, "Principles for Juvenile Detention," in Francis X. Hartmann, ed., *From Children to Citizens*, vol. 2: *The Role of Juvenile Court* (Springer Verlag, 1987), p. 350.

113. *Survey of State Prison Inmates* (Bureau of Justice Statistics, 1991), pp. 9, 10.

114. Tracy L. Snell, "Women in Prison," *BJS Special Report* (March 1994), pp. 1, 2.

115. Office of Juvenile Justice and Delinquency Prevention, *A Comprehensive Strategy for Serious, Violent, and Chronic Juvenile Offenders* (1993), p. 7.

116. Peter W. Greenwood, "Reforming California's Approach to Delinquent and High-Risk Youth," in James B. Steinberg et al., *Urban America: Policy Choices for Los Angeles and the Nation* (RAND, 1992), p. 221.

117. David M. Altschuler and Troy L. Armstrong, "Intensive Aftercare for the High-Risk Juvenile Parolee: Issues and Approaches in Reintegration and Community Supervision," in Troy L. Armstrong, ed., *Intensive Interventions with High-Risk Youths: Promising Approaches in Juvenile Probation and Parole* (Criminal Justice Press, 1991), p. 48.

118. David Whitman and David Bowermaster, "A Potent Brew: Booze and Crime," *U.S. News & World Report*, May 31, 1993, pp. 57–59.

119. Jeffrey Fagan, "Intoxication and Aggression," in Michael Tonry and James Q. Wilson, eds., *Crime and Justice Series: Drugs and Crime*, vol. 13 (University of Chicago Press, 1990), p. 292.

120. Philip J. Cook and Michael J. Moore, "Violence Reduction Through Restrictions on Alcohol Availability," *Alcohol Health and Research World*, vol. 17, no. 2, 1993, p. 151.

121. Alan R. Lang and Paulette A. Sibral, "Psychological Perspectives on Alcohol Consumption and Interpersonal Aggression," *Criminal Justice and Behavior*, vol. 16, no. 3, September 1989, p. 321.

122. Ibid., p. 301.

123. James A. Inciardi and Arnold S. Trebach, *Legalize It?: Debating American Drug Policy* (American University Press, 1993), p. 160.

124. Ibid.

125. Steven Jonas, "The U.S. Drug Problem and the U.S. Drug Culture: A Public Health Solution," in James Inciardi, ed., *The Drug Legalization Debate* (Sage Publications, 1991), p. 164.

126. Hannah Clayson, "Alcohol Policy and New York City: A Harm-Reduction Strategy," unpublished paper, Woodrow Wilson School, Princeton University, WWS 402d, May 10, 1994, p. 7, citing data from Tom Harford, "The Incidence of Alcohol and Other Drug Use," in Ura Jean Oyemade and Dolores Brandon-Moyne, eds., *Ecology of Alcohol and Other Drug Use: Helping Black High-Risk Youth* (U.S. Department of Health and Human Services, 1987), pp. 46–47.

127. *Seventh Special Report to the Congress on Alcohol and Health* (U.S. Department of Health and Human Services, January 1990).

128. Wesley G. Skogan, *Disorder and Decline: Crime and the Spiral of Decay in American Neighborhoods* (University of California Press, 1990), p. 4.

129. Cook and Moore, "Violence Reduction," p. 151.

130. Douglas Murdoch et al., "Alcohol and Crimes of Violence," *International Journal of Addictions*, vol. 25, September 1990.

131. James J. Collins and Pamela M. Messerschmidt, "Epidemiology of Alcohol-Related Violence," *Alcohol Health and Research World*, vol. 17, no. 2, 1993, p. 94, reporting data calculated from two 1988 studies and one 1991 study by the U.S. Bureau of Justice Statistics.

132. *Prisoners and Alcohol* (Bureau of Justice Statistics, January 1983), p. 15.

133. *Young Black Male Victims* (Bureau of Justice Statistics, December 1994), p. 1.

134. Alfred Blumstein, "Prisons," in James Q. Wilson and Joan Petersilia, eds., *Crime*, p. 412.

135. Robert Nash Parker, "Alcohol and Theories of Homicide," in Freda Adler and William S. Laufer, eds., *Advances in Criminological Theory*, vol. 4 (Transaction Publishers, 1993), pp. 113–42.

136. Patricia Ladouceur and Mark Temple, "Substance Use Among Rapists: A Comparison with Other Serious Felons," *Crime and Delinquency*, vol. 31, no. 2, April 1985, p. 272.

137. Helene Raskin White et al., "Alcohol Use and Aggression Among Youth," *Alcohol Health and Research World*, vol. 17, no. 2, 1993, pp. 144–50.

138. *Seventh Special Report.*

139. James J. Collins, "Alcohol and Interpersonal Violence: Less Than Meets the Eye," in Neil Allen Weiner and Marvin E. Wolfgang, eds., *Pathways to Criminal Violence* (1989), p. 50.

140. For example, compare Reginald G. Smart, "The Relationship of Availability of Alcoholic Beverages to Per Capita Consumption and Alcoholism Rates," *Journal of Studies on Alcohol*, 1977, pp. 891–96; and Brian R. Rush et al., "Alcohol Availability, Alcohol Consumption, and Alcohol-Related Damage: The Distribution of Consumption Model," *Journal of Studies on Alcohol*, 1986, pp. 1–18. The former study indicated that the relationships among availability, consumption, and problems weakened if one controlled for such socioeconomic variables as urban conditions and unemployment rates. But the latter and more sophisticated study incorporated those very factors as direct causes of aggregate alcohol consumption and as co-varieties of retail availability. As common sense would have it, the better model and research showed that availability increased consumption, and consumption increased problems. Likewise, see Philip J. Cook and Michael J. Moore, "Drinking and Schooling," *Journal of Health Economics*, vol. 12, no. 4, 1993, pp. 411–29, which finds that drinking and schooling do not mix (e.g., other things being equal, drinking in high school reduces the average number of years of schooling completed following high school).

141. Cook and Moore, "Violence Reduction."

142. Ibid.

143. Frank J. Chaloupka, "Effects of Price on Alcohol-Related Problems," *Alcohol Health and Research World*, vol. 17, no. 1, 1993, pp. 46–53.

144. Mark Temple and Patricia Ladouceur, "The Alcohol-Crime Relationship as an Age-Specific Phenomenon: A Longitudinal Study," *Contemporary Drug Problems*, 1986, pp. 89–116.

145. Chaloupka, "Effects of Price," p. 49.

146. Ibid.

147. Ibid., p. 52.

148. Henrick J. Harwood et al., *Social and Economic Costs of Alcohol Abuse and Alcoholism* (Research Triangle Institute, 1985).

149. For reports on estimates of the costs of violent crime, see Anne Morrison Piehl and John J. DiIulio, Jr., "Does Prison Pay? Revisited," *Brookings Review*, vol. 13, Winter 1995.

150. Paul J. Gruenwald et al., "The Relationship of Outlet Densities to Alcohol Consumption: A Time Series Cross-Sectional Analysis," *Alcoholism: Clinical and Experimental Research*, vol. 17, no. 1, 1993, p. 38.

151. Ibid.

152. Ibid., p. 45.

153. Paul J. Gruenwald et al., "Alcohol Availability and the Formal Power and Resources of State Alcohol Beverage Control Agencies," *Alcoholism: Clinical and Experimental Research*, vol. 16, no. 3, May/June 1992, p. 592.

154. Jerome Rabow et al., "Alcohol Availability, Alcohol Beverage Sales and Alcohol-Related Problems," *Journal of Studies on Alcohol*, vol. 43, no. 7, 1982, pp. 767–801.

155. Gruenwald et al., "Alcohol Availability," pp. 591–97.

156. Ibid., p. 596.

157. Jerome Rabow et al., "Alcohol Beverage Licensing Practice in California: A

Study of a Regulatory Agency," *Alcoholism: Clinical and Experimental Research*, vol. 17, no. 2, 1993, p. 245.

158. Ibid., p. 244.

159. Robert Nash Parker and L. A. Rebhun, *Alcohol and Homicide: A Deadly Combination of Two American Traditions* (SUNY Press, forthcoming, 1995), draft p. 60.

160. James Q. Wilson and George Kelling, "Broken Windows: The Police and Neighborhood Safety," *Atlantic Monthly*, March 1982, pp. 29–38.

161. Skogan, *Disorder and Decline*, pp. 10–11, summarizing the Wilson-Kelling "broken windows" thesis.

162. Parker and Rebhun, *Alcohol and Homicide*, draft pp. 60–61.

163. Travis Hirschi, *The Causes of Delinquency* (University of California Press, 1969); Marvin D. Krohn and James L. Massey, "Social Control and Delinquent Behavior: An Examination of the Elements of the Social Bond," *Sociological Quarterly*, 1980, pp. 529–43; Anne C. Case and Lawrence F. Katz, "The Company You Keep: The Effects of Family and Neighborhood on Disadvantaged Youths," NBER Working Paper No. 3705 (National Bureau of Economic Research, 1991).

164. Stanley I. Orenstein and Dominique M. Hanssens, "Alcohol Control Laws and the Consumption of Distilled Spirits and Beer," *Journal of Consumer Research*, September 1985, p. 208.

165. Case and Katz, "The Company You Keep."

166. Parker and Rebhun, pp. 55–56.

167. Cook and Moore, "Violence Reduction," p. 155.

168. Parker and Rebhun, p. 133.

169. F. Wittman, *Zoning Ordinances, Alcohol Outlets, and Planning: Prospects for Local Control of Alcohol* (Medical Research Institute, 1982); and F. Wittman and M. Hilton, "Uses of Planning Ordinances to Regulate Alcohol Outlets in California Cities," in H. D. Holder, ed., *Advances in Substance Abuse: Behavioral and Biological Research 1987*, pp. 337–66, as cited in Clayson, "Alcohol Policy and New York City," which argues persuasively in favor of reducing the density of liquor outlets and limiting liquor advertising in New York City.

170. Wittman, *Zoning Ordinances*, p. 13, as cited in Clayson, "Alcohol Policy and New York City."

171. As quoted in Clayson, "Alcohol Policy and New York City," p. 21.

172. David Whitman with David Bowermaster, "A Potent Brew: Booze and Crime," *U.S. News & World Report*, May 31, 1993, pp. 57–59.

173. Ibid.

174. Clayson, "Alcohol Policy and New York City," p. 22.

175. Philip J. Cook and George Tauchon, "The Effects of Minimum Drinking Age Legislation on Youthful Auto Fatalities, 1970–77," *Journal of Legal Studies*, 1984, pp. 169–90.

176. J. Tom Morgan, Memorandum, Metropolitan District Attorneys, May 16, 1995, summarizing data from the 1995 report of the U.S. Advisory Board on Child Abuse and Neglect.

177. Mark S. Fleisher, *Beggars and Thieves*, pp. 103–5.

178. Joe Klein, "The Predator Problem," *Newsweek*, April 29, 1996, p. 32.

179. Douglas J. Besharov, "Child Abuse Reporting," in Garfinkel et al., eds., *Social Policies for Children*, p. 259.

180. Ibid.

CHAPTER 3: RESTRAINING AND PUNISHING STREET CRIMINALS

1. James Rowen, "Before Deadly Spree, 92 Arrests," *Milwaukee Journal Sentinel*, January 28, 1996, p. 1.

2. *Criminal Victimization 1993* (Bureau of Justice Statistics, May 1995), p. 2; *Sourcebook of Criminal Justice Statistics 1993* (Bureau of Justice Statistics, 1994), tables 4.9 and 5.73; *Felony Sentences in State Courts, 1992* (Bureau of Justice Statistics, January 1995), tables 1, 2, 4.

3. Ibid.

4. Morgan O. Reynolds, *Crime in Texas* (National Center for Policy Analysis, February 1991).

5. Ibid. See also Morgan O. Reynolds, *Crime and Punishment in Texas: Update*, January 1996.

6. James Q. Wilson, "Crime in America: Reply," *Commentary*, February 1995, p. 20.

7. Calculated from *Profile of Inmates in the United States and in England and Wales, 1991* (Bureau of Justice Statistics, October 1994), p. 2.

8. Ibid., pp. 4, 6.

9. Ibid., pp. 7, 8.

10. *Imprisonment in Four Countries* (Bureau of Justice Statistics, February 1987), p. 2.

11. *The Public Perspective*, November/December 1991, pp. 5, 8, reporting data from a Roper Center poll.

12. *Americans Behind Bars: The International Use of Incarceration, 1992–93* (The Sentencing Project, September 1994), p. 2.

13. Mike Reynolds and Bill Jones, *Three Strikes and You're Out: A Promise to Kimber* (Quill Driver Books, 1996).

14. Charles H. Logan, "Who Really Goes to Prison?" *Federal Prisons Journal*, Summer 1991, pp. 57–59; *Who Goes to Prison?* (National Council on Crime and Delinquency, 1990; Tom Wicker, "The Punitive Society," *The New York Times*, January 12, 1991, p. 25.

15. *Pretrial Release of Felony Defendants, 1990* (Bureau of Justice Statistics, November 1992), tables 12 and 13.

16. *Weapons Offenses and Offenders* (Bureau of Justice Statistics, November 1995), p. 4.

17. *Prisoners in 1994* (Bureau of Justice Statistics, August 1995), p. 11.

18. Joan R. Petersilia, "Diverting Non-Violent Prisoners to Intermediate Sanctions," California Policy Seminar, unpublished paper, 1995, pp. 9–11.

19. Facts of the "pizza thief" case supplied by the California Department of Corrections, May 26, 1995; Michael E. Fletcher, "Study Tracks Blacks' Crime Concerns," *Washington Post*, April 21, 1996, p. A11. See also Andy Furillo, "Three Strikes: The Verdict's In" (a three-part series), *Sacramento Bee*, March 31–April 2, 1996, p. A1.

20. John J. DiIulio, Jr., and George Mitchell, *Who Really Goes to Prison in Wisconsin?* (Wisconsin Policy Research Institute, 1996).

21. John J. DiIulio, Jr., and Anne Morrison Piehl, "Does Prison Pay?" *Brookings Review*, vol. 4, Fall 1991, pp. 28–35; John J. DiIulio, Jr., and Anne Morrison Piehl, "Does Prison Pay? Revisited," *Brookings Review*, vol. 13, Winter 1995, pp. 21–25; Steven D. Levitt, "The Effect of Prison Population Size on Crime Rates: Evidence from Prison Crowding Litigation," unpublished manuscript, Harvard University, February 1995; and Thomas B. Marvell and Carlisle E. Moody, "Prison Population

Growth and Crime Reduction," *Journal of Quantitative Criminology*, vol. 10, no. 4, 1994.

22. *Prison Sentences and Time Served for Violence* (Bureau of Justice Statistics, April 1995), p. 2.

23. George Allen, "The Courage of Our Convictions," *Policy Review*, Spring 1995, pp. 4–7. Also see *Governor's Commission on Parole Abolition and Sentencing Reform: Final Report* (State of Virginia, August 1994).

24. *Prison Sentences and Time Served for Violence*, p. 2.

25. *Crime and Sentencing State Enactments* (National Conference of State Legislatures, November 1995); and *State Sentencing System and "Truth in Sentencing"* (National Conference of State Legislatures, April 1995).

26. John J. DiIulio, Jr., "Crime in America: It's Going to Get Worse," *Reader's Digest*, August 1995, p. 55.

27. *Probation and Parole Violators in State Prison, 1991* (Bureau of Justice Statistics, August 1995).

28. Joan R. Petersilia, "A Crime Control Rationale for Reinvesting in Community Corrections," *Spectrum*, Summer 1995, p. 19.

29. *Weapons Offenses and Offenders* (Bureau of Justice Statistics, November 1995), p. 5.

30. Julia Cass, "The Case of 'Mudman' Simon Has Made the Pa. Parole Board Cautious About Who Shall Be Released," *Philadelphia Inquirer*, December 18, 1995, pp. B1, B3.

31. Jeff Lean et al., "Crime and Punishment," *Miami Herald*, August 28–September 5, 1994, and December 18, 1994. Also see *Final Report of the Dade County Grand Jury* (Circuit Court of the Eleventh Judicial Circuit of Florida, May 11, 1994).

32. Dave Neese, "Plenty of Crime, Little Punishment in Jersey," *The Trentonian*, August 15, 1994, p. 3.

33. For example, see *Sourcebook of Criminal Justice Statistics 1993* (Bureau of Justice Statistics, 1994), table 6.77.

34. *Child Rape Victims, 1992* (Bureau of Justice Statistics, June 1994), p. 1: "Thirty-six states responded that they did not keep such statistics. . . ." Also see Andre Henderson, "The Scariest Criminal," *Governing*, August 1995, pp. 35–38.

35. Twenty-nine states do not retain such data on murderers; most other states retain only some such data for selected years. Brookings Institution, Homicide Information Project, phone survey and correspondence, Summer 1995.

36. For example, Anne Morrison Piehl, *Probation in Wisconsin* (Wisconsin Policy Research Institute, August 1992), p. 11: "The Wisconsin Division of Probation and Parole is uncomfortable thinking in terms of summary statistics and, therefore, does not record how many probationers go to prison during the term of their supervision."

37. *Recidivism of Felons on Probation, 1986–1989* (Bureau of Justice Statistics, 1992), pp. 1, 6; and *Prisons and Prisoners in the United States* (Bureau of Justice Statistics, 1992), p. xvi.

38. President's Commission on Law Enforcement and Administration of Justice, *The Challenge of Crime in a Free Society* (Government Printing Office, 1967), p. 167.

39. Patrick A. Langan, "Between Prison and Probation: Intermediate Sanctions," *Science*, May 6, 1994, p. 791.

40. Joan Petersilia and Susan Turner, *Intensive Supervision for High-Risk*

Probationers: Findings from Three California Experiments (RAND, 1990), pp. ix, 98; and Susan Turner and Joan Petersilia, "Focusing on High-Risk Parolees: An Experiment to Reduce Commitments to the Texas Department of Corrections," *Journal of Research in Crime and Delinquency*, vol. 29, February 1992, p. 34. Also see Joan Petersilia and Susan Turner, "Intensive Probation and Parole," in *Crime and Justice: A Review of Research*, vol. 17 (University of Chicago Press, 1993), pp. 281–335.

41. Joan R. Petersilia, "A Crime Control Rationale for Reinvesting in Community Corrections," *Spectrum*, Summer 1995, p. 19.

42. Ibid., p. 1.

43. John J. DiIulio, Jr., *No Escape: The Future of American Corrections* (Basic Books, 1991), pp. 5, 102.

44. Patsy A. Klaus, "The Costs of Crime to Victims," *BJS Crime Data Brief* (February 1994), pp. 1, 2.

45. Ted R. Miller et al., "Victim Costs of Violent Crime and Resulting Injuries," *Health Affairs*, vol. 12, Winter 1993, pp. 193–94.

46. Mark A. Cohen et al., *Crime in the United States: Victim Costs and Consequences* (Research Report, National Institute of Justice, December 1995).

47. Neil D. Rosenberg, "Gunshots Shatter Lives, Cost Millions," *Milwaukee Journal*, March 14, 1993, p. 12.

48. David P. Cavanagh and Mark A. R. Kleiman, *Cost Benefit Analysis of Prison Cell Construction and Alternative Sanctions* (BOTEC Analysis Corp., 1990), p. 26; DiIulio and Piehl, "Does Prison Pay?" p. 34; and DiIulio and Piehl, *New Jersey Inmate Survey: Results and Implications* (New Jersey Sentencing Policy Study Commission, 1993).

49. Michael K. Block and Steven J. Twist, "Lessons from the Eighties: Incarceration Works," *Commonsense*, vol. 1, Spring 1994, p. 78.

50. Alfred Blumstein et al., ed., *Criminal Careers and "Career Criminals,"* vol. 1 (National Academy Press, 1986), p. 123.

51. Michael K. Block, Carey Herbert, and Steven J. Twist, "Deterrence: What We Know and What It Means," working paper, University of Arizona, 1994.

52. Patrick A. Langan, "Between Prison and Probation: Intermediate Sanctions," *Science*, vol. 264, May 1994, p. 792.

53. Patrick A. Langan, "America's Soaring Prison Population," *Science*, vol. 251, March 1991, p. 1573; Langan, "Between Prison and Probation," pp. 792–93.

54. For the raw data from the Wisconsin study, see John J. DiIulio, Jr., "Community-Based Policing in Wisconsin: Can It Cut Crime?" *Wisconsin Policy Research Institute Report*, vol. 6, October 1993. For an analysis of the Wisconsin data, see DiIulio and Piehl, "Does Prison Pay?" pp. 28–35. For the raw data from the New Jersey study and a preliminary analysis of it, see DiIulio and Piehl, *New Jersey Inmate Survey*.

55. Thomas B. Marvell and Carlisle D. Moody, Jr., "Prison Population Growth and Crime Reduction," *Journal of Quantitative Criminology*, vol. 10, no. 4, 1994, p. 136; Steven D. Levitt, "The Effect of Prison Population Size on Crime Rates: Evidence from Prison Overcrowding," Litigation Working Paper 5119 (National Bureau of Economic Research, February 1995).

56. Richard Bernstein, "Young Predators Caught in a Chaotic System," *New York Times*, March 13, 1996, p. C18.

57. Penelope Lemov, "The Assault on Juvenile Justice," *Governing*, December 1994, p. 30.

58. *Juvenile Justice: Juveniles Processed in Criminal Court and Case Depositions* (General Accounting Office, August 1995), pp. 2, 27.

59. *Sourcebook of Criminal Justice Statistics* (Bureau of Justice Statistics, 1994), p. 531.

60. Ibid., pp. 379–82.

61. We are grateful to Harry L. Shorstein, State Attorney, Fourth Judicial Circuit of Florida, for providing us with the data and information contained in this section.

62. William S. Bratton, "The New York City Police Department's Civil Enforcement of Quality-of-Life Crimes," *Journal of Law and Policy*, 1995, pp. 447–64.

63. Ibid., pp. 447–48.

64. *Police Strategy No. 2* (NYPD, 1994), p. 31.

65. *Police Strategy No. 5* (NYPD, 1994), p. 40.

66. Bratton, "The New York City Police," p. 464.

67. George L. Kelling, "How to Run a Police Department," *City Journal*, Autumn 1995, p. 41.

68. Fox Butterfield, "Police Chief's Success in Charleston, S.C., Is What's Raising Eyebrows Now," *New York Times*, April 25, 1995, p. A12.

69. Reuben M. Greenberg, "Less Bang-Bang for the Buck," *Policy Review*, Winter 1992, p. 56.

70. Ibid., p. 56.

71. Ibid., p. 58.

72. Gregory Childress, "Leaders Turn to Police Wizard: Charleston Chief Takes Criminals to Task for Crime," *Durham Herald-Sun*, March 20, 1994, p. A1.

73. Ibid.

74. Linn Washington, "Common-Sense Economy-Minded Sheriff Cuts Crime Rate," *Philadelphia Inquirer*, January 25, 1994, p. 5A.

75. Drawn from a speech by Sam Nuchia to the Federal Bar Association on September 27, 1995. See also "Houston Murders Lowest Since '73," *Milwaukee Journal Sentinel*, March 12, 1996, p. 8.

76. Katherine M. Skiba, "Zero Tolerance for Crime: Houston Moves to Sweep Up Gangs, Sees the Statistics Drop," *Milwaukee Journal Sentinel*, March 12, 1996, p. 1.

77. Ibid.

78. From a speech by Sam Nuchia to the Katy Area Chamber of Commerce on October 10, 1995.

79. Drawn from a speech by Sam Nuchia to the Federal Bar Association on September 27, 1995.

80. Sarah B. Vandenbraak, "Bail Humbug!" *Policy Review*, Summer 1995, p. 75.

81. The Gallup Poll News Service, April 25, 1994. According to the Gallup data, in both 1993 and 1994, 18 percent of poll respondents expressed a "great deal" or "quite a lot" of confidence in the U.S. Congress, versus 17 percent in 1993 and 15 percent in 1994 for the criminal justice system. But the police were an exception, enjoying over 50 percent public confidence in both years, on a par with organized religion and a distant third to the military.

CHAPTER 4: DRUGS, CRIME, AND CHARACTER

1. Robert Hanley, "In Paterson, a Family's Sordid Existence Brings Arrests and Calls for Change," *New York Times*, December 6, 1995.

2. Don Terry, "Detroit Family in the Jaws of a Monster," *New York Times*, December 4, 1995.

3. Nancy Lewis, "Video Lands Couple in Family Court," *Washington Post*, December 18, 1995.

4. Quoted in William J. Bennett, *The De-Valuing of America: The Fight for Our Culture and Our Children* (Summit Books, 1992), pp. 120–21.

5. National Institute of Justice, "Drug Use Forecasting, 1991, Annual Report" (on adult arrestees), December 1992, p. 21.

6. T. E. Feucht, R. C. Stephens, and M. L. Walker, "Drug Use Among Juvenile Arrestees: A Comparison of Self-Report, Urinalysis, and Hair Analysis," *Journal of Drug Issues*, vol. 24, no. 1, 1994, pp. 99–116, quoted in Eric D. Wish, "Drug Use Among Juvenile Detainees in Maryland," reprint from *Proceedings: Maryland Statewide Epidemiology Work Group May 1995 Meeting*.

7. E. D. Wish, T. A. Gray, and E. Levine, *Measuring Drug Use Among Female Juvenile Detainees: Estimates from Self-Reports, Urinalysis, and Hair Analysis*, 1995 (Center for Substance Abuse Research, forthcoming).

8. Kenneth Tardiff, et al., "Homicide in New York City: Cocaine Use and Firearms," *Journal of the American Medical Association*, vol. 278, no. 1, July 6, 1994, p. 46.

9. Ibid., p. 45.

10. Robert Davis, " 'Meth' Use in the 90's: A Growing 'Epidemic,' " *USA Today*, September 7, 1995, p. 7A.

11. John McCormick, "A One-Man Children's Crusade," *Newsweek*, April 25, 1994, p. 56.

12. *Foster Care: Parental Drug Abuse Has Alarming Impact on Young Children* (General Accounting Office, 1994), cited in Center on Addiction and Substance Abuse at Columbia University (CASA), *Legalization: Panacea or Pandora's Box* (1995), p. 25, note 83.

13. Daniel Patrick Moynihan, "The Children of the State: Welfare Reform, Congress and Family Responsibility," *Washington Post*, November 25, 1990, p. C1.

14. Nicholas Davidoff, "To Give or Not to Give: Inside the World of Beggars Who Cajole, Amuse, Shame—and Threaten—Their Way to $100 a Day and More," *New York Times Magazine*, April 24, 1994, pp. 36–41, 50–51.

15. The Gallup Poll, "A 1995 View of the Drug Problem in America" (September 1995), released December 12, 1995.

16. The four best discussions of the issue of drug legalization are William J. Olson, "Why Americans Should Resist the Legalization of Drugs," published by the Heritage Foundation (*Backgrounder, no. 993*, July 18, 1994); James Q. Wilson, "Against the Legalization of Drugs," *Commentary* (February 1990); CASA, *Legalization: Panacea or Pandora's Box*; and Herbert D. Kleber, "Our Current Approach to Drug Abuse—Progress, Problems, Proposals," *New England Journal of Medicine*, vol. 330, February 3, 1994, pp. 361–65. Many of the arguments in these works shaped this analysis.

17. David F. Musto, *The American Disease* (Oxford University Press, 1987).

18. Ibid., pp. 258–59. Also see Wilson, "Against the Legalization of Drugs," p. 22.

19. Robert E. Peterson, "The Success of Tough Drug Enforcement," PAE Report, January 1996, p. 5. Also: Bureau of Justice Statistics, *Prisoners in 1990, in 1991, in 1992* (note 9), and *in 1993* (p. 8), (U.S. Department of Justice, 1991, 1992, 1993, 1994 respectively).

20. Musto, *The American Disease*, p. 265.

21. Dana Eser Hunt and William Rhodes, "Characteristics of Heavy Cocaine Users, Including Poly Drug Use, Criminal Activity, and Health Risks" (Abt Associates for ONDCP, Spring 1993), released by ONDCP, August 9, 1993, as "Characteristics of Heavy Cocaine Users: A Research Paper," p. 1.

22. Associated Press, March 3, 1988.

23. Office of Applied Studies, Substance Abuse and Mental Health Services Administration, U.S. Department of Health and Human Services, "Preliminary Estimates from the 1994 National Household Survey on Drug Abuse (1994 NHSDA)" (Advance Report Number 10, September 1995).

24. Press release by the University of Michigan's Institute for Social Research, "Monitoring the Future Study" (January 31, 1994), table 3.

25. Christine Smith and William Rhodes, "Drug Use by Age Cohorts Over Time" (Abt Associates, unpublished, quoted draft, August 11, 1992), p. 3. This is one of several contracted studies done for ONDCP. Some, like this one, have not been released by ONDCP, but the office now wants them to be available to interested individuals.

26. 1994 NHSDA, tables 6–10.

27. Office of Applied Studies, Substance Abuse and Mental Health Services Administration, U.S. Department of Health and Human Services, "Preliminary Estimates from the 1992 National Household Survey on Drug Abuse (1992 NHSDA)" (Advance Report Number 3, June 1993).

28. University of Michigan's Institute for Social Research, "Monitoring the Future Study," December 15, 1995, table 4.

29. Reuters, "Elders Reiterates Her Support for Study of Drug Legalization," *Washington Post*, January 15, 1994, p. A8.

30. On February 9, 1993, the White House announced that ONDCP would be cut from 146 staff members to 25. For more detail on drug czardom under the Clinton administration see Bryon York, "Clinton's Phony Drug War," *The American Spectator*, February 1994, pp. 40–44.

31. See Michael Isikoff, "Reno Has Yet to Make Mark on Crime," *Washington Post*, November 26, 1993, pp. A1, A10, A11. For a thorough analysis—and refutation—of the Clinton administration claim that the prison population contains an excessive number of nonviolent or "low-level" drug offenders see Richard K. Willard and Shannen W. Coffin, "Prison Capacity and 'Low-Level' Drug Offenders," Working Paper Series No. 60 (Washington Legal Foundation, February 1995).

32. Senate Committee on the Judiciary, *Losing Ground Against Drugs* (December 19, 1995), pp. 9–10.

33. From $1.960 billion in FY 1992 to $1.293 billion in FY 1995 in current dollars: ONDCP, *National Drug Control Strategy: Budget Summary* (February 1995), p. 235.

34. Tim Golden, "Tons of Cocaine Reaching Mexico in Old Jets," *New York Times*, January 10, 1995, pp. A1, A8.

35. H. G. Reza, "Border Inspections Eased and Drug Seizures Plunge," *Los Angeles Times*, February 13, 1995. An NBC *Dateline* report by Fred Francis, February 24, 1995, focused on the same problem.

36. Charles Rangel, *CNN News*, January 31, 1994.

37. Press release by the University of Michigan's Institute for Social Research, "Monitoring the Future Study" (also known as the National High School Senior

Survey—HHS) for 1995 (December 15, 1995), for 1994 (December 8, 1994), and for 1993 (January 31, 1994).

38. CASA, *Legalization: Panacea or Pandora's Box*, p. 37.

39. Office of Applied Studies, Substance Abuse and Mental Health Services Administration, U.S. Department of Health and Human Services, "Annual Medical Examiner Data, 1993: Data from the Drug Abuse Warning Network (DAWN)" (Statistical Series: Series I, Number 13-B, 1995).

40. The data cited are from Office of Applied Studies, Substance Abuse and Mental Health Services Administration, U.S. Department of Health and Human Services, "Preliminary Estimates from the Drug Abuse Warning Network: 1994 Preliminary Estimates of Drug-Related Emergency Room Episodes" (Advance Report Number 11, November 1995).

41. Ibid.

42. *National Drug Control Strategy*, 1995, pp. 45–48, 146 (table B-16).

43. ONDCP, "Pulse Check: National Trends in Drug Abuse," Fall 1995, p. 3.

44. *CNN News* October 30, 1995, 8:17 P.M. ET.

45. Quoted in Bennett, *The De-Valuing of America*, p. 120.

46. Orrin G. Hatch, *Congressional Record, Senate*, September 25, 1995, p. S14307.

47. William F. Buckley, Jr., "The War on Drugs Is Lost," *National Review*, vol. 48, no. 2, February 12, 1996, p. 35.

48. Ibid., p. 36.

49. Ethan A. Nadelmann, "The War on Drugs Is Lost," p. 38.

50. *National Drug Control Strategy*, 1995, p. 139 (table B-4).

51. CASA, *Legalization: Panacea or Pandora's Box*, p. 36.

52. "Preliminary Estimates from the Drug Abuse Warning Network, 1994," p. 3.

53. ONDCP, "Pulse Check: National Trends in Drug Abuse," December 1994, p. 10.

54. CASA, *Legalization: Panacea or Pandora's Box*, p. 37.

55. "Preliminary Estimates from the 1994 National Household Survey on Drug Abuse," pp. 58, 78 (table 22a), 80 (table 23A), 82 (table 24A), 86 (table 26a), and 56 (table 5A).

56. CASA, *Legalization: Panacea or Pandora's Box*, p. 12.

57. Kurt Schmoke, "The War on Drugs Is Lost," p. 41.

58. "Preliminary Estimates from the Drug Abuse Warning Network, 1994," multiple tables.

59. ONDCP, *National Drug Control Strategy: Budget Summary* (February 1995), pp. 235–38; and ONDCP, *National Drug Control Strategy* (February 1995), pp. 112–13.

60. L. D. Johnston, J. G. Bachman, and P. M. O'Malley, *Monitoring the Future: Questionnaire Results from the Nation's High School Seniors, 1995* (Institute for Social Research).

61. Partnership for a Drug-Free America, *1995 Partnership Attitude Tracking Study* (February 20, 1996).

62. Ibid., p. 4.

63. Information provided by Community Anti-Drug Coalition of America.

64. Ibid.

65. Ibid.

66. ONDCP, *National Drug Control Strategy: Strengthening Communities' Response to Drugs and Crime*, February 1995, p. 139 (table B-4).

67. Hunt and Rhodes, "Characteristics of Heavy Cocaine Users," p. 7; and David Boyum and Ann Marie Rochleau, "Heroin Users in New York, Chicago, and San Diego," Office of National Drug Control Policy (November 1994), p. 5.

68. Hunt and Rhodes, "Characteristics of Heavy Cocaine Users," p. 10.

69. Boyum and Rochleau, "Heroin Users in New York, Chicago, and San Diego," p. 5.

70. For a thorough discussion of drug treatment and the elements of effective treatment programs see ONDCP, "Understanding Drug Treatment," June 1990.

71. Treatment funding from: *National Drug Control Strategy, Budget Summary*, p. 187. Estimated treatment capacity from: *National Drug Control Strategy (1994)*, p. 103, table B-8.

72. Some advocates of greater federal treatment spending have asserted that while the federal government increased drug treatment spending, state and local governments cut such spending. There is no evidence to support this claim for treatment spending nationally. In fact, a study released by ONDCP last year, done by the U.S. Census Bureau, found that spending by state and local governments on all aspects of anti-drug programming increased between 1990 and 1991 (the two years measured) —*and treatment spending (under the category health and hospitals) increased 28.1 percent for state governments and 25.2 percent for local governments between 1990 and 1991*. See ONDCP, *State and Local Spending on Drug Control Activities: Report from the National Survey of State and Local Governments* (October 1993), p. 5.

There is also an effort under way by the federal government bureaucracy to discredit its own data showing a decline in persons treated as spending on treatment dramatically increased. In a memorandum dated January 25, 1995, the administrator of the Substance Abuse and Mental Health Services Administration (SAMHSA) at the U.S. Department of Health and Human Services (HHS) argues for a new methodology—that produces increases in persons treated as spending increases, of course— substituting a one-day count of persons treated, rather than an estimate of persons treated per year by treatment providers and *including both drug and alcohol treatment in the total*. This highlights the problem rather than resolving it, however. It strongly suggests that funds requested and appropriated to provide drug treatment have been shifted to alcohol treatment. In addition, the memorandum openly concedes that treatment providers "change the classification of clients in response to changing, legal, regulatory or policy priorities" and, apparently, neither SAMHSA nor HHS has any intention of altering this situation.

73. *National Drug Control Strategy, 1995*, p. 139 (table B-4), p. 143 (table B-9).

74. The criminal justice system is probably the single greatest cause of addicts entering treatment today. "Drug courts" and so-called diversion programs give less violent addicts a choice of entering and completing treatment or going to jail for an extended period. Washington, D.C., mayor Marion Barry may be the most well-known example of this practice.

75. In remarks before the 1993 National Summit on U.S. Drug Policy (May 7, 1993), Dr. Mitchell S. Rosenthal, president of Phoenix House and one of the nation's foremost drug treatment authorities, noted that what he called "disordered drug abusers" (others might call them "hard-core addicts") require long-term, drug-free, residential treatment. This means 18 to 24 months of treatment within a therapeutic community. There are only an estimated 11,000 such slots nationwide and they cost

an estimated $17,000 to $22,000 per year (Mitchell S. Rosenthal, "Asking the Right Questions About Treatment," May 7, 1993). President Clinton's drug strategy completely ignores this problem.

76. Yih-ing Hser, M. Douglas Anglin, and Keiko Powers, "A 24-Year Follow-up of California Narcotics Addicts," *The Archives of General Psychiatry*, vol. 50, July 1993, pp. 577–84. Quotation from p. 577.

77. Bayum and Rochleau, "Heroin Users in New York, Chicago, and San Diego," p. 19.

78. Hunt and Rhodes, "Characteristics of Heavy Cocaine Users."

79. Jeff Leen and Don Van Natta, Jr., "Drug Court: Favored by Felons," *Miami Herald*, August 29, 1994, p. 1A.

80. Jeff Leen and Don Van Natta, Jr., "Controversial Drug Court," *Miami Herald*, December 18, 1994, p. 24A.

81. National Opinion Research Center at the University of Chicago, "Evaluating Recovery Services: The California Drug and Alcohol Treatment Assessment (CALDATA)" (April 1994), p. 11.

82. Edwin W. Zedlewski, *Making Confinement Decisions* (National Institute of Justice Research in Brief, 1987). We note only that high cost-benefit claims have been made for prisons. We do not believe the 17-1 ratio is correct.

83. C. Peter Rydell and Susan S. Everingham, "Controlling Cocaine: Supply Versus Demand Programs" (RAND, 1994). The quotation is from the RAND press release on the report, June 13, 1994, p. 1.

84. ONDCP, Statement of Fred W. Garcia, Deputy Director for Demand Reduction, White House Office of National Drug Control Policy, on the RAND Studies' "Controlling Cocaine: Supply Versus Demand Programs" and "Modeling the Demand for Cocaine," June 13, 1994, pp. 1–2.

85. Rydell and Everingham, "Controlling Cocaine," p. 20.

86. William Rhodes, Paul Scheiman, and Kenneth Carlson, "What America's Users Spend on Illegal Drugs, 1988–1991" (Abt Associates, February 23, 1993), released by ONDCP, August 23, 1993, p. 10, table 1. This study has been updated with the data published in the *National Drug Control Strategy*, 1995, p. 145 (table B-14).

87. Coca is the bush whose leaves are processed to extract cocaine.

88. U.S. Department of State, *International Narcotics Control Strategy Report* (INCSR), 1995. Figures 4-17 to 4-21 are based on the INCSR data and unpublished analyses and a cocaine production model prepared by the staff of ONDCP's Office of Research during the Bush administration.

89. Note that the 1994 estimate of cocaine available in the United States employs an estimate of federal seizures based on projecting a 12-month total from the available data for the first six months of the year.

90. Unpublished results of an ONDCP-funded analysis of data from the DEA's System to Retrieve Information from Drug Evidence (STRIDE). The analysis was conducted by Abt Associates.

91. Ibid.

92. Office of Applied Studies, Substance Abuse and Mental Health Services Administration, U.S. Department of Health and Human Services, "Estimates from the Drug Abuse Warning Network: 1992 Estimates of Drug-Related Emergency Room Episodes" (Advance Report Number 4, September 1993), p. 45.

93. ONDCP, "Price and Purity of Cocaine: The Relationship to Emergency Room Visits and Deaths, and to Drug Use Among Arrestees" (October 1992).

94. *National Drug Control Strategy, 1995*, p. 139 (table B-4).

95. The decline in heavy cocaine use in the face of increased price indicates an important difference between casual and addictive use. As long as cocaine is easily obtainable, it seems that casual users not deterred by prevention efforts are unlikely to be deterred by even moderate increases in street prices. This is probably because they are spending so little of their disposable income on the drug that such price increases do not affect their ability to obtain it. Many heavy users, on the other hand, are using most of their disposable income to purchase cocaine (crack). When the price goes up they generally have to make do with less of the drug. This leads some of them to enter detox and treatment and apparently reduces the rate at which those who continue using suffer the health problems that cause them to appear at emergency rooms.

96. "Estimates from the Drug Abuse Warning Network: 1992 Estimates of Drug-Related Emergency Room Episodes," p. 45; "Preliminary Estimates from the Drug Abuse Warning Network, 1994," multiple tables; and STRIDE unpublished.

97. The record of Colombia's failure has been detailed in a wide variety of reports in addition to its treatment in the 1995 *INCSR*; see David L. Marcus, "Drug Traffickers' Grip on Colombia Tightens," "Colombian President in Drug Lords' Pocket, Officials Say," "Heroes and Victims: Cocaine Trade Brings Highest Earnings, Deadliest Toll to Colombia," "Killer Drugs: Narcotics Trade Destroys Everyday Life in Colombia," "Only the Good News: Censorship Bars Press from Reporting on Drug Trade," "Fight for Clean Flights," "Steep Price, Low Return: U.S. Wastes Millions in Colombia Drug Fight, Officials Say," "Drug Money's Influence on Constitution Seen," *Dallas Morning News*, February 26, 1955, pp. 1A, 32A, 33A, 1J, 10J, and February 27, 1995, pp. 1A, 6A, 1D, 4D, 1H; Majority Staff Report on Colombia's anti-drug performance, Committee on Foreign Relations, United States Senate, February 27, 1995; John P. Sweeney, "Colombia's Narco-Democracy Threatens Hemispheric Security," *Backgrounder* (Heritage Foundation, March 21, 1995); Jim McGee, "The Cocaine Connection, the Cali Cartel in America: Drug Smuggling Industry Is Built on Franchises," "The Cocaine Connection, Murder as a Management Tool: Violent Streak Raises Cali Cartel's U.S. Profile," "The Cocaine Connection, Lawyers Under Scrutiny: Cartel-Related Probe Focuses on D.C. Law Firm," *Washington Post*, March 26, 1995, pp. A1, A20; March 27, 1995, pp. A1, A12; March 28, 1995, pp. A1, A8.

98. Attorney General Dick Thornburgh prepared a report something like this that he released August 3, 1989 ("Drug Trafficking: A Report to the President of the United States"). But it was not made a strategic plan for federal drug enforcement.

CHAPTER 5: ABOUT MORAL POVERTY: SOME THINGS WE NEED TO DO

1. *The Challenge of Crime in a Free Society: Introduction*, A Report by the President's Commission on Law Enforcement and Administration of Justice (Government Printing Office, February 1967), p. 1.

2. Calculated from *The Challenge of Crime*: 1 robbery per 1,630 equals 1.2 per 2,000.

3. Calculated from *Criminal Victimization 1994* (Bureau of Justice Statistics, April

1996), pp. 2, 3: the robbery victimization rate per 1,000 was 6, and 55 percent of robberies were reported, for a rate of 6.6 robberies per 2,000.

4. *The Challenge of Crime in a Free Society*, p. 211.

5. Ibid., p. 213.

6. Ibid., p. 6.

7. Ibid., p. 12.

8. Ibid., emphasis added.

9. *Violent Crime: The Challenge to Our Cities* (George Braziller, 1969), p. 82.

10. Daniel Patrick Moynihan, "Toward a National Urban Policy," *The Public Interest*, no. 17, Fall 1969, pp. 3–20.

11. Daniel Patrick Moynihan, "The Underclass: Toward a Post-Industrial Policy," *The Public Interest*, no. 96, Summer 1989, pp. 16–27.

12. Daniel Patrick Moynihan, "Defining Deviancy Down," *The American Scholar*, vol. 61, no. 1, Winter 1993, pp. 17–30.

13. Cited in Daniel Patrick Moynihan, "Toward a New Intolerance," *The Public Interest*, no. 112, Summer 1993, p. 122.

14. David Popenoe, "American Family Decline, 1960–1990: A Review and Appraisal," *Journal of Marriage and the Family*, no. 55, August 1993, p. 528.

15. U.S. Department of Health and Human Services, *Vital Statistics of the United States, 1991*, vol. 1, "Natality" (Government Printing Office, 1993).

16. Congressional testimony of Lee Rainwater, Harvard University, in George Will, "The Tragedy of Illegitimacy," *Washington Post*, October 31, 1993.

17. David Blankenhorn, *Fatherless America: Confronting Our Most Urgent Social Problem* (Basic Books, 1995), p. 1.

18. David Blankenhorn, "Fatherless America," *Certain Truths*, Center of the American Experiment (Minneapolis, Minn.), 1995, p. 91.

19. James Q. Wilson, "The Contradictions of an Advanced Capitalist State," *Forbes*, September 14, 1992, p. 112.

20. Daniel Yankelovich, "How Changes in the Economy Are Reshaping American Values," *Values and Public Policy* (Brookings Institution, December 1993), p. 22.

21. Allan Bloom, *The Closing of the American Mind* (Simon & Schuster, 1987), p. 173.

22. William Galston, "Beyond the Murphy Brown Debate: Ideas for Family Policy," speech delivered before the Institute for American Values Policy Symposium, New York City, December 10, 1993.

23. Maggie Gallagher, "Why Murphy Brown Is Winning," *Wall Street Journal*, June 3, 1996.

24. Newton N. Minow and Craig L. Lamay, *Abandoned in the Wasteland: Children, Television, and the First Amendment* (Hill and Wang, 1995), p. 32.

25. See U.S. Department of Education, *The Condition of Education 1993*, pp. 351–52; and Diane Ravitch, *National Standards in American Education: A Citizen's Guide* (Brookings Institution, 1995), p. 82.

26. *Kids Count Data Book: State Profiles of Child Well-Being* (Center for the Study of Social Policy, Annie E. Casey Foundation, 1993), p. 13.

27. Urie Bronfenbrenner, cited by Chester E. Finn, Jr., in "Ten Tentative Truths," *Certain Truths*, p. 31.

28. Sally Fitzgerald, ed., *The Habit of Being: The Letters of Flannery O'Connor* (Farrar, Straus & Giroux, 1988), p. 229.

29. Walker Percy, *Sign-Posts in a Strange Land* (Noonday Press, 1992), p. 393.

30. Patrick F. Fagan, "Promoting Adoption Reform: Congress Can Give Children Another Chance," *The Heritage Foundation Backgrounder*, May 6, 1996, p. 5.

31. Albert R. Hunt, "A Good Mother's Day Gift: Pass the Adoption Bill," *Wall Street Journal*, May 2, 1996 (citing the National Council of Adoption).

32. Conna Craig, "What I Need Is a Mom," *Policy Review*, no. 73, Summer 1995.

33. Edmund Burke, "Letters on a Regicide Peace" (1796), *The Works of Edmund Burke* (London, 1909–1912), vol. 5, p. 208.

INDEX

ABOUT THE AUTHORS

William J. Bennett served as Director of the Office of National Drug Control Policy under President Bush and as Secretary of Education and Chairman of the National Endowment for the Humanities under President Reagan. The author of numerous bestselling books, he is a fellow of the Heritage Foundation and co-Director of Empower America. He lives in Chevy Chase, Maryland.

John J. DiIulio, Jr., is Director of the Brookings Institution Center for Public Management, as well as Professor of Politics and Public Affairs at Princeton University and a member of the Council on Crime in America. He lives in Montgomery County, Pennsylvania.

John P. Walters, Executive Director of the Council on Crime in America, is President of the New Citizenship Project, and former Deputy Director for Supply Reduction, Office of National Drug Control Policy. He lives in Washington, D.C.